PRAISE

Exploring Fait

MW00966277

"Smart, well-informed... lucid, engaging... Glass delivers a superb exposition of Darwinian theory and a meticulous, sharply reasoned discussion of the evidence that supports it. His logic is impeccable when he insists that evolutionary theory does not rule out the existence of God."

—Kirkus Reviews

"Glass has provided a thorough look at the evidence and the processes of evolution, alongside a compelling case for its compatibility with Christianity. His theological analysis is very sound as he addresses several of the commonly perceived points of tension between the Christian faith and evolution. For a thorough understanding of these issues, this book is among the very best resources available."

—Peter Enns, Ph.D. (Harvard), Professor of Christian Studies at Eastern University, author of numerous books, including *The Evolution of Adam*

"As a non-scientist, I found that *Exploring Faith and Reason* presents an accessible, fascinating, and compelling presentation of evolution. As a biblical scholar, I appreciate Bruce Glass' grasp of theological issues and the biblical text. His conclusion that evolution and Christianity are compatible is a crucial message for the church today."

—Tremper Longman III, Ph.D. (Yale), Robert H. Gundry Professor of Biblical Studies at Westmont College, author of numerous books on the Old Testament

"Glass tackles a historically controversial topic with finesse. Wherever one may be on the issue of evolution, Glass' superb scholarship and unbiased commentary on issues of faith does not disappoint."

—Reverend Jordan Ogden, Lead Pastor, Antioch Community Church, Dallas

"This book is superb. Bruce Glass' summary of the science is thorough and accurate, yet easy for non-scientists to follow. His analysis is sharp, his tone is winsome, and his approach to contentious issues is fair. This book is a valuable resource for those who want to understand how evolution and evangelical Christianity can be harmonious."

> **—Loren Haarsma, Ph.D. (Harvard), Associate Professor of Physics at Calvin College, co-author of *Origins: Christian Perspectives on Creation, Evolution, and Intelligent Design***

"Bruce Glass has provided a thought provoking look at the most significant theological issues arising from the advent of evolutionary science. Whatever their conclusions, readers will find Mr. Glass' treatment a welcome reminder of the richness and depth of God's Word, as well as a fresh perspective on God's glorious creation."

> **—Reverend Dr. Kristin Huffman, Associate Pastor, Memorial Drive Presbyterian Church, Houston**

"For Christians who want to know more about evolution and its implications for Christianity, Glass offers a clear, informative, and thought-provoking tour through the marvels of modern biology, carefully identifying its faith-enhancing possibilities. A must read for anyone who thinks that evolution is incompatible with faith, or that faith is incompatible with evolution."

> **—Joseph Bulbulia, Ph.D. (Princeton), Professor of Religious Studies at Victoria University (New Zealand)**

"*Exploring Faith and Reason* includes some of the finest exposition of Christian theology I have ever read in so short a space, with a clarity and exactness that is worthy of some of the best works of Joseph Ratzinger and of Thomas Aquinas. The book's unbiased and thorough examination of the pertinent theological issues is most impressive."

> **—Father Clifford J. Stevens, Senior Priest, Father Flanagan's Boys Home (Boys Town)**

"Glass writes with clarity, wisdom, and sensitivity. *Exploring Faith and Reason* is a must read for anyone who desires a thorough engagement with the issue of 'The Reconciliation of Christianity and Biological Evolution'. I highly recommend it."

—Reverend Dr. Tony Metze, Senior Pastor, St. Paul's Lutheran Church, Columbia, SC

"Well written, thoroughly researched, and honestly fair... The book's thorough and eminently readable scientific explanations provide general science readers with a lucid understanding of this complex subject."

—ForeWord Clarion Reviews

"*Exploring Faith and Reason* is an enticing read for anyone who wants a more complete understanding of their faith and meeting it with science. Highly recommended."

—The Midwest Book Review

"This is a fine, clear exposition, permeated by an irenic spirit. ... If you want to understand what 'natural selection' means, this is the best explanation I know of."

—J. Richard Middleton, Ph.D., Professor of Biblical Worldview and Exegesis at Northeastern Seminary and Adjunct Professor of Theology at Roberts Wesleyan College, author of several books, including *A New Heaven and a New Earth*

"In *Exploring Faith and Reason*, Bruce Glass has emerged as a fresh voice for the reconciliation of head and heart. Couched in the language and theology of conservative evangelical Christianity, Mr. Glass' book provides a welcomed bridge between an evidential worldview and traditional Christian conviction. Believers and non-believers alike will find much of value in these pages."

—Reverend Michael Dowd, author of *Thank God for Evolution*, endorsed by 6 Nobel Prize-winning scientists and by religious leaders across the spectrum

Exploring
Faith and Reason

The Reconciliation of Christianity and Biological Evolution

Bruce Glass

PUBLISHING

For information, write to DBG Publishing at 7700 Meadowglen Lane, Houston, Texas 77063, or visit www.exploringfaithandreason.com.

ISBN-13: 978-0-578-11047-9
ISBN-10: 0578110474

LCCN: 2012948298

Manufactured in the United States of America
First Edition

Contents

A Note From The Author

This book is not an account of personal religious conversion or
discovery. Nor is it a description of my own personal religious
views customized to align with evolutionary science. In fact, it is not
about me at all. As an agnostic I have no personal stake in the outcome
of any debate concerning Christianity's concordance with the findings
of science. My interest is as an impartial observer who, nevertheless,
laments the widely held misconceptions among the general public
concerning evolutionary science's compatibility with Christianity—
misconceptions often resulting from inadvertent and even deliberate
misinformation propagated by atheists and by creationists alike.

The following text is also not about the manipulation or
modification of Christianity so that it will comport with evolution. It is
only concerned with very basic and indeed conservative, evangelical
Christian theology, and how that orthodoxy may be seen in light of the
scientific discovery of the natural world. The basic tenets of Christianity discussed herein are, I believe, generally common to all mainstream Christian denominations. Naturally, as is customary among
Christians, one might take exception to one detail or another. I can only
request that the reader reasonably consider the, often overlooked,
intellectual depth of the Christian faith as it is aligned with the natural
world in which we live.

Introduction

S ome years ago, as I would sit in city traffic I began to notice little chrome emblems in the shape of a fish on the back of a few cars. As the emblems became more numerous, I learned that the particular representation of a fish that was being mounted on those cars was an Ichthys (often spelled "Ichthus") symbol—a symbol derived from the Greek word for "fish" as an acronym that was used by first-century Christians to signify their faith in Jesus of Nazareth as the Christ and as the Son of God. Christians were rediscovering the Ichthys symbol and using it on their cars and elsewhere to publicly declare their faith in Jesus Christ.

As time passed I began to notice little fish-shaped emblems that had feet. Then, occasionally emblems with the name "DARWIN" inside the outline of one of those fish with feet could be observed. More recently, I have seen emblems with the design of a fish containing the word "TRUTH" consuming a smaller fish containing the name "DARWIN." Evidently some of these car owners are using the little chrome emblems mounted on their cars to publicly express their conclusion that the truth of Christianity and the truth of Darwinian evolution are mutually exclusive—that a belief in God precludes a belief in evolution, and that a belief in evolution precludes a belief in God.

This is nothing new, of course. Perceptions of incompatibility between Christianity and biological evolutionary science have engaged passionate public debate for at least a century and a half with no popular consensus. For many decades tracking polls have consistently shown that about 45 percent of Americans believe that human beings were created in their present form within the last 10,000 years, while another 45 percent believe in evolution.

The disrespectful and mocking attitude of those who would insert Darwin's name and put feet on an Ichthys symbol is symptomatic of a contemptuousness that has often emerged in the ongoing debate, among some, regarding human origins that began with the 1859 publication of Charles Darwin's *On The Origin of Species*. Some have simply dismissed the findings of science and argued that all we need to know about the creation of the world is plainly spelled out in the Bible's book of *Genesis*. Others, on the other hand, have insisted that the discovery of the vastness of the cosmos and the Earth's relative position in it, along with the discovery of the age of the Earth and the natural processes of biological evolution have not only nullified the Bible's creation stories, but have demonstrated that any belief in God at all is nothing more than a "delusion."

Several Christian political advocacy organizations and individuals continually work on a number of fronts to affect public school curricula, public policy, and general public sentiment in the belief that the findings of science are a threat to their understanding of Christianity, and indeed, a threat to the very moral fabric of our society. A number of "creation science" museums and theme parks have even been established that promote a view of creation consistent with a very literal understanding of *Genesis*. Contrary to that which is well known to scientists, these parks even proclaim the historic interaction of human beings with dinosaurs. A bill introduced in the Louisiana legislature some years ago went so far as to prohibit state agencies from distributing any information at all about radiometric dating because the findings of this widely accepted method of determining the age of geologic strata contradict one particular Biblical interpretation of the age of the Earth.

Largely in response to the terrorist attacks of September 11, 2001, a number of authors calling themselves "New Atheists"—most notably, Richard Dawkins, Daniel C. Dennett, Sam Harris, and Christopher Hitchens—have written aggressively in opposition to religious belief, which they see as an abandonment of rational thought and which they believe has contributed to the evils of fanaticism. Instead, they

argue, Naturalism is a more rational and stable foundation for understanding and coping with the world.

While mostly well intentioned, these efforts on both sides of
the debate tend to unnecessarily foster conflict, confusion, and most
unfortunately, a far too limited understanding of the nature of God.

In his book *The God Delusion*, for example, renowned evolutionary biologist, atheist, and Oxford University professor Richard
Dawkins cited humankind's discovery of the universal laws of nature
as the best evidence of God's inexistence. Since we have discovered
natural causes for how much of the world works, especially biological
evolution by means of natural selection, Dawkins argued, we no longer
have any need for a God. Similarly, well-known Christian writer Lee
Strobel reported in his book *The Case for a Creator* that the study of
evolution in high school had prompted him to become an atheist. Mr.
Strobel's subsequent return to Christianity then led to his writing a
book that alleges the fallacy of the reported findings of science.
Perhaps these men, among many others, simply sell God short.

The implication of professor Dawkins' and Mr. Strobel's conclusions is that the existence of God is contingent upon the ineffective-
ness of the natural world in fulfilling God's plan. They offer the very
unsatisfying paradoxical suggestion that the best evidence of God's
existence could only be found in the incompleteness or the deficiency
of God's creation.

Sometimes people simply give Christianity too little credit for
its capacity to stand firm in the light of scientific discovery. Of course
God did not disappear with the discovery that the Earth is spherical and
that it orbits the sun. Nor did the discovery of the human circulatory
system or the discovery of germs or DNA portend the doom of
Christianity. Likewise, there is no reason to expect that the discovery of
biological evolution by means of natural selection should inhibit an
understanding of God as Creator.

Doubts about evolution are often founded less on a reasonable
assessment of the findings of science than they are on a denial of the
veracity of science to discover a reality that is consistent with a

preferred and especially narrow theological understanding. In addition, numerous authors have gone to great lengths in their attempts to discredit well-founded science because of what they perceive to be its pernicious social and moral implications. Thus, they devote a great deal more of their text to proclaiming why evolution *should not* be real than to why it *is not* real.

Of course it is not just Christians who sometimes rejected the idea of biological evolution. Ultra-orthodox Jews often insist on a literal understanding of the creation stories in *Genesis*, particularly when it comes to the creation of human beings. Islamic fundamentalists point to the six-day creation story in the Koran and express their certainty that it is a literal account of events. The Muslim author of *The Evolution Deceit*, Harun Yahya, has called the theory of evolution "nothing but a deception imposed on us by the dominators of the world system."[1] Polls consistently indicate, however, that skepticism of evolutionary science is more prevalent in the United States than in Europe and most prevalent among conservative evangelical Christians.

There are some very notable exceptions to this inclination among American Christians, however, particularly among those whose work in science has provided them with first hand knowledge of evolutionary processes. In fact, Darwin's *On the Origin of Species* was first introduced in the United States by botanist Asa Gray, who reviewed the book for *The Atlantic Monthly*. In addition to being a scientist, Gray was an evangelical Christian who saw no conflict between his faith and evolutionary processes. When someone likened Darwinian theory to a religion, he quipped that they might just as well have likened Christianity to botany. Gray wrote that Darwin's theory "can be held theistically or atheistically. Of course I think the latter wrong & absurd."[2] Prominent American geologists George Frederick Wright and James Dwight Dana, who actively promoted Darwin's work along with Gray, were also "committed evangelical Christians."[3] Scientist and devout Eastern Orthodox Christian Theodosius Dobzhansky immigrated to the United States from Russia in the 1920s and then published important volumes concerning the synthesis of

Darwinian theory and modern genetics in the 1930s. Dobzhansky famously entitled a 1973 essay, "Nothing in biology makes sense except in the light of evolution."

The ranks of scientists and educators whose work requires an understanding of evolutionary processes include a great many Christians today too. Dr. Francis S. Collins, formerly the Director of the Human Genome Project and more recently the Director of the United States National Institutes of Health, is an outspoken evangelical Christian who has written of his view that God, "who created the universe, chose the remarkable mechanism of evolution to create plants and animals of all sorts."[4] Evangelical Christian biology professor, Dr. Darrel R. Falk, at Point Loma Nazarene University noted that, "If the most predominant version of sudden Creation were true, the sciences of nuclear physics, astronomy, geology and biology would all be utterly wrong."[5] The Catholic author of *Finding Darwin's God*, Dr. Kenneth R. Miller, declared that, "A God who presides over an evolutionary process is not an impotent, passive observer. Rather, He is one whose genius fashioned a fruitful world in which the process of continuing creation is woven into the fabric of matter itself."[6]

Evangelical Christian and Kansas State University geologist, Dr. Keith B. Miller, published a collection of essays authored by twenty Christian academicians (mostly scientists) whose faith in God has been strengthened by their understanding of biological evolutionary processes. Dr. Miller explained:

> Evolution has been viewed by many theologically orthodox Christians, since the publication of *The Origin of Species*, as a positive contribution to understanding God's creative and redemptive work. For many, important theological truths concerning the nature of humanity, the goodness of creation, God's providence, and the meaning of the cross and suffering find renewed significance and amplification when applied to an evolutionary view of God's creative work.[7]

Some Christian educators and scientists are proponents of a type of theistic evolution which postulates that God has supernaturally guided evolutionary processes in order to achieve His intended outcome. This might very well be the case, but God has not provided any yet-discovered physical evidence of this and, as we will see in the following chapters, the transcendent nature of God could very well enable His creation of our world to have been implemented through purely natural processes. (That is, natural at least above the sub-atomic, sub-particle, sub-vibrating-string threshold where God may continually sustain the very existence of our physical universe.)

Recognition that the findings of science are consistent with an understanding of God as Creator is not limited to just those Christians who work in science. As scientific understanding has advanced, theological understanding has matured among laypeople and clergy alike. Just as we no longer have any need for Atlas to hold up the heavens or for Apollo to propel the sun across the sky, we are also learning that the existence and the relevance of the God of Abraham are not dependent upon what we do not understand about how the natural world works. He is far more than a "God of the gaps" in our knowledge of nature. We are also being reminded that He is not an easily explicable God whose acts of creation could be plainly documented in a text of human language.

In 1950, a statement by Pope Pius XII declared that, "the teaching of the church leaves the doctrine of evolution an open question." Building on this moderation of Church doctrine, Pope John Paul II, in a statement before a general audience in April 1986, suggested that,

> ...the theory of natural evolution, understood in a sense that does not exclude Divine causality, is not in principle opposed to the truth about the creation of the visible world as presented in the book of *Genesis*... The doctrine of faith, however, invariably affirms that man's spiritual soul is created directly by God. According to the hypothesis mentioned, it is possible that the human body, following the order impressed by the

Creator on the energies of life, could have been gradually prepared in the forms of antecedent living beings.[8]

Then in October 1996, the Pope declared in a formal statement to the *Pontifical Academy of Sciences* that, "Fresh knowledge leads to recognition of the theory of evolution as more than just a hypothesis."

Despite his assertion that such a conclusion was based on "fresh knowledge," perhaps it should not go unnoted that the Papacy is hardly well known for being ahead of the curve in accepting the findings of science. After all, it was only four years earlier, in 1992, that the Pope officially forgave Galileo for his endorsement of the Copernican view that the Earth orbits the Sun. Nevertheless, while there has been recurring controversy concerning some Christians' objections to teaching biological evolution in American public schools, evolutionary theory has been taught as a part of the biology curriculum in most Catholic schools for many years.

In his famous apologetic essay, *Mere Christianity*, twentieth-century Christian writer and theologian C.S. Lewis revealed a sophisticated understanding of God in relation to the natural world when he wrote:

Century by century, God has guided nature up to the point of producing creatures which can (if they will) be taken right out of nature... Until we rise and follow Christ, we are still parts of Nature, still in the womb of our great mother.

Lewis, drawing upon the works of Christianity's early theologians, wrote that it is primarily man's capacity to reason that constitutes our having been created in God's image. Our innate understanding of morality, our self-awareness, and our ability to reason, according to Lewis, are the best evidence of God's existence and our connection to Him. The point in time at which the ability to reason emerged in *Homo sapiens* within the historical framework of the physical universe is of little consequence.

In describing the essential miracle of Christianity—the incarnation of God as Jesus of Nazareth—Lewis again illustrated his understanding of Christianity as wholly consistent with the ancient and evolving world that we see around us. In his book *Miracles*, Lewis wrote:

> In the Christian story God descends to reascend. He comes down; down from the heights of absolute being into time and space, down into humanity; down further still, if embryologists are right, to recapitulate in the womb ancient and pre-human phases of life; down to the very roots and seabed of the Nature He has created. But He goes down to come up again and bring the whole ruined world up with Him.[9]

Though Lewis may have overstated the claim of embryologists, he nevertheless provides us with a realistic vision of how Christianity's validity need not be dependent on a denial of the evolving natural world in which we live. Indeed, we can see in Lewis' conception how a realistic understanding of natural processes can provide believers with an even deeper and firmer foundation for faith in God.

Given that so many very knowledgeable Christians see no real conflict between Christianity and the findings of science, we might wonder why perceptions of conflict are so pervasive. Of course it has to do with understanding the essential tenets of Christianity as they apply to the natural world, and with understanding the limits to the legitimate claims of science.

There are at least five generally perceived points of tension between Christianity and evolution. They can be expressed in these questions:

1) Doesn't the Bible's book of *Genesis* explicitly tell us about the creation of our world and its living inhabitants?
2) Doesn't the structural order of the universe—from stars, galaxies, and solar systems to the great complexity of living

cells and organisms—require *direct, special* creation by an "Intelligent Designer" and divine Craftsman?

3) How can the idea of a "fallen world" resulting from the transgressions of only two original human beings, Adam and Eve, be consistent with humans evolving as a population?

4) How can we reconcile the idea of "random" genetic variation and other seemingly random events that are associated with evolution with a providential, living God?

5) How can humans be special and unique among creatures if we and other creatures are descended from the same ancestral species?

The following chapters seek to satisfy each of these questions and to illustrate how our world has been shaped by amazing evolutionary processes—natural processes that are fully consistent with the essential tenets of the Christian faith.

We are often told, of course, that science and religion must be kept separated. They are indeed two distinct realms of inquiry—one of the natural universe, the other of the spiritual universe. There are very good reasons not to confuse these two paths to knowledge, as we will see in Chapter 4. But they need not be—in fact cannot be—in conflict. We need not abandon faith to appreciate the findings of science, and we need not abandon reason to believe in God. An ever-increasing body of knowledge of the natural world can never threaten any truly sound religious understanding. More than a century ago, American intellectual and evolutionist John Fiske attested to the stability of legitimate religion and to how faith can be affirmed through science when he declared: "Though science must destroy mythology, it can never destroy religion; and to the astronomer of the future, as well as to the Psalmist of old, the heavens will declare the glory of God."

Part 1

Christianity and Evolution

1

God's Word

E ver since the publication of Charles Darwin's *On the Origin of Species* in 1859, many religious leaders and religious laypeople have expressed skepticism of Darwin's theories because his assertions seemed to them subversive of their understanding of the creation stories found in the Bible's book of *Genesis*. Though Darwin's book did not introduce biological evolution—the idea is as old as ancient Greek philosophy and had been frequently discussed among naturalists for at least half a century prior to Darwin's work—it did offer the first scientifically valid explanation for how evolution could occur. The idea of "natural selection" came to both Charles Darwin and another English naturalist named Alfred Russel Wallace independently and more or less simultaneously. But Darwin had worked-out more of the details and offered more evidence in support of the theory. With the publication of *On the Origin of Species* Darwin became the best-known proponent of the theory of evolution through natural selection. His book brought the subject before a wider general public for the first time and offered a plausible explanation of life on Earth that substantially differed from a literal understanding of the accounts found in Scripture. Naturally, many God-fearing people, including Mrs. Darwin, were compelled to protest.

It had been long known that Scripture contains a great many passages that offer much greater depth of meaning when they are considered figuratively or allegorically, rather than literally. And the "official" Church's embarrassing insistence that the Earth is stationary and at the center of the solar system was still a fresh memory. But the creation stories are far too fundamental to be casually brushed aside. They are among the best-known passages in Scripture because they are crucial to so much that follows them throughout the Bible, and because they provide a rather satisfying explanation for the existence of the world, its diversity of creatures, and humankind's place within it.

The Bible's book of *Ecclesiastes* informs us, however, that we "cannot fathom what God has done from beginning to end." We cannot grasp the scope of God's works or His methods, nor can we fully comprehend the power and the glory of God Himself or His Kingdom of Heaven. This is why Scripture so often tells us that God or His power "is like..." or the Kingdom of Heaven "is like..." Many names and descriptions are attributed to God in the Bible. Each can offer only an incomplete impression of God's full character and capabilities. Even the most exalted descriptions fall short. As contemporary author Karen Armstrong explained in her book, *The Case For God*,

> ...God is One—but this term properly applies only to beings defined by numerical qualities. God is Trinity—but that does not mean that the three personae add up to any kind of triad that is familiar to us. God is nameless—yet He has a multitude of names. God must be Intelligible—and yet God is Unknowable.

Verbal descriptions always run the risk of giving us the impression that we can know what God is really like. We cannot. We can nurture a personal relationship with God within which we can gain insight for our own lives, and we can be comforted and buoyed by His love. We can know God in the sense of feeling His presence and having faith in His benevolent stewardship. But we cannot comprehend the real essence and complexity of His triune character nor the enormity of His power and capabilities. As thirteenth-century theologian Thomas Aquinas explained, "Man's utmost knowledge is to know that we do not know Him."[1]

Modern Bible translations usually refer to God by the titles "Lord" and "God" instead of the names Yahweh or Elohim at least in part as a result of a Jewish tradition beginning around the third century B.C. that regarded these personal names too sacred to utter. It is with an understanding of the limits of language in their pursuit of communion with God that monks sometimes opt for extended and complete silence.

Most Christians well understand that the extent of God's power and complexity far exceeds their own limits of comprehension, much less any description that could be articulated by means of human language. The full scope of a transcendent God's character and methods can only be hinted at, not definitively named or described.

As a result, Scripture can impart Biblical truth for the benefit of multiple depths of understanding, depending on the capacity and/or the propensity of the reader to grasp concepts of greater depth and complexity. The Bible has something to offer us as children as well as every other stage of life. For many, the simple truths found in the plain language of the texts are all that is needed, while for others, abstract truths of much greater profundity than that which can be seen on the surface can also be gleaned from the pages of Scripture. The influential Christian scholar of the early church, Origen, concluded that Scripture can be understood on three levels—"the literal sense, the moral application to the soul, and finally the allegorical or spiritual sense."[2] Until the Reformation, Origen's three levels of Scriptural meaning, along with a fourth eschatological dimension that was added by fourth-century monastic reformer John Cassian, were standard consideration in Biblical study.[3]

In his book *The Literal Meaning of Genesis*, acclaimed fourth-century theologian Augustine of Hippo expressed the idea of multiple depths of understanding Scripture when he asked of a particular passage if, in that instance, Scripture was speaking, "as is its habit, in a weak and simple style to the weak and simple, and yet all the same suggesting something more profound for those to grasp who have the capacity."[4] Despite his rather blunt manner of speaking, Augustine wisely expressed the importance of our not overlooking greater depths of meaning than that which can be deduced from merely a literal reading of many Scriptural passages.

Christians in particular are familiar with the Biblical use of allegory and parable because Jesus used those devices extensively as He communicated unfamiliar concepts to His followers. Indeed, the very foundational principle of Christianity is communicated to us by means of language that is not intended to be understood as literal. While Jesus is described as the "Son of God," we know that to believe God sired a son in the sense of a biological descendant, like Greek and Roman gods were once believed to have done, would be a violation of the monotheistic mandate of the First Commandment. We know that Jesus' appearance on Earth as the "Son of God" is to be understood as the earthly manifestation of the triune "God of Abraham" Himself—as only one side of the three-sided (triangularly revealed) deity that has been termed the Trinity. That is, just as a triangle exhibits three sides while remaining a single geometric figure, the deity that exhibits three characteristic "persons"—Father, Son, and Holy Spirit—remains the single entity that is God. As third-century theologian Tertullian put it, the Son is to God the Father just as a ray of sun is to the sun.

> When a ray of the sun is projected from the sun it is a portion of the whole sun; but the sun will be in the ray because it is a ray of the sun; the substance is not separated but extended. So from spirit comes spirit, and God from God as light is kindled from light...[5]

As the disciple John reported in his gospel, Jesus had explained, "I and the Father are one." (*John* 10:30) "Anyone who has seen me has seen the Father... Believe me when I say that I am in the Father and the Father is in me..." (*John* 14:9)

The word "Son" is used to describe Jesus because He was (and is) "begotten" by God the Father, *not created* like everything else in the physical universe. Though the Father, the Son, and the Holy Spirit can be thought of as the three "persons" of God, they cannot be understood to be separate and independent individuals in the same way that human fathers and sons are independent individuals.

Jesus would know best how to describe Himself to us, and since he spoke of the Father and of Himself as the Son, we can certainly expect that the terms He used provided the most appropriate descriptions available in human language. At the same time, however, we know that Jesus cannot be the carnal offspring of God because of the very first rule of Christianity, which holds that there can be only one God.

It is important to keep in mind the distinction between the Son as "begotten" and His "incarnation" as Jesus of Nazareth, when He became fully man while remaining fully God. The Son was not "begotten" at the moment of Mary's miraculous conception. He exists in conjunction with and because of the Father, but there can never have been a time before which the Son was begotten by the Father, because God in all aspects is eternal and immutable. He never grows, evolves, reproduces or otherwise changes His ultimate essence in any way.

The disciple John made reference to the eternal nature of the Son when he substituted "Word" for Son in his gospel: "The Word became flesh and made his dwelling among us." (*John* 1:14) That is, the same God's Word by which the world was created. "In the beginning was the Word, and the Word was with God, and the Word was God. He was with God in the beginning. Through Him all things were made." (*John* 1:1-3)

In his epistle to the Colossians (verses 1:15-17) the apostle Paul reaffirmed the description in John's Gospel of Jesus as eternal, as the earthly manifestation of God, and as the Creator, when he wrote: "He is the image of the invisible God, the first born over all creation. For by Him all things were created: things in heaven and on earth, visible and invisible...all things were created by Him and for Him. He is before all things, and in Him all things hold together." In *Hebrews* 1:3, Paul wrote that the Son is, in relation to the Father, "the exact representation of His being." In *1 Corinthians* 1:24, Paul described the Son as "the power of God and the wisdom of God."

Another term that has been interchanged with "Son" and "Word" is "Logos." Originating in Greek philosophy, Logos is defined in this context as "cosmic reason" and was believed to be the source of world order and intelligibility, or the "self-revealing thought and will of God."[6] (Jesus Christ, or "the Son," as Logos will be a very important concept to keep in mind as we explore an understanding of God as Creator in the following chapter.)

The difficult concept of the Trinity helps to remind us that the complete character of God is incomprehensible to human reason—that God is transcendent—and thus we might suppress idolatrous tendencies to reduce God to images of our own likeness and our own preferences. The complicated subject of the Trinity has filled numerous volumes and need not be fully explored here. It suffices to note that, though we may not usually think of it in this way, the phrase "Son of God" can be understood as more of a metaphorical than a literal description of that aspect of God that was manifested in the person of Jesus of Nazareth. Just as importantly, we should be keenly aware that greater depths of meaning are underlying many other Scriptural passages, perhaps most especially, some of the stories and the descriptions of God and His actions that are found in the Old Testament.

When the apostles Paul and Barnabas carried the Gospel to the Gentiles, a few of the Jewish Pharisee converts insisted that Gentiles could not become Christian until they had first converted to Judaism and were circumcised. The Council at Jerusalem (*Acts* 15) resolved the issue by, in effect, declaring that Christianity does not hinge on a strict adherence to the Law of Moses. Subsequently, the *Epistle of Barnabas*, a text that was part of Biblical Scripture in some of the early Christian churches, declared that the Law of Moses had never been meant to be taken literally. Early Christians followed the example of Jesus and the apostles in accepting the Old Testament as inspired Scripture. But they also found comfort and inspiration as they allegorized and spiritualized its ancient Hebrew stories and mandates.[7]

Second-century Gnostics, most notably a man named Marcion, pointed to differences between the descriptions of God in the Old

Testament and in the New Testament. Marcion claimed that the Old Testament God, who is characterized as jealous and often vengeful and who ordered genocidal war, was driven more by pride, bitterness, and anger than by love. Marcion insisted that the Old Testament God is incompatible with the Father of Jesus Christ who is described as merciful and filled with grace and love for all. The renowned Christian scholars of the early church, such as Origen in the second century, Tertullian in the third century, and Ambrose and Augustine in the fourth century, rebuffed Marcion's claims by expressing an understanding that great depths of meaning and Truth can be extracted from the coarseness of the Old Testament when allegorical and spiritual interpretations are applied.[8]

Periods of literalism came much later, beginning in the Dark and Middle Ages. Literalism was then bolstered, first around the seventeenth century as a reactionary response to the philosophical and scientific progress of the era that would be described as the "Age of Reason" or the "Age of Enlightenment," and then in the nineteenth and twentieth centuries as a response to modernity and the rise of liberal theology.

As the Dark Ages began, it was self-described "conservative" churchmen who flattened the Earth and brought the stars and the sky down low to be modeled after the tent that had been the Tabernacle of Moses.[9] Jesus' declaration that "the moon will not give its light" and "the stars will fall from the sky" at the end of time (*Matthew* 24:29) would seem perfectly plausible if the stars were small lights suspended from a crystalline vault that constituted the sky, as was supposed by ecclesiastical authorities. (It was believed that rain fell through little holes in the heavenly vault from a celestial cistern.) Today, of course, we know that Jesus' words, like much of Scripture, often utilized considerable poetic license. Early Christians knew it too. Like the Greek philosophers before him, Augustine (in the fourth century) well understood that the Earth is spherical, that the moon reflects the light of the sun, and that stars are like the sun but much farther away.[10]

Thus, the "official" Church's various revisions of the physical universe may have done more to undermine Christian credibility and to enable atheism than any other machination. Nevertheless, undeterred by the embarrassment that resulted from the Church's insistence that the sun orbits the Earth and other discredited ideas that had been based on erroneous literal interpretations of Scripture in the Middle Ages, an insistence on the plain text of the entire Bible persists among some Christians even today. This is likely due in part to the emergence of evangelicalism, but is more directly attributable to the advent of fundamentalism.

Beginning in England in the eighteenth century and then flourishing in the United States in the early nineteenth century, evangelicalism was primarily a reform movement. Furthering a trend that had begun with the Reformation, it sought to move away from a doctrinaire deferment to religious authority and tradition, while emphasizing a more individualistic and pragmatic approach to Christian living and a deep conviction in Biblical authority. Instead of being wholly reliant on a minister or a seminary education, small groups of believers could read the Bible together and instill virtue in their daily lives.[11] With it, however, came an unprecedented literalism in Scriptural interpretation.[12] For some, absolute Biblical authority meant that the plain text of Scripture was the whole Truth, as they simply overlooked many of the much deeper and more profound truths that can sometimes be gleaned from allegorical or spiritual interpretations.

The term "fundamentalism" was derived from a series of essays that were published in twelve volumes from 1910 to 1915 in the United States under the title *The Fundamentals: A Testimony To The Truth*. The essays were the culmination of a reactionary response to liberal, relativistic, and modernistic trends that were perceived by many to have been corrupting mainline Protestant denominations. They were intended to affirm the fundamental principles that their authors believed were essential to the Christian faith. Among these principles was the "inerrancy of the Scriptures," which many people took to mean the inerrancy of the literal text and phraseology of English Bible translations, dismissing most suggestions of greater depths of meaning through interpretation. (Ironically, several of the authors of *The Fundamentals*, including B.B. Warfield who wrote most forcefully of Biblical inerrancy, did not believe that Scripture needed to be understood as literal when it referred to nature, and they accepted evolution as a valid scientific explanation of God's creative activity.[13])

The modern idea that "each and every word in the Bible is literally true" of course overlooks the limits of the very "nuts and bolts" of how language works, particularly language that has been translated from one to another. In his popular book, *The Purpose Driven Life*, Dr. Rick Warren referenced fifteen different English language Bible translations. As Reverend Warren explained:

> First, no matter how wonderful a translation is, it has limitations. The Bible was originally written using 11,280 Hebrew, Aramaic, and Greek words, but the typical English translation uses only around 6,000 words. Obviously, nuances and shades of meaning can be missed, so it is helpful to compare translations.[14]

Even a comparison among various English translations will certainly sometimes fall short of conveying the real essence of the original text. The languages of ancient Hebrew, Aramaic, and Greek each had their own poetic patterns of expression that must be interpreted by modern human understanding as well as translated. For this reason, it may be useful to think of some Scriptural passages more *conceptually* than *literally*. That is, we ought to consider the general concept being conveyed without becoming bogged down with the literal meaning of a particular word or phrase (as we understand it in modern American English) when that literal meaning may seem to contradict other Scriptural passages.

Similarly, when we see Scriptural passages that seem to be contradicted by modern scientific discovery or which otherwise seem to defy our logical understanding of the world around us, we need not retreat from a conviction of the integrity of Scripture. Instead, we can endeavor to understand the literary methods employed in ancient texts and focus our attention on the limited purposes of those texts. This is particularly relevant to the ancient Hebrew texts of the Old Testament. In a footnote to his book entitled *Miracles*, C.S. Lewis offered an insightful way of understanding some of the Old Testament miracles and stories, suggesting that God's will and God's plan are revealed through evolving literary styles from the Old to the New Testament.

> ...just as, on the factual side, a long preparation culminates in God's becoming incarnate as Man, so, on the documentary side, the truth first appears in *mythical* form and then, by a long process of condensing or focusing, finally becomes incarnate as History. This involves the belief that Myth in general is not merely misunderstood history (as Euhemerus thought) nor diabolical illusion (as some of the Fathers thought) nor priestly lying (as the philosophers of the Enlightenment thought) but, at its best, a real though unfocused gleam of divine truth falling on human imagination. The Hebrews, like other people, had mythology: but as they were the chosen people so their mythology was the chosen mythology—the mythology chosen by God to be the vehicle of the earliest sacred truths, the first step in that process which ends in the New Testament where truth has become completely historical.

While history may become somewhat more explicitly focused and more literally described as we move through the Old Testament and into the New Testament, particularly in the book of *Acts*, the Scriptural use of symbolic and poetic language is of course continued throughout.

It is important to keep in mind how mythical stories were used in ancient cultures—not just in Hebrew culture, but in most all cultures—to impart important moral and societal truths. As Lewis suggested, the use of myth was neither a misunderstanding of reality nor an attempt to deceive. It was a literary device that could more effectively communicate complex ideas or universal moral truths.

In ancient cultures there were two distinct methods of pedagogic communication. *Mythos* and *logos*, as the Greeks called them, were both considered essential paths to knowledge, each with its own sphere of competence. *Logos* (lower case *l* meaning "reason," as opposed to upper case *L* meaning the "cosmic" or "divine reason" later associated with Jesus) was a pragmatic mode of thinking that enabled people to understand and cope with physical reality. *Mythos*, on the other hand, enabled people to, very often through song and symbolism, grasp more vague or abstract concepts, moral truths, and ultimately, to find meaning and purpose in life.[15] Complex realities or moral truths could be conveyed by the lessons imparted by mythical past occurrences. As historic stories were passed orally from generation to generation, what had actually happened was less important than what could be learned from the ultimate meaning of the events described.[16]

In the book of *Genesis* we find two such stories that, on the surface, appear to be intended to describe the physical events surrounding the creation of the universe and the human beings and other creatures that inhabit the Earth.[17] Though the suggestion is controversial, it appears that the two stories—one told in verses 1:1 through 2:3, and the other told in verses 2:4 through 2:25—came from different sources. It appears so because the two stories were written in very different styles, because God was referred to by different names ("Elohim" in the first story and "Yahweh" in the second), and because God behaved in very different ways. Most telling is that the two stories describe glaringly contradictory chronologies of events. Atheists tend to latch onto these discrepancies, among others, in their efforts to assail the veracity of Scripture, but in doing so they simply misunderstand the style and the point of the narrative.

There are at least a couple of explanations for why the two creation stories are so different. Though each is concerned with judgments of the extent of Mosaic authorship, neither requires a compromise of Biblical integrity.

Tradition holds that Moses was the author of the *Pentateuch* (the first five books of the Bible), also known as the Torah. Many Biblical scholars over the last three centuries, however, have concluded that it was the work of at least four sources and that the texts were written and combined after Moses' death. This idea began to take hold at the end of the eighteenth century and was then more fully developed in the nineteenth century among a group of German Bible scholars who utilized a new way of analyzing ancient texts. Using what is called a "historical-critical" methodology that, among other things, employed additional texts of the same or adjacent time periods for contextual comparisons, these scholars concluded that the *Pentateuch* was a compilation of the writings (or "documents") of at least four sources.

Linguists concluded that the language of the entire *Pentateuch* reflects the dialectic style of Hebrew in the first millennium B.C., long after the life of Moses.[18] And of course it was written in third person past tense. Included in these analyses, were comparisons of what are called "doublets" and "triplets" in the text, where the same events are described two or three times, often in quite different ways and sometimes with conflicting accounts, such as in the case of the two creation stories. Sometimes called "German higher criticism," this method of Scriptural analysis was not introduced to the general public until seven Anglican clergymen included its findings, often called the "Documentary Hypothesis," in their English publication of *Essays and Reviews* in 1860, the year after the original publication of Darwin's *On the Origin of Species*.

Since Jesus and several New Testament authors, as well as the Old Testament itself, made reference to Mosaic authorship of the Torah, among other reasons, many conservative evangelical Christians and others vehemently reject the idea of multiple authorship. But perhaps we need not choose between two, seemingly opposing, possibilities. Given the way ancient Scripture was handed down over many years and through many generations, we can easily imagine that perhaps both are actually true.

Though the Law of Moses was originally a written account of God's revelation to Moses as described in Scripture, it would then have been hand copied and, most commonly, orally transmitted through many generations among long separated populations of Jews. Of course from the ninth century through the seventh century B.C., the Israelites resided in two separate kingdoms—the Kingdom of Judah, with Jerusalem as its capital, and the larger and more prosperous Kingdom of Israel that bordered the Mediterranean Sea to the north. Then there was the Babylonian exile from the sixth century into the fifth century B.C., with groups of Israelites returning during three separate time periods. Naturally, as the traditions of Moses were orally handed down over many generations among separate populations who were also being influenced by the other traditions of the regions in which they resided, they could easily have taken on variously distinguishable characteristics. With this in mind, we can imagine that while the written accounts found in Scripture may have been compiled from multiple written sources, much of the history described and, even more importantly, the fundamental principles conveyed, remain the inherited sacred Law of Moses.

Scripture itself tells us that additions were made to the *Pentateuch* after Moses' death. For example, the book of *Joshua* (verses 14:25-26) tells us that Joshua added decrees and laws to the Book of the Law of God. *Deuteronomy* 34, which describes Moses' death, would also, naturally have been written by someone other than Moses.

Even if we set aside the Documentary Hypothesis, Moses himself would certainly have used several outside sources. In addition to his various mentors, such as his father-in-law Jethro as described in *Exodus* 18:17-26, Moses would likely have also drawn upon a number of ancient oral traditions. While much of the *Pentateuch* describes events that occurred during Moses' lifetime, *Genesis* in particular describes events that occurred long before his life. Scripture does not tell us precisely how each and every detail of the book of *Genesis* was revealed to him.

However we might conceptualize it, multiple authorship of the *Pentateuch* is not essential to the point being made here, so we can certainly reject it if we prefer. But it may help us to see why there are two very different creation stories and why we need not be troubled by their inconsistencies.

Since the exact identities of the four sources proposed by the Documentary Hypothesis were unknown, they were assigned the names "J," "E," "D," and "P." The "J" source was so named because that source used the personal name for God, Yahweh (the German equivalent being "Jahweh"), as was the practice in the southern Kingdom of Judah around the 900s B.C. The "E" source used the name "Elohim" when speaking of God, as was more commonly done in the northern Kingdom of Israel. The text attributed to the "E" source is thought to have been written about a hundred years after that of the "J" source. The designation "D" is for "Deuteronomists," who were a group of reformers in Jerusalem around 600 B.C. The "P" source, for Priestly Code, is believed to have been a group of priests during and shortly after the Babylonian exile, around 500 B.C. It is thought that the "J" and "E" narratives were combined around 750 B.C., and the "D" and the "P" texts were then added to the "JE" narrative sometime around 400 B.C.

It is believed that the creation story described in *Genesis* 2 was a "J" narrative from around the tenth century B.C., while the creation story told in *Genesis* 1 originated some 500 years later from the "P" source (developed during or shortly after the Jews' Babylonian captivity). The editors who compiled these and the other stories contained in *Genesis* simply had no reason to eliminate any apparent discrepancies in the two accounts of creation because their purpose had nothing to do with a scientific documentation of natural history. Instead, they tell us something that, for believers, is much more important. They tell us about God's sovereignty and about our relationship and our responsibility to Him.

The creation stories along with other stories in *Genesis* tell us that there is only one God, that He is the sole Creator of the universe, that He had a purpose for His creation, that the world is not autonomous from its Creator, and that the world is not transcendental (of the same stuff as God). The stories affirm that the world has been set in motion by God and is sustained only at the behest of God's will, but is nevertheless independent of God's direct control.[19] (It is worth noting that, in *Genesis* 1 [unlike *Genesis* 2] God's acts of creation are indirect. God simply allows creation to proceed as He commands: "Let..." certain things happen. In *Genesis* 2, of course, man is the product of the "dust of the ground," just as science has shown.)

Of course, the book of *Genesis* tells us even much more than that. Indeed, it is unquestionably the most important book of the Bible, since all that follows is based on the foundation that it establishes. Theologians and Biblical scholars have written countless volumes that purport to explain its meaning and lessons. We need not explore all of the many facets of the book or their various interpretations and implications here. It suffices to note that the fact that the creation stories in *Genesis* do not fully comport with what we now know about physics, cosmology, geology, and biological evolution does absolutely nothing to compromise the integrity of Biblical truth.

2

God's Creation

As we reflect upon the universe that we see around us—from its galaxies, solar systems, suns and planets, to oceans, continents, mountains, rivers, and especially its complex living organisms—it seems most apparent that our world was purposefully designed. The way many complex structures and systems in the natural world work in harmony to serve functions that provide for the function of other structures and systems suggests that they were deliberately designed and constructed in much the same way we human beings engineer structures and systems for our own benefit. With this in mind, in his 1802 treatise entitled *Natural Theology—or Evidences of the Existence and Attributes of the Deity Collected from the Appearances of Nature*, theologian William Paley offered the analogy of man-made objects that had been designed and manufactured in arguing that complex structures in nature provide compelling evidence of a supernatural Intelligent Designer. Paley began his monograph with the now famous passage:

> In crossing a heath, suppose I pitched my foot against a stone, and were asked how the stone came to be there; I might possibly answer, that, for anything I knew to the contrary, it had lain there for ever: nor would it perhaps be very easy to show the absurdity of this answer. But suppose I had found a *watch* upon the ground, and it should be inquired how the watch happened to be in that place, I should hardly think of the answer which I had before given, that for anything I knew, the watch might have always been there. Yet why should not the answer serve

for the watch as well as for the stone? Why is it not admissible in the second case as in the first? For this reason, and for no other, namely that, when we come to inspect the watch, we perceive—what we could not discover in the stone—that its several parts are framed and put together for a purpose. ...the inference, we think, is inevitable; that the watch must have had a maker.[1]

The *inference* clearly established with the example of the watch, Paley went on to cite specific examples of structures in nature that he believed were analogous to man-made objects. For example, "there is *precisely the same proof* that the eye was made for vision as there is that the telescope was made for assisting it. ...the reasoning is as clear and certain in the one case as in the other."

Paley was accused of plagiarizing the watch analogy from a follower of the renowned French mathematician and philosopher Rene' Descartes named Bernard Nieuwentyt, but Paley cited Nieuwentyt's work on several occasions as he developed a more detailed and more compelling version of the argument. Indeed, the watch analogy had been used by a number of philosophers before Paley and he addressed many of the objections that had previously been proffered as well as others that he anticipated.[2] Paley was evidently unaware, however, of a similar analysis that had been put forth by the Scottish philosopher David Hume some two decades earlier.

In his *Dialogues Concerning Natural Religion*, published in 1779, Hume's interlocutor Cleanthes offered a concise description of what has come to be known as the "argument from design" or the "design argument" for the existence of God.

Look around the world: contemplate the whole and every part of it: You will find it to be nothing but one great machine, subdivided into an infinite number of lesser machines, which again admit of subdivisions to a degree beyond what human senses and faculties can trace and explain. All these various machines, and even their most minute parts, are adjusted to each other with an accuracy which ravishes into admiration all men who have ever contemplated them. The curious adapting of means to ends, throughout all nature, resembles exactly, though it much exceeds, the productions of human contrivance; of human designs, thought, wisdom, and intelligence. Since, therefore, the effects resemble each other, we are led to infer, by the rules of analogy, that the causes also resemble; and that the Author of Nature is somewhat similar to the mind of man, though possessed of much larger faculties, proportioned to the grandeur of the work which he has executed. By this argument *é posteriori*, and by this argument alone, do we prove at once the existence of a Deity, and his similarity to human mind and intelligence.

The reason we might assume that Paley had not seen Hume's discussion of the subject is because he made no overt attempt to address Hume's objections. As it happened, Hume had put forth the "argument from design" simply so that he could then knock it down.

Hume argued that analogies between man-made objects or systems and those found in nature are not very reliable because natural objects and phenomena are too dissimilar to human artifacts—self-sustaining versus limited existence, changing or evolving versus fixed until decay, living versus non-living, etc. He quipped that the cosmos more closely resembled a living organism than a man-made machine.[3]

Hume's most forceful objections, however, addressed what such an argument ultimately says about God. The imperfections and the evils that can be seen in nature can imply an imperfect Designer. Most objectionable is that the design argument evokes an anthropomorphic conception of God—a conception of God employing the attributes of man—as Watchmaker and Craftsman. Such a conception, some have argued, is idolatry. Hume wrote:

But as all perfection is entirely relative, we ought never to imagine, that we comprehend the attributes of this divine Being, or to suppose, that his perfections have any analogy or likeness to the perfections of a human creature.

Hume also recognized the affronts to monotheism. Since man-made objects are the product of any number of designers, nature's complexities too could have been authored by any number of Designers. More importantly, if we were to concede validity of the design argument—the argument that organized complexities in nature can exist only if they have been directly engineered by a supernatural Intelligent Agency—then the Intelligent Agency itself (God) would require a similar explanation. God's existence could then only be accounted for by a separate, even more capable Intelligent Agency, and that Creator would of course require its own Creator, and on and on.

Hume argued that there are alternative explanations that can account for complexities in nature. Indeed, since we can identify numerous organized structures that are the result of natural causes, even something as simple as a rainbow, then that same possibility exists for all other structures in nature. This does not mean that all structures in nature must be the result of natural causes, but it does remove any legitimate claim that complex structures in nature are *necessarily* suggestive of a direct Intelligent Agency. The design argument for the existence of God simply cannot stand up to logical analysis.

Nevertheless, it represents a way of perceiving the world that has persisted throughout human history. The many gods of Egyptian, Greek, Roman, Incan, Mayan, and other cultures were created mostly as explanations for natural phenomena. Zeus was responsible for lightning and thunder, Atlas was responsible for holding up the Earth and the sky, and Poseidon presided over the seas, just as scores of other gods had their duties and proclivities. Of course as human knowledge of the natural world grew, the usefulness of each of these gods eventually faded.

The demise of those gods who became obsolete as a result of the expansion of human knowledge points to an error that has also plagued Christianity for centuries. That is, a tendency among some Christians to proclaim God's *supernatural* handiwork in relation to phenomena that are simply not yet understood, only to be forced into embarrassing retractions when such phenomena are ultimately determined by scientific discovery to be natural.

We can imagine numerous occasions throughout history when unexplained natural phenomena might have been cited as supernatural evidence of God's existence and God's providence. The beauty and order of a rainbow must have seemed an unquestionably supernatural sign of God's presence, particularly as it usually accompanies a rain shower, a seemingly obvious life-sustaining blessing from God. For some people, after having believed that it was a supernatural event, the discovery that a rainbow is merely the refraction of sunlight as it passes through water droplets in the atmosphere—the emergence of an orderly structure through a wholly natural process—could seem to diminish the significance of God. For others, it might even imply the absence of any God at all.

Such is the hazard of a "God of the gaps." Drawing on the writings of nineteenth-century evangelist Henry Drummond and twentieth-century theologian Dietrich Bonhoeffer, the Methodist lay-preacher Charles A. Coulson coined the term "God of the gaps" in his 1955 book, *Science and Christian Belief*. Coulson used the term as a dismissive description of that God whom many people imagine fills gaps in our knowledge of the natural world—gaps that, Coulson cautioned, "have the unpreventable habit of shrinking."

Just as indiscriminate preferences for literal interpretations of Scripture ultimately condemn Christianity to a persistent posture of retreat, relying on gaps in our knowledge of the physical universe to affirm a belief in God can provide only a tentative foundation for faith in God. And again, filling gaps in our knowledge of nature's properties and processes with explanations of God the Artisan, God the Craftsman, or God the Tinkerer requires an idolatrous conception of God based on the trades of men.

Nevertheless, there are those who cling to gaps in human understanding to prop up their faith in God even today. Gaps in the fossil record are most often cited as either evidence of God's direct involvement in evolutionary processes or even "proof" of the fallacy of evolutionary science altogether—gaps that are regularly being filled by new discoveries. The newly established so-called "Intelligent Design theory" is based primarily on the assumption that gaps in our know-ledge of natural processes are the best evidence that they are the direct creation of an "Intelligent Designer"—gaps that, again, have an "un-preventable habit of shrinking." (This and other difficulties with Intel-ligent Design theory are discussed at greater length in Chapter 10.)

Unquestionably, appearances of design can be seen throughout the visible universe. As we will see throughout this book, particularly in Chapter 6, much of what appears to have been designed has been discovered to be the result of natural processes. The parameters and the propensities of those natural processes are, of course, prescribed by the laws of physics. We are then left to wonder how the laws of physics came to be such that they could produce the kind of universe that we see around us—the kind of universe within which intelligent creatures could evolve to wonder about the universe and to know God as its Creator. Such ponderings are the purview of the "anthropic cosmo-logical principle," a term coined in the latter part of the twentieth century.

The anthropic principle can be roughly defined by the idea that our understanding of the character of the universe is contingent upon its favorability to human life. This is because, if the universe were other than the way we find it, then we would not be here to reach any understanding about it at all.

More precise definitions of the principle are elusive since its use tends to vary among those scientists and philosophers who make reference to it. In that regard, Australian theoretical physicist Brandon Carter described two variants of the principle, which he termed the

Weak Anthropic Principle (WAP) and the Strong Anthropic Principle (SAP). Perhaps most closely resembling the original concept, WAP essentially restates one of the most fundamental principles of scientific research. That is, it is crucial to take into account the limitations of one's measuring apparatus (in this case, the limited perspective of the observing intelligent creatures) when interpreting one's observations.[4] The SAP, on the other hand, suggests a teleological force. That is, those observant intelligent creatures "must play a key role in (if not be the goal of) the evolution of the universe."[5] As a result, the Strong Anthropic Principle is the one that has become popularly cited by believers who wish to proffer scientific evidence for the existence of God as Designer and Creator of the universe. And indeed there is a great deal of physical evidence that appears to support this idea.

Physicists and cosmologists have observed that several of the quantitative values attributable to the laws of physics within our universe appear to have been "precisely tuned" to allow for a universe within which intelligent life could emerge. If the values attributable to the strength of any one of the four known forces in the universe (i.e. gravity, electromagnetism, and the strong and weak nuclear forces), for example, were only very slightly different, the universe could not have produced life as we know it. If the strength of gravity had been slightly greater, it would have slowed the expansion of the universe and, as theoretical physicist Stephen Hawking put it, "If the rate of expansion one second after the big bang had been smaller by even one part in a hundred-thousand-million-million, the universe would have recollapsed [sic] before it ever reached its present size."[6] It would have collapsed long before life could have emerged. On the other hand, if the force of gravity was slightly weaker, the particles of matter produced by the Big Bang and its subsequent processes could not have coalesced into galaxies, stars, planets, and ultimately, human beings.[7]

Similarly, if the values of several other fundamental constants were different, life could not exist. The author of *Finding Darwin's God*, Kenneth R. Miller explained:

If the strong nuclear force were just a little weaker, no elements other than hydrogen would have been formed following the big bang. If it were just a little stronger, all of the hydrogen in the universe would be gone by now, converted to helium and heavier elements. Without hydrogen, no sun, no stars, no water.

If another fundamental force, electromagnetism, were just a little stronger, electrons would be so tightly bound to atoms that the formation of chemical compounds would be impossible. A little weaker, and atoms would disintegrate at room temperature. If the resonance level of electrons in the carbon atom were just four percent lower, carbon atoms themselves would never have formed in the interiors of stars. No carbon, no life as we understand it.[8]

Of course there are a multitude of variables that, had any one of them been different, would have rendered the universe unsuitable for life. For instance, the universe might have been only one or two-dimensional. Or it might have been three-dimensional, but without time, leaving it completely static and non-evolving. Contemplation of the nearly infinite number of scenarios by which we would not exist within the known universe or even without a universe at all simply leads us back to the age-old and seemingly unanswerable question of how we came to be here. At the same time, however, if our visible universe is the only universe in existence, when we consider the multitude of variables that have come together and the minute tolerances of numerous key values within the laws of physics that have all cooperated in creating a suitable infrastructure for the evolution of life on Earth, it seems apparent that a force, separate from and outside of our physical universe, has specifically designed our world in a way that would provide for the emergence and the development of intelligent life.

Before we declare proof of the Creator in the findings of cosmology and physics, however, we should always keep in mind that God-fearing man who believed that the order and the beauty of a rainbow provided supernatural proof of God's existence. It should not go unnoted that there are plausible alternatives to the idea that our universe was specifically designed for the purpose of producing life. None of these alternatives, however, do anything to exclude the possibility of God as the ultimate Creator.

For example, we cannot see the edge of our universe. We do not know if it is or is not spatially infinite. It is possible that there are a great many or even an infinite number of regions within the three dimensional universe that we perceive where the laws of physics are different from what we experience. In addition, we do not fully understand the spatial nature of our universe close to home. Scientists working in the realm of quantum physics (the tiniest bits of matter and energy) have discovered that our world is far more complex than is readily apparent. Among the things that have been detected is evidence of at least eleven additional spatial dimensions that we do not normally perceive. If it turns out that there are an infinite number of dimensions, which is entirely possible, then it could also be possible that our universe is spatially infinite even within the length of our arms. Of course, there is also the possibility that our physical universe is not the only universe in existence. There are several so-called "multiverse" hypotheses currently being considered and tested.

If there is an infinite amount of space and an infinite number of regions within our physical universe, each possessing different laws of physics, or if there are an infinite number of dimensions within our universe, or if there are an infinite number of physical universes, each with different laws of physics, not only would a universe like the one we experience be probable, perhaps it would be inevitable. Most relevant to this discussion, however, is that we need not and indeed we cannot exclude the possibility that such inevitability is merely the result of God's directive.

Of course we should not overlook the very essence of the original anthropic principle itself, which recognizes that our perception of the issue is skewed by our personal interest in the matter. For example, if any one of the pertinent cosmological values had been slightly different, the outcome would have been a universe that cannot sustain life as we know it, but that outcome is no less improbable than the one with which we are familiar. In fact, there could have been an infinite number of possible outcomes for the universe, and each one would be equally improbable. The reason that a universe capable of sustaining human life seems to us such a very very lucky outcome is simply because we place such great value in that particular outcome. Only a God capable of producing all outcomes could *objectively* value one over another.

Even with all of those cosmological values firmly in place that have resulted in our sort of universe—a universe capable of producing and sustaining life—we can still imagine that intelligent creatures capable of pondering such questions might not have evolved but for the slimmest of chances. Since natural evolutionary processes and evolutionary outcomes are driven, in part, by somewhat random events, the emergence of human beings can quite easily be attributed to a mere accident of nature. We can point to innumerable contingencies in the history of natural events that, had any one of them resulted in only a very slightly different outcome, we would not be here. If we were to simply "rerun the tape of life," as evolutionary scientist and Harvard University professor Stephen J. Gould argued in his book *Wonderful Life*, through the colossal chain of events occurring over the course of three and a half billion years by which life has evolved from simple organic chemistry to amebas, to invertebrates, to fishes, to amphibians, to reptiles, to mammals, and ultimately to human beings, then the world would undoubtedly be very different. Among its features, Gould proclaimed, would almost certainly be an absence of intelligent beings. Gould's assertion was that human beings are merely the result of an enormously long line of accidental occurrences, and had any one event in that long series of occurrences happened differently, then all subsequent events would certainly have followed a path to a starkly different ultimate outcome.

At the same time, however, we can point to several indications that the Earth's natural environmental infrastructure encompasses, not only the possibility, but also a *propensity* to produce certain kinds of plant and animal forms. One such indicator is provided by the many instances of "convergent" evolution. Discussed at greater length in the following chapters, convergent evolution is where sometimes strikingly similar organisms are the product of lineages that have evolved completely independently of each other in separate but comparable ecological environments. The similarities between some marsupial and placental mammals, for example, provide strong evidence that environmental infrastructures—deserts, swamps, grasslands, for example—affect the forms of their living inhabitants. Just as specific cosmological constants within the laws of physics allow for the evolution of a universe that is capable of sustaining life, the natural environments within which organisms evolve dictate certain parameters in evolutionary development.

In a rebuttal to Professor Gould, Cambridge University evolutionary palaeobiologist Dr. Simon Conway Morris has pointed to the ubiquity of convergent evolution around the world. In his book, *The Crucible of Creation*, the professor wrote:

> What we are interested in is not the origin, destiny, or fate of a particular lineage, but the likelihood of the emergence of a particular property, say consciousness. Here the reality of convergence suggests that the tape of life, to use Gould's metaphor, can be run as many times as we like and in principle intelligence will surely emerge.[9]

Along with professors Miller and Conway Morris, the scientists associated with the BioLogos Foundation—most notably Francis S. Collins, Karl Giberson, and Darrel R. Falk—have also emphasized the importance of seeing the apparently "fine-tuned" properties of the universe and the resulting convergences of evolutionary processes as evidence of God's creative work. This is indeed an important consideration—a way in which we can envision God's creative order. But, as we have seen, we must be wary of emphatically declaring that the properties of the universe are "scientific proof" of God or of His work.

The assertions of evolutionists regarding the contingencies of happenstance have long been of keen interest to Christians because these kinds of assertions seem to take God out of the equation in the creation of life. This apparent denial of God has induced some, in defense of Christianity, to deny the legitimate findings of science. Yet, it is clear that those who deny the existence of God based on what we know about cosmology and evolution, as well as those who deny the findings of science in their defense of Christianity, tend to, once again, confuse the God of Abraham with a simplistic "God of the gaps." Both appear to underestimate the transcendent character and the immeasurable capabilities of God.

Any discussion of the probability of a universe that can sustain life or the multitude of contingencies encountered over the course of biological evolutionary history, and thus, the probability of the emergence of intelligent life in the natural world, ultimately have no bearing on an understanding of God as Creator of the universe. This is because God is unencumbered by the constraints of space and time. The essential reality is this: *A God that is outside of space and time is not constrained by any sequential probabilities that can be calculated in our world.* Such a God already knows the beginning, the end, and all of the many contingencies that may arise in between. God is omniscient and He is omnipotent. No method of creation is beyond His capabilities. And no multitude of variable contingencies can result in any outcome that would be a surprise to Him.

We cannot fully know God or His methods, but we can be aware of certain characteristics that help us to reconcile a conviction of God's providence with the natural processes that we can see in the world. Though Augustine is popularly credited with being the first Christian theologian to conclude that God is outside of time, he almost certainly adopted the idea from Plato, who discussed just such a concept in his dialogues, *Parmenides* and *Timaeus*. Nevertheless, Augustine was on firm Scriptural ground in placing God outside of space and time. The Bible does not specifically tell us so, but its description of God as immutable and eternal leaves no other possibility. Also, there are a number of Scriptural passages that speak of God "before time began," and God being outside of time helps to explain how the Biblical prophets' visions of the future could have been revealed to them.

Of course language that speaks of "before" or "outside" of space and time is inadequate. The word "before" suggests a sequence of time, whereas God is not subject to any sequential parameters. The word "outside" suggests a particular location, whereas God is ubiquitous. Though it has its limitations too, the word "transcendent" is generally considered a more apt description of God's relationship to our world. Yet, for many, the notion of "outside" may be easier to visualize. Space and time are merely worldly characteristics of God's creation of the physical universe. God certainly could not be constrained by His own creation.

Since He is outside of time, each and every moment of time in human history and indeed all the history of our physical universe—past, present, and future—occurs simultaneously from the perspective of God. So, while from our perspective it was about 10 to 20 billion years after the initial creation of our visible universe, about 4.6 billion years after the formation of the Earth, and about 3.7 billion years after life first appeared on Earth that man eventually gained the capacity to reason and was thus created in the image of God, from the perspective of God it was instantaneous (in a sense)—more precisely, it simply was and is.

Scripture suggests that it should be no surprise that we cannot find definitive "proof" of the existence of God by a scientific examination of the natural world. As Jesus explained to His disciple "doubting" Thomas, "blessed are those who have not seen and yet have believed." (*John* 20:29) In his first epistle to the Corinthians, the apostle Paul told the parishioners that he would not use persuasive words "so that [their] faith might not rest on men's wisdom, but on God's power." He described God's "secret wisdom" that is intentionally "hidden" from all but those who receive it through the Spirit. (1 *Corinthians* 2:5-13) The sixteenth-century reformer Martin Luther often wrote of the "masks of God" by which God performs His work and makes Himself known spiritually, while remaining hidden from our direct observation.[10]

There are a number of ways in which God might work to affect the course of nature without our detection. For example, the Director of The Center for Theology and the Natural Sciences, Robert John Russell, and others have pointed to the "ontological indeterminacy" that is inherent in quantum physics, as articulated by the Heisenberg uncertainty principle. Dr. Russell noted that what appear to us to be random sub-atomic processes provide an opening in nature for God to act without any apparent violation of the laws of physics. In this way God could control the raw materials (gene mutation) upon which evolutionary natural selection operates. Citing the work of Thomas Tracy and others, Dr. Russell concluded:

Quantum mechanics allows us to think of special divine action as the 'providential determination of otherwise undetermined events.' Moreover, though pervasive in its effects on the world's structure, God's action will remain hidden within that structure. God's action will take the form of realizing one of several potentials in the quantum system, not of manipulating sub-atomic particles as a quasi-physical force. Meanwhile we are still free to think in terms of divine action at other levels of nature, including God's interaction with humanity and God's primary act of creating and sustaining the world.[11]

How God's providence and His will may be recognized in the processes of the natural world without any direct "proof" can perhaps be illustrated by an essential component of Christian living. Most Christians are fully aware that an answer to prayer need not be miraculous (supernatural), and that it is never possible to prove empirically that a given, non-miraculous event was or was not an answer to prayer. In fact, according to C.S. Lewis, the impossibility of empirical proof in such cases is a spiritual necessity, since knowing that a particular event had been directly caused by one's own prayer could easily "turn the head and corrupt the heart."[12] Instead, the Christian is to believe that all events are answers to prayer in the sense that, whether granted or refused, prayers are always heard and taken into account and woven into the chain of (usually natural) events that constitute the whole of God's will. This does not mean that God does not answer the prayers of individuals. It simply means that it is not for us to *know and direct* God's will. Rather, we are to have *faith* in His benevolent stewardship.

When we consider that God transcends space and time, we come to realize that an answer to prayer can be integrated into the natural course of the universe from its very beginning. As C.S. Lewis pointed out, there is no reason that we cannot pray to affect past occurrences. (If God were to grant our wishes in such cases we would never know it, of course.) Similarly, God could affect the course of nature through direct action in any number of ways and at any time over the course of the history of the universe. As discussed in the following chapter, we know that God does not directly dictate every-thing that happens in the world because of the evil that we can see within it. But this does not nullify God's ultimate providence or His participation in our lives and in the world's evolving creation. Though the natural processes that we can detect and evaluate may appear to be godless and purposeless from a scientific perspective, there can be no basis to conclude that their outcomes are the least bit unexpected or purposeless to God.

We can envision any number of ways in which God might direct the course of nature, but it seems quite clear that God has no intention of our discovering them. God's direct action, whether in affecting the course of nature or in affecting the course of each of our lives, is not to be conquered and understood by scientific analysis, but is to be discerned through *faith*—faith in Jesus Christ as the Son, the

Logos, the Creator of the universe and the source of its continuing rational order.

It is solely through the faithful belief in God's appearance on Earth as Jesus of Nazareth that the Christian can know God and have faithful knowledge of His purpose for individual lives and for all of creation. And it is through this understanding—this spiritual insight—that the believer can attribute the beauty and the order of nature to the work of God's "invisible qualities" (*Romans* 1:20). In that sense, of course, nature can shout the existence of God.

However we might declare a line between what Thomas Aquinas called "first cause" (supernatural creation) and subsequent natural processes, we clearly need not conceded that a natural environment which can support the spontaneous emergence of life and the systematic evolutionary development of complex organisms would require an ideological Naturalism or Materialism that excludes a living God. Just as we can reason that an answer to prayer through God's will can be realized through natural events, we can reason that God's creation can be realized through natural processes. As thirteenth-century Franciscan theologian Bonaventure aptly noted, the "Book of Nature," much like Scripture, has a spiritual as well as a literal meaning, with the beauty and order of nature elegantly evoking its spiritual essence.[13] Even if we cannot prove the handiwork or the existence of God through scientific analysis—even if all we can find are natural processes that account for the emergence and the evolution of living organisms—we certainly need not retreat from a conviction of God's providence and our marvel at the glory of God's creation.

3

God's Providence

There are a great many people who simply cannot abide by the notion that happenstance could play such a major role in the development of life on Earth as has been proclaimed by evolutionary theory—that mere chance and unintelligent forces, rather than the direct Hand of God, could determine the various characteristics of the many species of living organisms, especially our own. Yet, when we consider the central Christian doctrine concerning the free will of individual human souls, we find that the indeterminate processes that are associated with evolutionary natural selection are not only consistent with, but perhaps even essential to the necessary relationship between God and the physical universe that could provide the basis for our free will, and thus, our ability to choose Him. Naturally, if we did not live in a world like the one in which we do—one replete with contingency—then we would be unable to receive God's blessing as a result of confessing Jesus as our Savior.

As we look around we find that, in many ways, the world in which we live seems an ungodly place. It is filled with so much imperfection and so many hazardous circumstances and contingencies. We are subject to household, industrial, and all-manner of injurious accidents. We are subject to congenital abnormalities and a multitude of addictions and diseases. We are very often confronted with just plain "bad luck" in our personal aspirations, our careers, our relationships, and simple everyday living. Naturally, when we see the indiscriminate destruction of major natural disasters, or when we see children or otherwise clearly innocent people suffer from congenital deformity or other birth defects, accidents or disease, the randomness of these hazards seems most apparent. We are also, of course, sometimes subjected to the evil deeds of other people. One might be inclined to ask how a respectable God could have created such a world. How could a just God have created a world that is filled with so much evil?

Western Christianity teaches us that our suffering and our mortality are not the creation of God, but are the result of humankind's fall from grace—the result of the "original sin" of human beings.[1] Before we examine the concept and the implications of that original sin, however, let us first consider the character of the universe within which an "original sin" could have occurred in the first place. In at least one important way, it would be much like the one we find ourselves in today, with all of its many hazards and within which we are told that we can expect to prosper from a relationship with a living God. It would be a universe marked by contingency.

Even if we set aside, for now, the concept of "original sin," Christianity offers an explanation for the imperfection and the apparent randomness that we see in our world. It is an explanation that accompanies an account of God's purpose for the creation of the physical universe as well as an explanation of the evil deeds of human beings and fallen angels. And we may be heartened to know that Christianity's explanation is fully consistent with the ever-changing and evolving world that we see around us.

An important distinction between Pantheism and Christianity is the relationship between God and the physical universe. While Pantheism holds that the physical universe is a "part of" or "one with" God, Christianity declares that the physical universe is separate and apart from God. It is His creation, not simply a part of Him. At the same time, however, the physical universe and all that it contains and all that happens within it remain the providence of God. So then the question remains, how can we reconcile the idea of a living God—a benevolent God, an omnipotent God, a providential God—with a world that includes so much evil, along with random events and unintelligent forces such as those that are associated with biological evolution?

Christianity's answer is that God's plan requires the free will of human beings. It requires a universe much like the one in which we find ourselves—a universe that, even though its existence may be maintained only at the behest of God's will, is nevertheless independent of God's direct control. It requires a universe that is not static—a universe within which free will can be duly exercised, and where the resulting choices will have consequences. In order for our choices to have consequences, we must live in a universe within which those choices, along with all other events, will produce contingent effects— inevitably, a universe that is constantly changing, evolving.

When we consider that God is outside of (transcends) time, we know that the outcomes of the souls of individuals as well as the whole of humankind are known to Him, and that His will has been, is, and will be done. (That is, the creation of the ultimate good and happiness, as manifested by love and by our worship of Him.) God's eternal knowledge and God's providence, however, do not preclude random processes and random effects within a creation continually called into existence by His will.

In his *Shorter Summa*, Thomas Aquinas separated what he termed "first cause" and "secondary causes." God is said to be the first cause because God created the physical universe from nothing. Yet, within that creation, things can happen as a result of secondary causes. Saint Thomas explained:

> Although all events, even the most trifling, are disposed (as we have shown) according to God's plan, there is nothing to prevent some things from happening by chance or accident. An occurrence may be accidental or fortuitous with respect to a lower cause when an effect not intended is brought about, and yet not be accidental or fortuitous with respect to a higher cause...[2]

In reference to how so much of what occurs in our world is contingent upon other events as the world evolves while serving the purposes of God's plan and His will, Saint Thomas continued:

> The efficaciousness of the divine will demands not only that what God wishes will happen, but that it will happen in the way

that He wishes. But He wills that some things should happen necessarily and that other things should happen contingently; both are required for the perfection of the universe.[3]

And the latter is required for the existence of the free will of human beings, which of course is at the heart of God's plan.

An evolving universe where events, circumstances, and our choices will produce contingent effects is not only required for the full exercise of our free will. Such a universe is also necessary if supernatural intervention by a living God is to have any relevance or any continuing effect on the world. As Dr. Kenneth Miller has noted, our use of the word "random" to describe evolutionary processes can, for some, be somewhat misleading. While events on a sub-atomic level, and thus on an atomic, molecular, bio-chemical, and genetic level, are in fact prone to "random" variation, this does not mean that anything can happen. The randomness of these variations is confined to the limits set by the laws of physics that define our universe. Therefore, Miller suggested, perhaps a better word to use in describing the processes of genetic mutation as well as other natural events is "indeterminate." In connection with this observation, Miller also wisely pointed out that the only real alternative to the indeterminate processes that characterize our evolving world would be a "strict, predictable determinism,"[4] and therefore a universe that would be set on an unchangeable course, precluding both the free will of human beings and any possibility of God's participation or intervention. A continually evolving universe, on the other hand, allows for the existence of our free will, and it also enables a supernatural intervention, such as the incarnation of God as Jesus of Nazareth, for example, to produce contingent effects—to forever thereafter affect the hearts of men. That is, to affect the evolution of an evolving world.

Even as we understand that God is, in a way, separate and apart from the physical universe, we are still left with the question of why His creation could contain so much evil. According to Saint Augustine and C.S. Lewis, Christianity separates the evil in our world into two categories. First there is the everyday imperfection (from our perspective) of the physical universe, and secondly there is the depravity of human beings and fallen angels. In reference to the first of these, Lewis suggested that:

> ...the Christian answer (I think) is that God, from the first, created her [nature] such as to reach her perfection by a process in time. He made an Earth at first 'without form and void' and brought it by degrees to its perfection. In this, as elsewhere, we see the familiar pattern—descent from God to the formless Earth and re-ascent from the formless to the finished. In that sense a certain degree of 'evolutionism' or 'developmentalism' is inherent in Christianity.[5]

As Augustine explained it, "every defect comes from nothing..." That is, the absence of Divine Goodness. In his treatise *On Free Choice of the Will*, Augustine began by presenting the classic question: If God created everything in our world from nothing, "isn't God the cause of evil?" His answer was that God did not create evil. God created a free and independent world within which our perception of evil and injustice is the result of humankind's separation from God as a result of our disobedience to the calling of God's Eternal Truth. Just as sin is the result of turning away from God, all defects in nature, as perceived by us, are indicative of our distance from the Divine Order of Eternal Truth.

Christianity tells us that our ability to connect with God, and to therefore comprehend Eternal Truth and abide by what Augustine called Eternal Law, is facilitated by a capacity to reason that is unique to and innate in the human soul. So then, where do we imagine that the human soul comes from, and how is it unique from that of other creatures?

Despite the suggestion of Pope John Paul II, as seen in the introduction, that "man's spiritual soul is created directly by God," Christianity is not dependent on such a claim. Saint Augustine listed four views regarding the origin of human souls: "(1) they come into being by propagation; (2) they are created individually for each person who is born; (3) they already exist elsewhere and are sent by God into the bodies of those who are born; (4) they sink into bodies by their own choice."[6] Unlike the Pope, Augustine appeared to lean toward a conclusion that souls are propagated. He pointed to Scriptural references to sin having entered humankind through Adam (*Romans* 5:18-19) as evidence that souls, as the prerequisites to sin, are propagated through generations. He cautioned that suggestions of God's direct creation of individual human souls could appear to implicate God as the "author of sin."[7] Ultimately, however, Augustine believed that the origin of the soul is of no real importance when compared to the more substantive issues of faith, of obedience to God, and ultimately, of eternal salvation.

Though we sometimes hear people suggest that humans have souls while other animals do not, Christianity is not dependent on this idea either. The word soul, much like the word consciousness, can mean different things in different contexts, and it can encompass a variety of concepts, depending on the context as well as depending on the user. In any case, most Christian theologians have not excluded the idea of a "soul" being attributable to an animal. Christianity merely holds that humans have souls of a higher order than do other animals — a soul that possesses the capacity for a direct spiritual connection to God.

Congruent with this common conception of the soul, it is also sometimes suggested that humans possess the capacity for morality while other animals do not. Again, Christianity is not dependent on such a claim. Christianity merely asserts that humans are capable of a higher order of moral reasoning—a morality that transcends nature— one that is derived from a direct spiritual connection to God through a soul that is, whether bestowed or evolved, uniquely capable of facilitating such a connection.

We can observe apparent codes of ethics (or at the very least, codes of social conduct) among many other species of animals, from ants to birds to porpoises to the higher non-human primates, and perhaps most especially among chimpanzees and bonobos,* our closest living relatives. In addition to the highly disciplined social cooperation that is exhibited by ants, bees and other insects, behaviors of "proto-morality" and even apparent altruism have been observed among a variety of animals, particularly mammals.

Beginning with the almost universal trait among animals of protecting their own offspring, we see a variety of behaviors where one animal protects the interests of another in the absence of a direct reciprocal benefit to itself. Elephants and giraffes are just two of numerous species that work to save injured members of their own families from predators. Whales too have been known to put themselves in harm's way in order to protect a wounded family member. Entire herds of grazing animals will often work together in protecting each other from predators. Vampire bats are among several species that share food between individuals when one has been less fortunate in acquiring a portion. Porpoises will push a sick member of their pod to the surface so it can breath. A recent study at the University of Chicago demonstrated that rats have empathy for fellow rats that have been trapped and will work to free them.[8] Several species of non-human primates will often comfort members of their group who have been emotionally upset. Chimpanzees and bonobos have even been known to intervene in disputes between unrelated individuals when there is no apparent direct benefit and sometimes considerable risk to the interventionist.

Primatologists Jessica Flack and Frans de Waal, who have studied proto-moral behaviors in non-human primates extensively, have observed that, in primates, "moral sentiments such as sympathy, empathy, and community concern, engender a bond between individuals, the formation of which facilitates and is facilitated by cooperation." They found that monkeys and apes are capable of learned

---

* Once thought to be a subspecies of chimpanzee, bonobos are now understood to be an entirely separate species with some rather striking differences in behavior. Interestingly, each of these species shares many, but different, behavioral characteristics with humans.

adjustment, and note that evidence suggests that apes, like humans, are capable of cognitive empathy.[9] Their conclusions suggest that the behaviors they have observed are indicative of the precursors from which higher moral reasoning may have evolved in human beings. At the same time, however, they expressed a reluctance to claim that there is sufficient scientific evidence to show that any animal other than humans are "moral beings" in the sense of possessing a capacity for truly abstract moral reasoning.

In his book *What Evolution Is*, evolutionary biologist Ernst Mayr described three levels of altruism that are produced by the evolutionary process of natural selection. Just as importantly, Mayr also noted a fourth level of altruism among human beings that is not the result of natural selection—that is, altruism that is the product of social and religious development.

First is the altruism that benefits an individual's immediate offspring, which would certainly be favored by natural selection. Animals that do not sufficiently protect their own young (or that do not produce offspring in sufficient numbers to surpass the odds of destruction) are obviously much less likely to survive as a species.

Second is the altruism that favors immediate family members or close relatives, which would similarly be favored by natural selection. This kind of altruism extends beyond an individual's direct offspring to brothers, sisters, parents, and perhaps even cousins who have grown up together and who have remained in a group.

Third is the altruism that extends to the members of a wider group or flock or herd. Naturally, when individuals of a species are inclined to protect members of their group, the resulting safety in numbers benefits the individual and thus the survival of the species as a whole.

Altruism described by these three categories is called "reciprocal altruism." Though the individuals that exhibit these kinds of altruistic behaviors do not benefit directly from their own actions, they nevertheless reap the benefits of these traits as they are instilled in the instinctual behavior of all the members of their species. These traits are thus embedded into the genotype (the genetic make-up of a species) as they are favored by natural selection.

Instances of altruism between members of different species are relatively rare and are almost always instances of reciprocal altruism. The "cleaner fishes" that clean large predator fishes, for example, benefit the large fish by ridding them of external parasites, while the cleaner fishes do their work in exchange for food and protection.[10] Only reciprocal altruism can be engendered by natural selection and reciprocal altruism usually only occurs within a species or within a cohesive social group.*

There is an additional level of altruism, however, that is exhibited by human beings. It is altruism toward outsiders, where any benefit to the provider is far enough removed that the behavior could not be induced by instincts that are the consequence of natural selection. It is a conceptual altruism that is the product of a higher order of moral reasoning that has been and continues to be developed through cultural and spiritual progress.

Observations of chimpanzees by primatologist Jane Goodall revealed that, though chimpanzees exhibit remarkable altruistic tendencies toward members of their own group, they are nevertheless sometimes prone to wage brutal war against chimpanzee tribes of adjacent regions. Of course human beings too have a long history from which we continue the struggle to extract ourselves, of committing genocide against people of other nations and other races. Altruism toward outsiders is generally not instinctive. It must be learned.

---

* Though instinctual moral behaviors that are instilled by natural selection are usually species specific, once those instincts are embedded in the animal, they may be applied across species. For instance, our family dog is fully aware that we are not dogs, but he nevertheless adopts us as family and treats us with the respect of hierarchy, just as he would a family of dogs. He will also sometimes risk his own life for our protection. Similarly, when a dog and a cat live in the same household, they often treat each other as family. We know that the dog knows that the cat is a cat because of the aggressive way in which he behaves toward those cats that are not members of his family. Such examples are aberrations of nature and are, in these cases, instances where multiple species are found in a close family group.

Discrimination and belligerence against outsiders, whether they are nations, races, socio-economic classes, or any variety of other distinctions, is a condition of humanity that has engaged philosophers as well as civic and religious leaders throughout recorded history. In humans, altruistic morality toward outsiders has evolved over many centuries and remains a central element of humankind's continuing moral reflection.

We can even see the evolution of how outsiders are thought of and dealt with over the course of history as it is presented in the Bible. From the acts of genocide that were favorably presented in the Old Testament we are brought to the lessons of Jesus to love our neighbors and our enemies alike. Jesus' interaction with the Samaritan woman at the well (*John* 4:7-13) and the lesson of His parable concerning the Good Samaritan's altruism toward an outsider (*Luke* 10:30-37) were conspicuous departures from long-standing Jewish custom.[11]

Scripture tells us that Jesus said He had not come to supersede the authority of the Old Testament. He came to fulfill its promise. In doing so, however, His teachings clearly brought a higher order of moral reasoning than that which had been previously known to the Jews. The Sermon on the Mount, for instance, introduced new ways of moral thinking about a number of circumstances in our lives.

Many have wondered why Jesus appeared on Earth only two thousand years ago. Why not three thousand years ago, or at the time of the exodus, or at the time of Noah, or even closer to the beginning of civilization? This question is a part of the even larger question of why life's handbook (the Bible) was not available from the beginning of civilization—why were its information and choices not made available to humankind from the beginning? We know that God could not have failed to foresee the events described in Scripture for which He had to make adjustments. He is omniscient. He would have seen it all from the start.

Perhaps the answer is that the world had to first be made ready through the process of evolution with which the Hebrew Scriptures were created—through the more than 2500-year history of the Jewish people, the recording of events and revelations, and the completion of the Hebrew Scriptures. Thus, the world was made ready to receive Jesus of Nazareth and the resulting addendum to the Hebrew Scriptures. Unquestionably, with the addition of the New Testament, the ancient Hebrew Scriptures of the Old Testament evolved to reveal, through Jesus, an additional dimension of moral truth and understanding. Just as God's message to humankind through the written Word of Scripture was made ready by means of an evolutionary process over time, it is apparent that the creatures intended to receive that message and fulfill its promise have been similarly made ready by means of evolutionary processes.

Biological evolutionary theory persuasively suggests a continuity of all mental powers between humans and the ancient ancestors from whom we evolved, including social morality and even the fundamentals of altruism. In the scope of human morality, where natural forces left off, cultural and spiritual forces have taken over. Though there may remain some debate over the role of spirituality in social ethics, such questions are outside of the reach of evolutionary science. It is only the natural processes involved in the evolution of cognitive reason and proto-morality that can be studied and largely understood by science. Most importantly, evolutionary theory and evolutionary science cannot and do not preclude a higher order of moral reasoning in humans that is, firstly, derived from an inherent spiritual connection to God, and secondly, enhanced by an actively nurtured relationship with God.

Among the key factors of the human soul or intellect that are most relevant to Christian thought are our self-awareness and our ability to understand concepts that are outside of our own experience. We know what we know, and we know that we know what we know. We are capable of abstract reasoning. We are capable of thought that transcends our earthly experience.

While chimpanzees, bonobos and other animals may know right and wrong in the context of the social structures in which they thrive, Christianity teaches us that human beings are capable of understanding a moral code that transcends the natural world—the Eternal Law that is derived from the Eternal Truth of God. It is this ethical understanding that enables us to overcome and rise above the distorted temporal desires and cravings that are the result of our experience in the natural world.

Since we are aware of ourselves and of our own knowledge, we are also aware that our knowledge is incomplete. We are therefore instructed to seek wisdom through the Word of God. Saint Augustine explained:

> But most important, He gave them the power of judgment, by which every soul knows that it should ask for knowledge where it is hindered by ignorance; that it must strive persistently in dutiful labors to conquer the difficulty of acting rightly; and that it must implore its Creator for help in its struggle.

Augustine suggested that much of what ails us in this world is what he called "inordinate desire." This was a characterization of our untoward cravings for the temporal pleasures that can corrupt our moral purity, and that in the end leave us unfulfilled and unhappy.

Anyone who owns a dog is aware that animals too are sometimes inflicted with inordinate desires of various sorts. A dog, of course, is merely acting on the instinct that has been bequeathed to him by many thousands of years of evolutionary development, even though his instinctual inclinations may be misplaced given his position in the modern world. He does not know that his desires may sometimes be inordinate or unhealthy for him. In fact, we usually consider the behavior of any animal, even deadly behavior, to be simply instinctual, and therefore, the animal is held blameless as a matter of moral responsibility.

Human beings, on the other hand, are thought to be evolved to a state where inordinate instinctual inclinations can be mitigated by the calling of Eternal Truth. We are expected to recognize our inordinate desires and we are expected to, with humility, submit to the Eternal Word of God for our own safety and happiness, as well as for a higher ethical order of love and caring for others. It is left up to us, through our own free will, to subdue our pride and to turn to the Light of God.

In his letter to the Romans (8:5-9), the Apostle Paul explained:

> Those who live according to the sinful nature have their minds set on what that nature desires; but those who live in accordance with the Spirit have their minds set on what the Spirit desires. ... You are controlled not by the sinful nature but by the Spirit, if the Spirit of God lives in you.

One area where our earthly ancestral roots are pretty clearly revealed by human inclination is the nature of our attraction to the opposite sex. Most animals, including humans, are sexual creatures. In the animal world mates are instinctively chosen on the basis of the optimum partner for propagation—a partner that will result in the production of the healthiest and strongest offspring. It is an instinct that has been instilled by natural selection. Though humans are, for the most part, no longer subject to natural selection, and though we are taught by societal ideals and Biblical morality that our choice in a mate should be based more on moral character than on physical characteristics, we nevertheless find that ancient and natural human instincts for propagation persist. In fact, clinical studies have confirmed that our propensity is to be attracted to individuals on the basis of particular physical attributes (upper body muscularity, breast size, firmness and roundness of the buttocks, particular waist to hip size ratios, etc.) and is grounded in our ancient instinct to strive for successful reproduction. Clearly, our natural inclination is to be attracted to a person of the opposite sex first as a consequence of their physical attributes, and only subsequently as a consequence of their personality and moral character.

Similarly, we must also sometimes wrestle with a natural inclination for sexual promiscuity, particularly among men. Just as we are driven by instinct to choose a mate that will produce the healthiest offspring, we also have an instinctual drive to produce lots of offspring. It is a perversion of this natural instinct that so often results in unhealthy sexual promiscuity—in what we have come to understand as "inordinate desire," given our now long-developed sense of moral reasoning.

Such examples are among many that may serve to illustrate how we can benefit from our use of the power of judgment—the power of our free will—to choose a course that will free us from the bondage of earthly inclinations. After all, it can only be from the platform of the natural world from which we have evolved that we might use our free will to rise up and seek, as well as to comprehend, a higher order of moral truth, whether by simple reason or by means of a spiritual connection to God and His Eternal Truth.

Along with instruction on how we might use our free will to rise above inordinate natural and instinctual inclinations, Western Christian tradition and thinking includes the idea that humankind's moral compass is simply broken—that the good world that God created has turned away from Him and has, as a result, gone horribly wrong. And there is certainly a great deal of evidence to support this idea.

When we consider the enormous atrocities committed in the name of whole societies such as those committed by Hitler, Stalin, or Pol Pot, we can see that our free will has been used to engage in a level of evil that is far removed from that which we might expect from natural inclinations. The meanness and cruelty exhibited by rapists, pedophiles, and other criminals are symptoms of a misuse of free will by creatures that are both self-aware and capable of acting on their own horrible conceptions of evil. Even a great many of the lesser evils that we all tend to engage in from time to time are indicative of our conscious resistance to using our free will for selfless acts of humility and graciousness. Western Christianity teaches us that our capacity for such evil, large and small, is the legacy of the "original sin" of humanity.

Many may wonder how we might associate the Scriptural story of Adam and Eve's original sin with real, historic events. Thomas Aquinas wrote that he well understood how, "by sharing in the same species, many men may be thought of as one man" and "there are many persons in one human nature."[12] Of course, the word "adam" or "adham" is the Hebrew common noun for "human" (or "humankind"), while adhamah, the word from which adham was likely derived, is Hebrew for earth. The use of the name Adam in *Genesis* and in *I*

Chronicles 1:1 as the proper name for the first man may simply suggest the unity of humankind.

C.S. Lewis indicated that he did not really understand a real-world historical connection to Adam and Eve and original sin, but he nevertheless offered an interesting idea that may be worth noting here. In his 1940 book, *The Problem of Pain*, Lewis suggested that perhaps there were once creatures on this Earth who possessed, even if only for a brief moment in time, the capacity to know God but had not yet selfishly turned away. It was the corruption of these pious creatures, Lewis proposed, that resulted in the creation of our sinful forefathers from whom we have inherited our own sinful nature.

Obviously our prehistoric ancestors would be considered by modern standards to be brutish savages, almost certainly prone to violent hostility toward each other under a variety of circumstances. But perhaps such standards are misplaced, given our limited understanding of such a prehistoric mind. Even more importantly, we should remember that the "original sin" was not a social sin. It was not a sin against neighbor. It was (as it continues to be) a sin against God. It was a sin that was made possible only with the emergence of self-awareness, along with an accompanying awareness of the larger universe and of God—an awareness of time, beauty, righteousness, and of course, evil.

Lewis suggested that perhaps a new human species was formed as a consequence of "The Fall"—that is, the sinful modern human beings that we are today. Paleontological and archaeological evidence, however, pretty well demonstrates that it was us, *Homo sapiens*, who were transformed from innocence into self-awareness and spirituality, and thus, ultimately into depravity. Scientists have uncovered a great deal of evidence that points to a fairly specific time in history—60,000-30,000 years ago—when self-awareness along with conceptions of God (and perhaps the accountability of genuine free will) emerged within the consciousness of the human mind.

Artifacts that have been found alongside the many fossil remains of the "pre-human" and the "early-human" species of our ancient ancestors have helped scientists to roughly track the evolution of the human mind. (A more detailed description of the nearly two dozen species of known human ancestors and their relatives will be discussed in Chapter 8.) From the crude stone tools that were used by our pre-human ancestors, to the simple hand-axes that were used by early human species such as *Homo erectus*, to the more sophisticated tools of the Neanderthals and early *Homo sapiens*, progress in sophistication of design and the usefulness of those tools and weapons reflects the increasingly sophisticated cognitive aptitude of their makers. The most rapid advancement in cognitive capabilities and resulting technology, however, is reflected in the history of our own species, modern *Homo sapiens*.

There were two very important periods of cognitive and technological progress among *Homo sapiens* that occurred well before the beginning of recorded history (which of course was a mere 5,000 years ago). In comparison to the very protracted and ancient timescales usually associated with most significant evolutionary changes, these two periods of human transformation happened very rapidly and very recently. Around 10,000 years ago humans began the practices of agricultural food production and the domestication of plants and animals. This sea change in human behavior marked the beginning of a dramatic acceleration in population growth, leading to the formation of cities and, ultimately, to great societies. Well before the development of agriculture and domestication, however, an even more significant transformation in human consciousness took place that set the stage for our understanding of what it means to be human. It was the emergence of contemplative self-awareness and spirituality.

This climax of the evolution of human cognitive ability occurred between 60,000 and 30,000 years ago and has been called the "cultural explosion." During this period, in addition to achieving advancements in utilitarian tools and weaponry, humans began making jewelry with materials such as snail shells and bird claws, indicating a newly developed appreciation for aesthetics. Sculpted icons were also being made, and artistic painting and symbols began to appear on the walls of caves. Some of these imaginative creations included chimerical images of human beings merged with a variety of animals, as well as various totemic images representing priests, sorcerers, demons, and gods. These artistic expressions reflected a new understanding of the universe that was emerging in the human consciousness.

This period in history might also best correlate with C.S. Lewis' conception of creation and of "original sin." It was the time when man became man as we know him. It was the time when man discovered beauty, art, goodness, evil, the larger universe, and most significantly, himself and his own free will. It was the time when an understanding of God and conceptions of spirituality emerged within the human soul.

Archeologist and author of *The Prehistory of the Mind: The Cognitive Origins of Art, Religion and Science*, Steven Mithen, has called this period of history the "big bang of human culture." Professor Mithen explained:

> ...when the first modern humans, *Homo sapiens sapiens*, appeared 100,000 years ago they seem to have behaved in essentially the same manner as Early Humans, such as Neanderthals. And then, between 60,000 and 30,000 years ago— with no apparent change in brain size, shape or anatomy in general—the cultural explosion occurred. This resulted in such a fundamental change in lifestyles that there can be little doubt that it derived from a major change in the nature of the mind. ...this change was nothing less than the emergence of the modern mind—the same mentality that you and I possess today.

Regardless of how we might associate actual historic events with the ancient Hebrew story of the creation of Adam and Eve, their fall from grace, and their subsequent realization of good and evil, we know that their sin, the "original sin," is the fundamental sin of humankind. That is, the sin of pride. Though the original sin is often thought of as disobedience to God, it was pride that prompted that disobedience. In the case of Adam and Eve, it was their prideful desire for excellence, a desire to be like little gods themselves, a desire to rule their own personal universe, which ultimately induced them to succumb to temptation and to "turn away from the light of wisdom"[13]—to disobey God's instruction. Again, C.S. Lewis:

> According to Christian teachers, the essential vice, the utmost evil, is pride. Unchastity, anger, greed, drunkenness, and all that, are mere fleabites in comparison: It was through pride that the devil became the devil: Pride leads to every other vice: It is the complete anti-God state of mind.

The sin of pride is largely what separates us from other creatures. It derives from the source of our accountability—self-awareness. Only creatures that are self-aware and that are capable of consciously exercising a free will to worship themselves are enabled to commit the sin of pride.

The original sin is fundamental and it is timeless. It is committed for the first time daily across the world by maturing young children, and it is attributable to every individual human life. We can rather easily trace the nature of most modern human motivations and human depravity to the legacy of that original sin.

It cannot be suggested that God did not foresee the fall of man. God could not have been taken by surprise with a resulting compromise of His plan. God would necessarily have seen it all from the beginning of creation—the Big Bang, the formation of nebulas, galaxies, stars and planets, the evolution of life, the rise of humanity, the fall of man, the rise and fall of the Egyptian, Roman, and Mayan Empires, the crucifixion of Jesus, as well as the ultimate fate of all souls and the fate of humankind in its entirety. According to Scripture, God's plan was and is complete and perfect, regardless of any number of contingencies that may arise within it.

Those contingencies are the result of the necessary character of God's creation. The original sin and all other sins are possible because we have the capacity to choose our behavior and to choose the way we think about any number of things, whether temporal or eternal. We sin because we have free will. But, if free will enables sin, why would God create free will? The Christian answer is that the creation of the ultimate good and perfection—God's objective—is only achieved with man's *voluntary* embrace of God's love. This naturally requires the availability of the alternative.

Scripture teaches us that, by means of a spiritual connection to God through our souls, we can use our free will to accept the eternal truth of God for the benefit of our happiness on Earth and, ultimately, for the benefit of our receiving God's gift of eternal salvation. Augustine described our acceptance of and submission to God's will as the only true path to the ultimate freedom of our human souls. Quoting Jesus from the Gospel of *John* (verses 8:31-32), Augustine wrote:

> This is our freedom, when we are subject to the truth; and the truth is God Himself, who frees us from death, that is, from the state of sin. For that Truth, speaking as a human being to those who believe in Him, says, 'If you abide in my word, you are truly my disciples. And you shall know the truth, and the truth shall make you free.'

The tenets of Christianity are based upon God's revelation through divinely inspired Scripture and through God's historical performance of miracles on Earth. Our response to God and our adherence to those tenets, on the other hand, are carried out within the context of the natural world in which we were born and in which we live our lives. Each of us was born of the flesh of our ancestors in that natural world. As the Reverend Michael Dowd aptly noted, "We were not thrust into the Universe, we were born out of it."[14] We are the product of an inheritance bequeathed to us by ancestors. Yet, we are not carbon copies of either one or both of our parents. Each of us is a new and unique individual, possessing our own free will, not copied but evolved from our predecessors. Because of this reality, each of us as individuals bear our own accountability and responsibility to ourselves, to others, and to God.

Christianity teaches us that the natural world, therefore, is the foundation or the platform from which we must rise and exercise our free will in accepting and obeying the call of Eternal Truth.

Of course Christianity is also based on an understanding that God is a living God. He is active in the world and, most importantly, He is active in our own lives when we invite Him into them. But we know that God is not in direct control of everything that happens in the world or in our own lives because such a notion would implicate Him as an accomplice to the evil that we see around us and that we perpetrate. Instead, God's creation is a free and independent world, the natural world that resulted from the singular act that Thomas Aquinas described as "first cause"—God's primary act of divine creation from which all of the natural world and all natural consequences have emanated.

Regardless of how each of us may come to an understanding of other tenets of faith, or an understanding of how our natural world conforms to those tenets, we can undoubtedly see that the concept of the free will of individual human beings is foremost among Christianity's essential doctrines. We can also reason that our ability to choose or reject such concepts and our ability to choose or reject the mandates of God can occur only within a physical universe much like the one in which we find ourselves. That is, a universe where those choices have consequences—a universe where our choices and our behavior, along with all other events, will necessarily produce contingent effects—a universe that is, inevitably and continually, undergoing the processes of evolution.

Part 2

The Theory of Evolution

4

Layers of Understanding

I n the early 1980s several advocacy groups—most notably, Jerry Falwell's Moral Majority—enjoyed some success in arousing public discussion regarding the practice of teaching evolutionary science in public schools without the counterbalance of also teaching the Biblical creation stories as natural history, or so-called "creation science," as an alternative theory. It was in that context that, during his 1980 presidential campaign, Ronald Reagan was asked what he thought of the teaching of evolution in public schools. "Well," began Mr. Reagan in his famously disarming manner, "it's a theory." He then went on to explain: "It is a scientific theory only, and it has in recent years been challenged in the world of science and is not yet believed in the scientific community to be as infallible as it was once believed." The view expressed by Mr. Reagan was and continues to be a rather commonly held one—that biological evolution is "just a theory," that it is just one among several (perhaps equally plausible) explanations for the diversity of life on Earth. This commonly held view, however, is a commonly held misconception. It is a misconception born, in part, of a misunderstanding of the way the term "theory" is used in the world of science.

Scientists use the terms "hypothesis," "model," "theory," and "law" in ways that are often rather different from the way the general public tends to use them. To better understand how these terms are used in science, we will need to have a basic understanding of what is referred to as the "scientific method."

In the realm of science there can never be any absolute claim of certainty. In science, all knowledge is tentative. All of the "facts" that we know about our world can, in principle, be superseded or altered by new information at any time. This, of course, does not mean that we cannot have a great deal of confidence in much of what has been learned about the world through scientific discovery. Indeed, the human condition has greatly improved as a result of knowledge gained through science. Discoveries in engineering, physics, electronics, chemistry, agriculture, biology, medicine and many other fields account for our increasingly long life expectancy and constantly improving standard of living. Everything that we know in each of these fields, however, is always subject to refinement or revision, and the scientific method of discovery and analysis always necessarily assumes that possibility.* When used in the context of scientific discovery, therefore, the terms "hypothesis," "model," "theory," and "law" assume this requisite and reflect various levels of understanding and an organizational means of interpreting our world.

Scientific discovery very often begins with a hypothesis. We tend to think of a hypothesis as anything from just idle speculation to an intelligent guess. The *Oxford American Dictionary* defines a hypothesis as "a supposition or proposed explanation made on the basis of limited evidence as a starting point for further investigation." This is indeed how the term is used in science, however, usually with the addition of a subtle caveat. That is, a proper scientific hypothesis should be testable.

---

* Paradoxically, it is the very fact that scientific consensus and orthodoxy is always subject to challenge that ensures our ability to have a great deal of confidence in those scientific principles and theories that have been developed over time. Contrary to the myth that scientists are inclined to suppress evidence that runs counter to generally accepted assumptions (as claimed by some in regard to the politics of climate change, for example), it is precisely those scientists who successfully challenge orthodoxy that make a name for themselves. Just as competition ensures the greatest efficiency in economics, competition in science ensures excellence and veracity.

Testability is the hallmark of the "scientific method." Any scientific hypothesis, law, or theory must be testable and it must be falsifiable. In science, nothing can be definitively proven to be "true," but it can certainly be proven false. This is the essential dividing line between scientific and non-scientific proposals and understanding. This is generally what separates science and theology or spirituality. Science cannot affirm or deny spiritual truth because spiritual truth cannot be tested in the natural world—it is, by design, a matter for faith. The scientific method can only assess the physical properties and processes of the natural world.

The term "model" is used in at least two ways. First, a model can be an analogy that helps us to understand the character of a given process. For example, the "billiard ball model" is used to describe the kinetic character of gas molecules, as they elastically collide with one another like billiard balls while spontaneously expanding to fill an available space.

Causing some confusion, however, the term "model" is occasionally used interchangeably with the term "hypothesis" and, even more often, with the term "theory." Apart from its use as an analogy, "model" is most appropriately used to describe a collection of ideas, some of which may not be particularly well established, but nevertheless, when fit together may offer a viable explanation of complex and/or multifaceted processes. In a sense, a model is an idea or a set of ideas that we can "try on for size" to see how it fits as a solution to a question. A scientific model is very often a complex construct that includes some well-established assumptions along with elements of conjecture, which, when taken as a whole, can undergo sufficient testing to learn if the model might gain enough evidentiary support to become a viable scientific theory.

Perhaps the most confusion surrounds the use of the term "theory." Many of us tend to use the term as if it were interchangeable with "hypothesis" or to describe an unsubstantiated supposition or just "a hunch." Contributing to the confusion, scientists have sometimes been known to use the term in this way too. But when used properly, in the realm of science the term "theory" describes a construct that is much more than merely an educated guess. In science, a theory is supported by evidence—sometimes, as in the case of evolutionary theory, a substantial body of evidence.

There are at least two ways in which the term "theory" is used in science, both of which apply to how it is used in connection to biological evolution. First, "theory" is used to describe an umbrella, under which a collection of ideas, theories, laws, principles, and/or unanswered questions about a particular subject may be associated. Some examples are quantum theory, gravitation theory, language theory, game theory, atomic theory, gene theory, and cell theory. This use of the term "theory" is meant to signify, not that these things may or may not exist, but the inclusion and organization of all the theories, principles, laws, and/or any uncertainties that can be associated with the properties and/or the functions of these things. Webster's New Riverside University Dictionary, defines "theory" as:

> Systematically organized knowledge applicable in a relatively wide variety of circumstances, esp. a system of assumptions, accepted principles, and rules of procedure devised to analyze, predict, or otherwise explain the nature or behavior of a specified set of phenomena.

Under the very large umbrella of "evolutionary theory" there are a great many theories regarding the details of the various components and processes of evolution. For example, various theories concerning the origin of life, hereditary theory, gene theory, cell theory, natural selection theory, common descent theory, plate tectonic theory, and many others are all relevant to the larger umbrella of evolutionary theory. Evolutionary theory has been called "the grand unifying theory of biology" because so much of what we see in all aspects of biology is explained by what we know about evolution.

A second way in which the term "theory" is used is based on the notion that any thing or any phenomenon that we cannot see directly, even if it is very well understood as a result of deductive reasoning, is theoretical. For example, the idea that the Earth orbits the sun, rather than the other way around, is theoretical because no one has directly seen it occur. We can nevertheless have a great deal of confidence that it is the Earth that orbits the sun because of many things we can directly observe that suggest the theory is reliable. Our confidence in the theory is further enhanced by its predictability and testability. For example, if the Earth along with the other planets in our solar system actually do orbit the Sun, we should be able to predict the seasonal relative positions of the planets according to their orbits. And of course, we can. We can have confidence that it is the Earth that orbits the sun, not because of *direct* empirical evidence, but through the process of deductive reasoning.

Though we can directly see evolution at work on a very limited scale (in insect and microorganism adaptations, and in plant and animal domestication, for example), most of what we know about evolution, like our understanding of the Earth orbiting the sun, has been learned by the process of deductive reasoning. The notion that today's species of living organisms are evolutionary descendants of previously existing species is indeed, as we will see in Chapters 7, 8, and 9, as thoroughly supported by evidence as is the idea that the Earth orbits the sun.

We rely on the veracity of a great many theoretical concepts for important applications in our world. Albert Einstein's analysis and description of what he called Special Relativity is a theory. Yet, global positioning satellites would not work without calculations that are based on the truth of Special Relativity. We would certainly be hard pressed to convince the survivors of Hiroshima and Nagasaki that Einstein's theory of Relativity is only an unsubstantiated supposition. Even the existence of the Earth's molten iron core is theoretical. Yet, for many years mariners and Boy Scouts have relied on the magnetic field that it generates to assist them with navigation.

In science, the use of the word "theory" can suggest that a given process, set of processes, or system of inquiry or characterization may not be fully understood and/or, while being true, may not necessarily be the whole truth. For instance, unlike all of the other planets, Mercury's orbit cannot be accurately predicted with the use of calculus based on Isaac Newton's laws of motion and gravity—it requires calculations based on Einstein's General Relativity (and a deeper understanding of gravity than Newton had imagined). And while Relativity's calculations work well in predicting the physics of planets, stars, and most of the universe as a whole, they begin to break down when applied to the realm of quantum physics (the tiniest bits of matter, energy, space and time). So while Newton's theory of gravity and Einstein's theory of General Relativity are both true, they are not the whole truth.

This is an important way of seeing the world for scientists and for Christians alike. Just as various levels of understanding can be gleaned from the study of Scripture, there are very often additional layers of reality in the natural world that are beyond the reach of our contemporary capabilities of detection or understanding. Responsible and prudent scientists are always wary of drawing conclusions that exceed the scope of substantial evidence and testing. While we may know a great deal about how the laws of physics and many of the world's natural processes work, there are very often additional layers of reality that may be eventually uncovered. Indeed, it is our understanding of such layers of reality or layers of understanding that can provide a basis for our accepting the findings of science without the slightest waiver in our faith in God as Creator.

Consider the illustration to the right, for example. It seems pretty simple—two lines with the lower ends being about three times further apart than the upper ends. But suppose we are told that these two lines are in fact parallel. What could we make of that? The reality that we can see right in 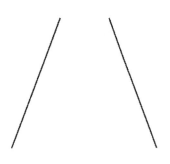 front of us on this page is that the lines are not parallel. But suppose there is a deeper reality that we do not immediately see? If the two-dimensional image that we see here on the page turns out to be only an incomplete glimpse—an illusionary representation—of a three-dimensional reality, it becomes clear. As the upper ends of the lines project into that third dimension, they only appear to converge, much like railroad tracks do as they recede into the distance. An additional layer of understanding has revealed a whole new reality. It was only the limits of the two-dimensional medium by which we perceived the lines that led us to conclude that they were not parallel.

Another illustration of "layers of reality" that can perhaps help to show how biological evolution can fit under the larger umbrella of divine creation is an account of how Isaac Newton's seventeenth-century theory of gravity can be seen in light of Albert Einstein's twentieth-century theory of gravity. It may be useful to examine the nature of these theories for a couple of reasons. First, because the two theories are completely different explanations of the same thing and, yet, they are largely compatible. Second, because a discussion of gravity can help to remind us that our universe, even an aspect of it that is as close to each of us as gravity, is not nearly as simple as it might appear from the point of view of our everyday lives. The gravity that we simply take for granted is the result of a truly astounding reality that permeates everything, from entire clusters of galaxies to the book you are now holding.

Isaac Newton's theory of gravity described the physical characteristics that he called the "universal law of gravity." Newton observed that every object in the universe exerts an attractive force on every other object. With an analysis of his three laws of motion, he was able to conclude how gravitational force acts between two objects. Newton showed that the force is directly proportional to the product (multiplication) of their two masses and inversely proportional to the square of the distance between their centers. With the use of his newly developed method of mathematics that would later be called calculus, he was able to demonstrate his findings to others, and to show how the law of gravity could reliably predict the movement of objects such as planets and various other heavenly bodies. Indeed, it was only with a thorough understanding of Newton's theories of motion and gravity, and with the use of his calculus that the United States was able to land men on the surface of the Moon and to then bring them home again.

Nearly three and a half centuries after Newton's discoveries, however, Albert Einstein developed a completely different theory of gravity. While it was a starkly different theory, Einstein's theory did not nullify Newton's theory. It merely explained an aspect of gravity that Newton probably could not have imagined. In addition to how gravity works, Einstein's theory explained why it works the way it does.

Newton understood that there would have to be a third agency through which one body of mass could affect another body of mass. But he had no idea what it could be. In the process of answering that question, Einstein supplanted only one aspect of Newton's understanding of gravity. Newton believed that the force of gravity of one body upon another was instantaneous and constant. In discovering Relativity, Einstein showed that the speed of light is constant but limited and, in doing so, he demonstrated that the speeds of all forces along with their effects in the universe are also limited. So the effects of gravity are not instantaneous, as Newton had thought. Aside from this important detail, Newton's theory of gravity—the theory which first proposed that the force that causes an apple to fall from a tree to the ground is the same force that dictates the orbits of planets and moons, and which accurately predicts the properties of that force—fits rather nicely within the larger framework of Albert Einstein's theory of gravity.

Einstein deduced that mass (physical matter) distorts or warps space and time. We do not know precisely which, but it appears that either, space and time are constantly collapsing into bodies of mass or mass constantly accelerates into space and time. The effect is that relatively small objects, such as ourselves, are overwhelmed by the gravitational force of much larger objects, such as the Earth, as space and time are constantly accelerating past us. It is essentially the same effect as being pressed against the seat of an accelerating car, or airplane, or rocket. It is like being pressed against the inner wall of one of those spinning Tornado rides found in amusement parks. (Centrifugal force is a form of acceleration. An object is accelerating if either the speed or the direction of its motion changes.) While Einstein's explanation of gravity may be somewhat difficult for many of us to truly comprehend, numerous tests have demonstrated that it is almost certainly an accurate description of reality.

As we begin to comprehend how gravity works, we can appreciate that our world is not even nearly as simple as it might seem to our ordinary senses. Indeed, recent discoveries in quantum physics have revealed that the fundamental inner workings of our universe are, as apposed to the standpoint of our usual perception, truly bizarre. As noted in Chapter 2, within the behavior of sub-atomic particles scientists have detected indications of at least eleven spatial dimensions in addition to the three that we normally perceive. Furthermore, it has been shown that a single electron can move along more than one path (in fact, an infinite number of paths) simultaneously.[1] Trillions upon trillions of virtually massless particles called neutrinos that emanate mostly from the nuclear reactions within the sun are constantly passing through our planet and everything on it, including us. There are even some sub-atomic particles that come into and then out of existence again (existence as we understand it) in as little as 0.0000000000-00000000000001 second.[2] Scientists examining the intersection of particle physics and cosmology have even concluded that the matter and energy that we can directly see is a mere 4 to 5 percent of what is actually there—the other 95 or 96 percent being what has been termed "dark matter" (about 26 percent) and "dark energy" (70 percent). It is merely in the translation to the atomic level of physical substances and objects that the world behaves in the way with which we are familiar. It is evident that our physical universe, whether considered from the perspective of its great expanse of space, matter, energy and time, or considered from a perspective that encompasses no more than our own fingertips, is an immeasurably complex, mysterious, and wondrous creation, the true scope of which we have only begun to comprehend.

Just as Newton's theory of gravity reliably told us how gravity works, but did not tell us why it works the way it does, biological evolutionary theory tells us a lot about how evolution works, but does not tell us why our universe happens to be the way that it is—why our universe is conducive to the emergence and the evolution of intelligent life in the first place, and what purpose may be attributed to the existence of intelligent beings. Most significantly, it is important for us to keep in mind that the first of these considerations is a matter for scientific discovery, while the latter is a matter best left to philosophers, theologians, and the Scriptures.

The example of how Newton's and Einstein's theories of gravity are so different and, at the same time, both accurate descriptions of reality may help us to visualize how evolution can fit into a larger framework of divine creation. It is important to keep in mind, however, that there is a very important difference in these two associations. Both Newton's and Einstein's theories are scientific theories that can be tested. Our understanding of divine creation, on the other hand, does not come from empirical evidence, and it cannot be tested in the natural world. It is an understanding that is not applicable to the scientific method. It is an understanding that comes to us by tradition (Scripture) and by spiritual insight. The spiritual guidance of Scripture and the spiritual insight fostered by a personal relationship with God constitute wholly different ways of knowing about our world and knowing about the relevance of our own lives within it. That is, wholly different layers of understanding.

The distinction between spiritual knowledge and scientific knowledge has not always been so well defined, and the importance of that distinction has only in very recent centuries become fully appreciated. It was Augustine of Hippo, in the fourth century, who first attempted to reconcile Christian dogma with the ancient Greek philosophy of Plato and with much of what can be observed in the natural world. Augustine's efforts helped to legitimize Christian dogma in the minds of intellectuals such as himself by reconciling it with the natural world through the application of reason. The result was a richer and a deeper Faith that exalted the wondrous complexity and the glory of God and His creation.

Augustine's contributions to Christian theology remain highly important to the intellectual depth and richness of the faith (and are in fact referred to repeatedly in this volume), but his influence was used by several of the leading thinkers of the Medieval era in a way that proved damaging to any realistic quest for philosophical truth and, ultimately, to Christianity itself.

In the eleventh and twelfth centuries, a newly developing philosophical and theological way of thinking known as Scholasticism split into two branches. On one side were the Rationalists, advocating the application of reason to Scripture, much the way Augustine had done. Believing that the Rationalists had strayed too far from orthodoxy, conservative reactionaries on the other side, most notably Saint Anselm, along with Saint Peter Damian and Saint Bernard, condemned the use and what they considered the abuse of reason.[3] Instead of applying reason to Christian dogma in an effort to reach a greater understanding of its deeper meaning and ultimate truths, this branch of Scholasticism attempted to apply rigid religious dogma to reason. Consequently and unfortunately this pseudo-philosophy gained prominence and stifled debate for many centuries. Philosophical disagreements regarding Scriptural interpretation began to lead to charges of heresy and even, occasionally, a burning at the stake. It was a way of thinking in which Scriptural literalism reigned supreme and any seemingly contradictory observations in the natural world would be explained away with denials or elaborate contrivances. Sadly, it promoted neither a realistic understanding of the world nor the credibility of Christianity.[4]

In the thirteenth century Thomas Aquinas introduced Aristotelian logic into Christian theology. Just as was the case with Augustine, Saint Thomas' incorporation of Greek philosophy and logic into Christian theology was largely beneficial. But the theology of Thomas and the philosophy and science of Aristotle became distorted as they were adopted into Church orthodoxy. Thomas' "five proofs of

God," for example, have become an object of ridicule, in part, because they have been taken out of context. After his lengthily developed five points of logical argument demonstrated, according to Thomas, that God exists, he then went on to say (the part that is usually left out) that we have no idea what "exists" really means in this context. He had merely demonstrated that God is the best explanation for the resolution of certain mysteries—a God of the gaps, if you will. At the same time, however, Thomas well understood that we cannot learn anything substantive about God from the natural world.[5]

As the Church adopted Aristotelian logic, it also adopted pretty much everything that Aristotle had proposed. He had a lot to say about nature, but his understanding of nature included some rather glaring errors. For example, despite the realization by a number of earlier philosophers that the Earth orbits the sun, Aristotle insisted that the Earth was the center of the universe. It was also Aristotle who concluded that the universe was made of four primary elements: earth, air, fire, and water. As the official Church stubbornly insisted that the teachings of Aristotle were "The Truth," both science and Christianity suffered.[6]

After several centuries of stifling dogmatic constraint, conservative Scholasticism and the official Church's version of Aristotelian philosophy finally came under challenge. First, Copernicus in the fifteenth century, and then Galileo in the sixteenth century declared that the Earth orbits the sun, not the other way around. Physical evidence and sound deductive reasoning pointed to a heliocentric solar system, despite official Church doctrine that insisted otherwise. As the Earth was being removed from the center of the universe, philosophers and scientists began to recognize that all physical events and processes are governed by fixed natural laws, and that, whatever purpose God may have for it, the natural universe can be reliably analyzed and understood by means of a scientific method. The result was the emergence of the era that would become known as the "Age of Enlightenment" or the "Age of Reason"—an era also marked by a misguided theological movement away from Biblical revelation in favor of what has been termed "scientific religion."[7] This new way of thinking would lead to deism (in which God plays little or no active role in the world after creation) and then ultimately to, for the first time in history, an intellectual foundation for atheism.

In the seventeenth century, the French philosopher and mathematician René Descartes concluded that everything in the universe, including the existence of God, could be explained with the use of mathematics. Descartes had also supposed that, upon its creation, the universe had been set in motion with the guidance of God's laws of physics and that no further divine participation was needed. The English philosopher John Locke, among others, then suggested that there was no longer any need for Biblical revelation or "superstitious doctrines," since everything one needed to know about God could be seen in nature. A new form of religion was being developed based entirely on reason and natural science with the exclusion of Biblical revelation. Both deism and scientific religion as applied to more traditional Christian faith were bolstered by the work of Isaac Newton, particularly as he proclaimed that he had discovered scientific proof of God's existence.[8]

In discovering the laws of motion and gravity, Newton had synthesized Cartesian philosophy, Johannes Kepler's laws of planetary motion, and Galileo's laws of terrestrial motion. It was a monumental achievement in explaining the laws of physics that account for the properties and movements of celestial bodies as well as everything else that we see in the world. But there remained much that Newton did not understand. He did not know why objects are attracted to each other, and while he could explain why the planets move as they do and why they remain in their orbits, he could not imagine how the solar system could have been formed to begin with. He concluded:

> Though these bodies may, indeed, continue in their orbits by the mere laws of gravity, yet they could by no means have at first derived the regular position of the orbits by themselves from these laws. ... [The positions of celestial objects had been

positioned so precisely that they] could only proceed from the counsel and domination of an intelligent and powerful Being.[9]

Newton had also observed how the apparent design of the universe was conducive to the existence and the function of its living creatures. By means of reasoning that was facilitated by the Strong Anthropic Principle (though no such principle had yet been formally identified and named), Newton had discovered his own Intelligent-Designing God of the gaps.[*]

As noted in Chapter 2, a God that is rationalized by gaps in our knowledge of the physical universe is a precarious God. After Biblical revelation had been somewhat marginalized and displaced by a religion of scientific rationalization, the systematic filling of gaps in scientific knowledge by new discoveries naturally paved the way for the rationalization of atheism. It has been the scientifically justified God that emerged only some four centuries ago, along with a growing trend toward undue Biblical literalism among many people of faith, that has allowed scientific discovery to be presented as a sound intellectual basis for atheism.

Of course not everyone succumbed to the temptations of deism or even a more limited scientific rationalization for God. In an apparent rebuttal to Descartes and his followers, seventeenth-century French mathematician Blaise Pascal argued for the older idea—that of Augustine and Thomas Aquinas—of God as transcendent and undetectable in nature. He insisted that certainty about God could only come from the "heart," and that a God who was merely "the author of mathematical truths and of the order of the elements" could offer no comfort or wisdom for the trials and the aspirations of human life.[10] Similarly,

---

[*] Newton also believed that "Monstrous Legends, false miracles, veneration of reliques, charmes, ye doctrine of Ghosts or Daemons, and their intercession, invocation & worship and other such heathen superstitions" had corrupted what he called "fundamental religion." He held a rather odd belief that Noah had founded a faith based on the rational observation of nature, and that this faith had been corrupted by "ye nations." Newton saw no rationality in the doctrines of the Trinity and the Incarnation.

eighteenth-century German religious leader Nicholas Ludwig von Zinzendorf declared that faith in God emanates "not in thoughts nor in the head, but in the heart." Just as most believers well understand today, Zinzendorf knew that knowing God is not a product of reason, but "a presence in the soul."[11]

A scientific method that excludes the consideration of religious dogma does not proclaim that enlightenment is best achieved with the exclusion of religious belief. Rather, it utilizes the important recognition that spiritual knowledge and knowledge of the characteristics and the processes of the natural world are best sought independently of one another. Scientific understanding and spiritual insight are separate realms of knowledge that are acquired from separate sources. We need not insist, however, that science and religion must always be considered separately in our view of the world or in our understanding of our own role within it. Indeed, it is very clear that human beings are spiritual beings who live in a natural environment. And it is clear that each of these realms can greatly affect our comprehension of the other. It is incumbent upon each of us to come to terms with our own life as it is affected by both the spiritual and the natural aspects of our being. Experience has taught us, however, that our search for truth in each of these two aspects of our lives requires separate and different avenues of inquiry. Yet, let us be confident that truth and knowledge, wherever it may be found and wherever it may lead, will surely enhance the richness of our entire lives.

5

The Awakening of
Evolutionary Science

T he publication of Charles Darwin's *On The Origin of Species By Means of Natural Selection* in November 1859 is often described as a turning point in human history. Darwin's theory of evolution, it is said, offered a new way of thinking about the world and about humankind's place within that world and among its living inhabitants. Yet, biological evolutionary theory did not originate with Charles Darwin.

References to evolutionary concepts can be found in the writings of a number of ancient Greek philosophers, including Thales, Anaximander, Empedocles, Aristotle, Epicurus, and Lucretius. The second-century-B.C. Indian philosopher Patañjali, who is best known for his development of the philosophical and physical practices of yoga, also considered the idea of biological evolution.[1] Discussions of evolution then fell virtually silent for more than nineteen centuries, undoubtedly due in part, at least in the Western world, to the narrow and repressive doctrines of the "official" Christian Church.

Throughout much of the Dark and Middle Ages, the universe was considered by the official Church and most of society to be a closed and immutable system with human beings and the Earth at its center. Everything in the universe was essentially just as it had been in the beginning when it was created directly by the Hand of God, including each of the species of life. None had been lost and none had been transformed or altered. This generally accepted sentiment was expressed in naturalist John Ray's 1701 publication *The Wisdom of*

God Manifested in the Works of the Creation, in which he reiterated official Church doctrine, stating that all things, whether living or inanimate, were "created by God at first, and by Him conserved to this Day in the same State and Condition in which they were first made."[2]

Fossils were believed to be nothing more than stones that God had playfully created in a way that would mimic plants and animals. It was not until after it had become very clear that fossils represent an abundance of extinct species that Biblical literalists began to put forth the claim (contrary to Scripture) that Noah had failed in his mission to save "all living creatures," and that all of the extinct species that were being found around the globe were simply those that had been destroyed by the Great Flood.

In the centuries just prior to Darwin's work, however, the findings of Copernicus, Galileo, and Newton, and a new philosophical approach begun by Descartes, and further developed by Locke, Hume, and others, began the process of separating the natural sciences from unduly rigid religious conformity. Though Descartes, Newton and others allowed their scientific findings to affect their religious understanding in ways that many would find destructive, as we saw in the previous chapter, their recognition that natural processes are guided by immutable laws of nature began a scientific method that would eventually become wholly independent of Biblical revelation. In 1766, French mathematician and naturalist Georges-Louis Leclerc, the Comte de Buffon, helped to lay the foundation for modern biological evolutionary science in his thirty-six volume *Histoire naturale, generale et particuliere* (*Natural History, general and particular*) in which he completely separated religious and scientific study and argued that nature can be best understood simply by the systematic observation of natural processes.

Buffon recognized that the forces of nature, much like the practices of domestication, could modify the characteristics of many species of plants and animals. He noted that some animals retain vestigial structures that are no longer useful, and speculated that they were indicative of biological evolution. He even noted the similarities between humans and apes and mentioned the idea of common descent. But he then dismissed that idea as too heretical, concluding that the weight of evidence was against it. After his 1778 publication of *Les époques de la nature*, in which he postulated that the Earth was about 75,000 years old—much older than the 6,000 years proclaimed by the Church—Buffon was condemned by the Catholic Church in France and his books were burned.

Another significant development that preceded Darwin's work was the systematic and hierarchal classification of species. Beginning in 1735 with his first publication of *Systema Naturae* and further developed in subsequent editions, Swedish physician, botanist, and zoologist Carl Linnaeus created a system of classifying plants and animals based on their structural characteristics. The system grouped plants and animals according to their similarities into hierarchal classifications. Three *Kingdoms* represented the broadest categories under which organisms would fall. The kingdoms were then divided into various *classes*, and the classes were divided into *orders*, which divided into *genera*, which divided into *species*.

Like Aristotle before him, Linnaeus recognized that whales, including porpoises and dolphins, were not fishes but were instead mammals. Though Linnaeus did speculate that species of plants belonging to the same genus might have sprung from a common ancestor, he never proposed a theory of evolution as such. He was nevertheless accused of "impiety" by the Lutheran Archbishop of Uppsala for having placed human beings in the same genus as apes.

Linnaeus' system would later be recognized as an illustration of how evolution and speciation (the emergence of new species) produced a branching diversity of life on Earth. Additional levels of classification have been added for use by a few various scientific disciplines, and the classification of species according to their evolutionary relationships has become much more precise with the use of DNA analysis (as we will see in Chapter 10), but Linnaeus' basic system is still in use today.

Darwin's *On The Origin of Species* began with a section called "AN HISTORICAL SKETCH OF THE PROGRESS OF OPINION ON THE ORIGIN OF SPECIES..." Darwin dedicated several pages to crediting those botanists, zoologists, geologists, philosophers, clergy, and other naturalists who had, prior to his work, offered theories and observations regarding the gradual evolution of organisms. He limited his remarks to an account of those naturalists whose work concerning evolution had been published within only about seventy years prior to his own book, with the exception of this footnote containing a sample of the ideas found in Greek philosophy that had been expressed on the subject more than two thousand years earlier:

> Aristotle, in his 'Physicae Auscultationes,' after remarking that rain does not fall in order to make the corn grow, any more than it falls to spoil the farmer's corn when threshed out of doors, applies the same argument to organization; and adds, 'So what hinders the different parts [of the body] from having this merely accidental relation in nature? As the teeth, for example, grow by necessity, in the front ones sharp, adapted for dividing, and the grinders flat, and serviceable for masticating the food; since they were not made for the sake of this, but it was the result of accident. And in like manner as to the other parts in which there appears to exist an adaptation to an end. Wheresoever, therefore, all things together (this is all the parts of the whole) happened like as if they were made for the sake of something, these were preserved, having been appropriately constituted by an internal spontaneity; and whatsoever things were not thus constituted, perished, and still perish.' We here see the principle of natural selection shadowed forth, but how little Aristotle fully comprehended the principle, is shown by his remarks on the formation of the teeth.

Darwin accounted for about two-dozen authors who had previously offered a variety of explanations for the evolution of living organisms and/or the natural creation of species, along with a synopsis of each of their various hypotheses. He even briefly noted his own grandfather, Dr. Erasmus Darwin, a physician by trade, a botanist, and a reputed eccentric, who had been an embarrassment to Charles' father, and who had also been among only a few people in the eighteenth century to have expressed a belief in evolution. Erasmus had proposed that, by means of a process he called "transmutation," a species would simply change into a different species.

Among the many naturalists Darwin mentioned, the work of French biologist and botanist Jean Baptiste de Lamarck had previously received the most public notice. In 1801, Lamarck first published his views concerning natural organic evolution. By 1809, he had fully formulated the first comprehensive theory of biological evolution. Just as Darwin later came to understand, Lamarck believed that all species, including human beings, are descended from antecedent species.

Among several mechanisms that Lamarck proffered as the impetus of evolutionary change, the primary one was described by his *theory of the inheritance of acquired characteristics*. This theory proposed that plants and animals change their forms as a result of pressures exerted on them by their immediate environment. For instance, appendages, organs, and muscles tend to grow and become stronger when they are used more frequently, while those that are used little or not at all tend to become weaker and eventually wither away. These changes, it was believed, would become more and more pronounced as they were passed on to subsequent generations, eventually resulting in a transformation of species.

For example, Lamarck believed that the long necks of giraffes were the result of a change in their environment and their habits. As they would reach higher and higher to get to the tender leaves of trees, their necks would stretch just a little. Then, as they passed this acquired trait on to their offspring, generation after generation, the necks of giraffes as a species became the very long necks that exist today. Similarly, for many years, people believed that the Negroid peoples of central and southern Africa had dark skin because they had been exposed to the tanning effects of the tropical sun for many thousands of generations. Even Darwin thought there was some merit to the idea of the inheritance of acquired characteristics as a cause of small variations, but he did not believe that it could sufficiently account for the diversity of life found around the world.

The "theory of evolution by means of the inheritance of acquired characteristics," also known as "transformationism," was much more widely accepted than Darwin's theory until at least the 1890s. It even held sway among a few scientists until the 1930s. As it turned out, with the advent of molecular biological research in the twentieth century it was discovered that "no information can be transmitted from the proteins of the body to the nucleic acids of the germ cells [sperm or egg cells]."[3] In other words, an inheritance of acquired characteristics cannot occur.

Charles Darwin has become known as the father of evolutionary theory because of what he offered that Lamarck did not. Darwin provided an even more comprehensive theory that included a much more plausible and logical explanation for the primary mechanism that causes evolutionary change. Darwin also included explanations of several interrelated issues, and he offered a great deal of well-documented evidence to support his claims in a book that was easily accessible to general readers.

On the Origin of Species did not simply introduce a new theory suggesting that organisms evolve and that disparate species share common ancestors. Those ideas had been around for a long time. Darwin showed us *how* species evolve and how the processes of evolution can logically account for the diversity and the various characteristics of life on Earth. In doing so, Darwin outlined numerous theories. Of those, the five most important ones are:[4]

1) The basic theory that organisms evolve—that the characteristics of plants and animals are not constant and unchanging.
2) Speciation—The bifurcation of species.

3) The theory of common descent—that all organisms share a common ancestor.

4) Gradualism—The gradualness of evolutionary change. No discontinuity or sudden large-scale mutations. (No so-called "saltation")

5) Natural Selection—The process that guides evolutionary change.

Natural selection is the primary mechanism that causes and guides the evolution of organisms. It is by far the most important of Darwin's discoveries. It is important to note, however, that Charles Darwin was not the only naturalist to discover the operation of natural selection and its central role in the processes of evolution.

Many years had passed between Darwin's initial formulation of his theories and the first publication of *On the Origin of Species*. There were two reasons for this. The first was Darwin's propensity for thoroughness. He wanted to be sure that he had worked-out as many of the related issues as possible, and he wanted to have answers to the many objections that he anticipated might arise. Darwin wanted to cover all the bases, so to speak, and to compile enough evidence to overwhelm any skeptics.

The second reason for the delay was that his conclusions resulted in an unavoidable sense of dread. Darwin was a timid man who loathed confrontation, and he well knew that his ideas would likely stir great controversy. Discussions of evolution had already been frequently attacked as heretical. For example, in 1844 an anonymous author published a book entitled *Vestiges of the Natural History of Creation*. The book began with a description of the laws of physics and the chemistry involved in the formation of the Earth, the solar system, and the surrounding stars, as those things were understood at the time. The Earth's geology and the fossils that it contains were also described. The author noted that with the progression of geologic time the fossils of more and more complex forms of life had been deposited in the strata. These observations led to what was described as an obvious question. If God had made the heavenly bodies by means of the natural laws of physics, "what is to hinder our supposing that the organic creation is also a result of natural laws, which are in like manner an expression of His will?"[5]

The arguments offered in *Vestiges* were weak and very often based on erroneous assumptions, but the most scathing criticisms were not concerned with the science. They were accusations of heresy. Even the renowned geologist Adam Sedgwick offered a powerful rebuke. Sedgwick declared that if the book were true, "religion is a lie; human law a mass of folly and a base injustice; morality is moonshine."[6]

It was clear to the shy and reserved Darwin that the publication of his observations would probably invite virulent attacks, so he was not all that anxious to publish his findings—at least not yet. Darwin's procrastination was finally interrupted, however, when he received a most unexpected letter from Alfred Russel Wallace.

Wallace was a young naturalist who had read Darwin's book describing his world voyage many years earlier, and had set out on his own voyages of discovery. Wallace had read *Vestiges* and was looking for evidence to support the concept of the upward evolution of life and the mechanisms that could cause it. As a way to finance his travels, Wallace gathered insect and bird specimens and forwarded them to dealers, collectors, and scientists in England. Darwin was a customer, and the two would occasionally exchange letters.

Darwin had encouraged Wallace in his endeavor and had even mentioned that he had some ideas about how evolution worked. Wallace then decided he would write to Darwin to explain his own ideas. When Darwin read Wallace's letter, he was shocked to see much of his own long-developed theory being proposed by Wallace. The two theories were not identical, but the central principle was essentially the same. It was as though Alfred Russell Wallace had discovered natural selection while Charles Darwin was still dotting his "i"s and crossing his "t"s.

Darwin's friends, geologist Charles Lyell and biologist Joseph Hooker, scurried to help Darwin establish the precedence of his ideas, but Darwin saw to it that Wallace would receive proper credit for his discovery. He arranged for the Linnaean Society to receive a paper on Wallace's work along with his own. Though the discovery is usually attributed to Darwin, in the annals of science Charles Darwin and Alfred Russel Wallace share credit for the discovery of natural selection.

When the reports to the Linnaean Society attracted little notice, Darwin concluded that the time had come for him to present his full argument to a scientific journal. Over the years, Darwin's notebook (that he had entitled *Natural Selection*) had swelled to an enormous volume, containing hundreds of thousands of words. It contained everything he had learned on the subject over many years of research. When he tried to summarize his work for publication in a scientific journal, he had difficulty editing it down to the customary length. He was reluctant to remove many of the evidentiary examples that he had accumulated over the years, and which he imagined would counter many of the criticisms that he expected. After he had edited his massive essay down to the length of a normal book—a mere 490-page "abstract" of the origin version—the journal publisher agreed to publish it as a separate volume. It would be entitled *On the Origin of Species by Means of Natural Selection; or, the Preservation of Favored Races in the Struggle for Life*.

Darwin's book on evolution was the culmination of nearly a lifetime of studying the natural world. As a boy from a comfortable family, Charles spent much of his time collecting and studying pebbles, insects, and birds. As a teenager, he and his brother built a laboratory where they experimented with chemicals and crystals. Like his older brother, his father, and his grandfather before him, Charles was expected to attend medical school and become a physician. But the young man had no stomach for medicine. He was particularly horrified by surgical operations, usually performed without anesthesia. So he kept himself busy with his study of natural history.

When Charles announced that he would not be a doctor, his very disappointed father insisted that he instead become a member of the clergy. Charles agreed and attended Cambridge University in pursuit of a degree in theology. But his passion remained the study of nature. He read the books of the world's leading naturalists, many of whom had traveled extensively, and he too wanted to travel to far-away places and learn about the processes of nature.

Eventually, Darwin received an offer through one of his professors at Cambridge. It was an opportunity that would change his life and would ultimately forever change the world's understanding of biology as well. He would accompany Captain Robert Fitzroy on a voyage around the world that was assigned to test a new generation of precisely engineered clocks and to map the coastline of South America, particularly its harbors. In that era, Navy Captains did not socialize with their crews and Captain Fitzroy decided he needed a companion to mitigate the solitude that would ensue on the five-year voyage. The companion would also act as an unofficial naturalist with the charge of documenting the geology along with the plants and animals that would be encountered around the world. Darwin set sail with Captain Fitzroy and his crew aboard the *H.M.S. Beagle* in December 1831.

In the beginning of the voyage Darwin was enthralled by a new book called *Principles of Geology* by Charles Lyell. Building on the observations of a Scottish gentleman farmer named James Hutton fifty years earlier, Lyell suggested that the Earth often experiences various states of flux and is constantly changing and evolving as a result of natural forces. Lyell illustrated how the present character of the Earth and its geological features could be explained by its historical evolution. In those days, the idea that the Earth' geology had changed or evolved, since its creation, was as radical as the idea of the evolution of species.

Encountering earthquakes and active volcanoes, along with the lava flows and the rifts of previous geologic events, Darwin could see Lyell's principles at work right before his eyes. Darwin would later write:

The very first place which I examined, namely St. Jago in the Cape de Verde islands, showed me clearly the wonderful superiority of Lyell's manner of treating geology, compared with that of any other author, whose works I had with me or even afterwards read.[7]

This new understanding of geology would eventually enable Darwin to envision how the interplay between plants, animals, and the ever-changing geology of the Earth could account for the dispersion of species that he found on the voyage.

As the *Beagle* surveyed South America's coasts and its harbors, Darwin had ample time to explore the mainland and the islands they encountered. Darwin spent most of his time on land, taking excursions inland for many weeks at a time. He even climbed the Andes Mountains and rejoined the *Beagle* as it progressed north, up the west coast. Everywhere he went, Darwin asked lots of questions about the history of the land, its geology, and its flora and fauna. He saw an abundance of new species unlike anything in Europe, and he and the ship's crew gathered a great many specimens, especially birds, to be sent back to England.

In Argentina, Darwin found the fossilized teeth and bones of several mammals that were unusually enormous. He guessed that perhaps they were the remains of giant ground sloth and rhinoceroses that had long ago gone extinct as a result of the Biblical Flood. He had the fossils shipped home to England ahead of the *Beagle*, though he did not yet realize the significance of his find. At that time, very few fossils had been preserved for study. In fact, until then, there had been only one specimen of an extinct mammal in all of England. Darwin sent so many unusual specimens back to England that, by the time he returned, he had already gained a prominent reputation as a naturalist.

By the end of his journey, Darwin had become a more mature and independent thinker with a better understanding of how to study the natural world with the use of disciplined scientific methods.[8] The five-year expeditionary voyage of the *Beagle* was to become the foundation upon which Darwin's understanding of the natural world would flourish. But it was not until after he had returned to England that Darwin began to truly understand the significance of what he had seen.

As he sorted and catalogued the bird collections he began to see distinctive patterns of biogeography. In the geographically isolated Galapagos Islands[*], for example, he found many similar species of finches that were each differently adapted to fill ecological roles (such as insect-eaters or seed-eaters, etc.) that would normally be filled by birds like warblers, woodpeckers, and parrots. Since these other birds were not present on the islands, the finches had evolved in a way that enabled them to take advantage of opportunities in each of those ecological niches.

Similarly, with the help of James Gould, one of England's leading ornithologists, Darwin came to realize that each of several islands was inhabited by separate species of mockingbirds and finches. As it had been initially unclear to Darwin whether they were just different varieties or separate species, he began to consider the idea of the transformation of species. He would later write that, as he compared the birds from each of the islands of the Galapagos archipelago, "both with one another and with those of the American mainland, I was much struck how entirely vague and arbitrary is the distinction between species and varieties." Also, since the environment on each of the islands was very similar, Darwin began to think that the only reason the islands would contain unique and different species was if each of those separate species had evolved independently of the others.

At first, as the evidence of evolution began to accumulate, Darwin was horrified. Could his grandfather have been right after all? Darwin's timidity and terrible fear of controversy was manifested by

---

[*] The Galapagos Islands were, and continue to be, a fruitful place to study evolution because they were never connected to the nearby continent of South America. They were formed, like the Hawaiian Islands, as a result of volcanoes rising up out of the sea. As a result, many species have been isolated on the islands for many centuries to evolve independently of the nearby species of South America.

heart palpitations and stomachaches. He knew that the laws of nature that governed plants and animals also governed human beings, and he knew the reaction that such ideas tended to elicit. He nevertheless plodded forward. In July 1837 Darwin began his first organization of notes on the "Transmutation of Species." He would later write:

> During the voyage of the *Beagle* I had been deeply impressed by discovering in the Pampean formation great fossil animals covered with armour like that on the existing armadillos; secondly, by the manner in which closely allied animals replace one another in proceeding southward over the continent; and thirdly, by the South American character of most of the productions of the Galapagos archipelago, and more especially by the manner in which they differ slightly on each island of the group; none of these islands appearing to be very ancient in a geological sense.
>
> It was evident that such facts as these, as well as many others, could be explained on the supposition that species gradually become modified; and the subject has haunted me. But it was equally evident that neither the action of the surrounding conditions, nor the will of the organisms (especially in the case of plants) could account for the innumerable cases in which organisms of every kind are beautifully adapted to their habits of life...

Darwin concluded that evolution was a reality. He continued to gather evidence as he tried to understand the processes involved. He particularly needed to find the cause or the mechanism by which evolution could be produced. He thought Lamarck's theories to be inadequate, so he worked to find a more plausible explanation.

After about fifteen months, it finally came to him in September 1838. Darwin had read a rather dreary book written in 1798 by Thomas Malthus called *An Essay on the Principle of Population*. The book was a warning about human overpopulation that spoke about the inevitability of exponential population growth if unchecked by war, disease, or "moral restraint." The book induced Darwin to realize the significance of the populations of most all plants and animals producing many more offspring than conditions can usually sustain. It then occurred to him that this struggle to survive is naturally characterized by some individuals within the populations having a greater chance of survival and reproduction than others, depending on certain traits, whether behavioral or physical.

Naturally, the properties of those individuals that survive and reproduced will be passed along to their offspring, thus preserving those favorable traits in the species population more and more over time. As environmental conditions change, adaptations will occur through the process of favoring the reproduction of individuals exhibiting variations that benefit their function in the new environment, while the genes of disadvantaged individuals are passed along to the next generation at a reduced rate. All the while, the general trend (while not being a strict rule) will gravitate toward increased complexity for more resilience and more favorable traits of adaptability. In his autobiography, Darwin explained how the concept had come to him:

> I happened to read for amusement Malthus on Population, and being well prepared to appreciate the struggle for existence which everywhere goes on from long-continued observation of the habits of animals and plants, it at once struck me that under these circumstances favorable variations would tend to be preserved, and unfavorable ones to be destroyed. The result of this would be the formation of new species. Here, then, I had at last got a theory by which to work.[9]

Darwin called the process described by his new theory *Natural Selection* as a corollary to the man-made selection that occurs in the process of modifying or improving domesticated plants and animals. When we hear references to "Darwin's theory," it is not the theory of evolution. That is not really his. It is the theory of Natural Selection.

Indeed, the term "Darwinian evolution" refers to evolution by means of natural selection, not merely evolution.

It was not until more than twenty-one years after his initial conception of the theory, and after the accumulation of an enormous volume of documented observations and experimental data, that Darwin finally published *On the Origin of Species*. He received praise from some reviewers—particularly his friends and allies. Physician, surgeon, and zoologist Thomas Henry Huxley in particular became a vocal supporter of Darwin and his theories. But just as Darwin had anticipated and feared, his work was met from some quarters with virulent criticism and accusations of heresy. Though he did not include any assertions regarding the evolution of human beings, the implication was plain enough.

The Quarterly Review proclaimed that Darwin's theory "contradicted the revealed relation of the creation to its Creator," and that it was "inconsistent with the fullness of His Glory." The review that Darwin found most disturbing came from the famous anatomist Richard Owen, whom Darwin had admired for many years. Owen declared that Darwin's thesis was an "abuse of science." Owen was not opposed to the idea of evolution so much as he abhorred the idea that biological processes could be driven by what he considered to be the blind materialism described by Darwin. It is believed that much of Owen's animosity was driven as much by professional jealousy as it was by any legitimate scientific concern. His review deliberately distorted the facts in an effort to discredit the new theory. It is also believed by many that Owen wrote his unusually harsh review out of anger at both Darwin and Darwin's friend and ally Thomas Henry Huxley, who had made it a practice to antagonize Owen because of what he (and others) perceived to be Owen's arrogance.

Despite the vigorous support of Darwin's closest associates, of the five major theories that Darwin put forth in *Origin of Species*, only two were initially accepted by a significant majority of the scientific community—the theory of *evolution* and the theory of *common descent*. In fact, by around 1870 the general idea of biological evolution had gained near universal acceptance among scientists. Darwin's other three, and much more novel theories—*gradualism, speciation,* and *natural selection*—would not be generally accepted for many years.

Darwin's primary theory about how evolution worked, natural selection, turned out to be difficult for many people to truly comprehend. Moreover, for those that did understand it, the concept tended to evoke notions of a philosophical materialism that excluded God in ways that were unthinkable. As a result, several evolutionary theories that were loosely based on long-held and competing philosophical ideas persisted until well into the twentieth century.

Two such theories, as noted earlier, were *transmutationism* (based on "saltations" or sudden large-scale mutations, where a species could instantly mutate into a different species), and *transformationism* (evolution through the inheritance of acquired characteristics). A third theory is *orthogenesis,* also called *finalism* (evolution by means of a teleological force). The first two of these theories—*transmutationism* and *transformationism*—were largely influenced by a philosophical understanding of the universe, called *essentialism,* that had been widely accepted since its original development in ancient Greece by the Pythagoreans and by Plato.[10]

Essentialism holds that each thing in the universe is characterized by its unique "essence." This fixed and immutable essence defines the "class" within which each thing can be categorized. Plato suggested that the universe is composed of fundamentally unalterable ideas and forms, and that each object in the physical universe is merely a reflection of a particular, permanent essence—an intrinsic nature that underlies the object and is unaffected by superficial variation. For instance, chairs may differ from one to another, but the essence of a chair—the distinct "type" that is a chair—remains fixed.

When applied to nature, essentialism precludes the possibility of speciation. Though the individuals of a given species may differ from one to another, and though they will tend to differ from one generation to the next, they nevertheless remain the reflection of an underlying immutable essence. Any variations are merely superficial and are ultimately limited to the parameters dictated by that organism's underlying essence.

As noted in the beginning of this chapter, the idea of essentialism is consistent with and has been facilitated by the Jewish, Christian, and Muslim belief that was held for many years, which proclaimed that God created all things "in the beginning" just as we see them today. All living members of each species, therefore, would be the direct descendents of the first pair of a specific "kind" or "type," just as they had been originally created directly by God and given their name by Adam in the beginning.

Accordingly, a widely accepted understanding of the universe in the medieval and post-medieval world was based on the "scala naturae" or "great chain of being." This idea proclaimed that everything in the universe, from earth, stones, and minerals to plants and animals, could be categorized within a hierarchal gradient beginning with the lowest and most material things and progressing upward toward the highest, most complex, and spiritual things. This "scale of nature" was the manifestation of God's will, and it could not change without God's direct intervention. It was also believed that none of these "essences" or "kinds" could ever cease to exist, because such an interruption of the "great chain of being" would be a violation of God's divine plan.[11]

Naturally, as evidence accumulated over many years that revealed the continual evolution of the Earth's geology, its living inhabitants, as well as the entire cosmos, the concepts of essentialism and the "great chain of being" were almost universally abandoned. Despite the disintegration of these philosophies, however, several evolutionary theories that were strongly influenced by a philosophical bent toward the principles of essentialism persisted until they were finally shown to be hopelessly unworkable by the scientific discoveries of the late nineteenth and early twentieth centuries.

Some remnants of the principle of essentialism have even persisted within human culture to this day. Tragically, it is the basis of belief behind many stereotypic and racist attitudes—drawing on the assumption that individuals of a particular "kind" will necessarily possess all of the (often erroneously assumed) characteristics that define that "kind." Fortunately, what we now know about Darwinian evolution and genetics completely undercuts the notion that a species or an ethnic race can be defined by any underlying immutable essence.

Another ideology that affected pre-Darwinian ideas about evolution was *finalism*. Originating with Aristotle, finalism separates "final causes" from "efficient causes." An efficient cause is the mechanism or the "natural" cause of an event. The "final cause," on the other hand, is the intended goal or the purpose of that event. Much like essentialism, finalism was consistent with most Christian thinking because of the long-held Christian belief that there is a final cause—a direct purpose, according to God's plan—for everything that exists and everything that occurs.

As the evidence of biological evolution began to accumulate in the nineteenth century, the concept of finalism was then applied to the reasoning for a mechanism that would drive evolutionary change. Several theories were based on the idea of evolution being driven by a purposeful force. These various theories, referred to as "orthogenetic" or "autogenetic" theories, suggested that plant and animal species are steadily changed by a teleologic (purposeful) force and intrinsic drive toward greater complexity and improvement. All such theories were abandoned, however, when they could not be supported by evidence of either the mechanisms that produce change or a consistent advance toward complexity or improvement. (As we heard from Thomas Aquinas in Chapter 3, of course, the mere fact that there is no teleologic *force* at play in the mechanisms that drive evolutionary change certainly does not preclude the possibility that the seemingly purposeless mechanistic processes that do drive evolutionary change could, nevertheless, ultimately serve God's ends.)

With the religious and philosophical objections and diversions aside, there were a few scientifically based objections with which Darwin had to contend. A significant obstacle concerned the question of how complex structures, such as an eye, an inner ear, or bird or bat wings, could have been formed through incremental steps when the rudimentary beginnings of such structures could not have offered the same selective benefits to the organism that the fully formed structures do. If in fact the building blocks of evolutionary change are composed of small inheritable variations that occasionally produce beneficial novelties, how could the slight beginnings of structures which could only much later serve the functions with which we are familiar be advantageous enough to the organism to be naturally selected?

Darwin's answer was that such rudimentary structures could be advantageous to the organism in ways that are not directly related to those functions that might proceed after further development. For instance, bird feathers are believed to have evolved from the scales of dinosaurs initially as a means of more efficient heat insulation. They obviously could not have evolved *in anticipation* of flight. Another example is that the air-breathing lung is thought to have evolved from the swim bladder of fish. The lungfishes of Africa, Australia, and South America offer examples of intermediate forms. These fishes live in muddy oxygen-depleted waters. Darwin's answer to this question has stood the test of modern research and analysis, and it is still regarded as the best explanation. (The systematic development and refinement of complex structures will be discussed at greater length in the following chapter.)

Among the scientific objections that were raised concerning Darwin's theories, there were three that gave him serious trouble. The first of these was the lack of representative "intermediate types" in the fossil record. In Darwin's era, the collection and preservation of fossil remains had just begun, so there were a great deal fewer specimens to work with than are available today. Darwin also did not fully appreciate the often abruptly varying speed of evolutionary changes. Modern paleontologists have accumulated overwhelming evidence indicating that species sometimes remain stable for long periods and then undergo relatively rapid and significant evolutionary changes. The issue of "gaps" in the fossil record remains perhaps the greatest *perceived* weakness in the evidence for evolution. But a great many gaps have been filled since Darwin's era and, as we will see in Chapter 8, such gaps continue to be filled on a regular basis.

The second issue that gave Darwin so much trouble concerned the age of the Earth. In order for Darwinian evolution to have time to have produced the diversity of life that exists today, the Earth would have to be much older than was generally believed in the mid-nineteenth century. Geologists had already begun to recognize that the Earth was much older than the 6,000 years proclaimed by the Church, but Darwin's theory required a span of time that seemed almost inconceivable. Darwin supposed that the Earth must have been at least 100 million years old. Darwin's contention suffered a serious blow, however, when the respected physicist Lord Kelvin estimated the age of the Earth by calculating the amount of time that it would take for a mass the size of the Earth to cool from its initial molten state. Kelvin eventually refined his findings down to an estimate of about 24 million years—much younger than Darwin had supposed. Kelvin's calculations, however, did not account for the heat-producing radioactivity of the Earth's molten core that was discovered at the end of the nineteenth century. We now know, based on several methods of analysis, that the Earth is very much older than even Darwin had imagined—about 4.6 billion years.

The third objection was the most troublesome, since it seemed to undermine the very basis upon which natural selection could work. In 1867, a Scottish engineer named Fleeming Jenkin pointed out that any beneficial novelties that might arise in an individual organism would soon be dispersed and diluted as the individual bred with "normal" members of the population.[12] That is, since the exact same novelty is very unlikely to arise in other individuals, it would soon be extinguished by dilution.

Faced with the very powerful and logical objections of both Kelvin and Jenkin, Darwin began to lose confidence in his own theory. As a result, he felt it necessary to introduce a supplementary mechanism that could expedite evolutionary change. Darwin then published a two-volume book illustrating his new theory of *pangenesis*. The theory offered a detailed explanation of hereditary processes that justified the reintroduction of the old Lamarckian idea of the inheritance of acquired characteristics, which was gaining wide acceptance among scientists. We now know, of course, it was completely wrong.

To his great credit, Alfred Russel Wallace, the co-discoverer of natural selection never wavered. Wallace was one of perhaps only two prominent scientists who remained steadfastly loyal to the principle of natural selection—completely rejecting the idea of the inheritance of acquired characteristics. The other one was a German biologist named August Weismann whose research led him to the conclusion that acquired traits could not be transmitted to offspring through germ cells (reproductive cells).

The irony in Darwin's great blunder of introducing *pangenesis* is that the answer to Jenkins objection had been sitting on Darwin's bookshelves all along—evidently unread. An Austrian monk named Gregory Mendel had published a paper that served as a clear answer to the issue raised by Jenkin less than a year after Jenkin's objection had been published. And Mendel had sent a copy to Darwin.

Jenkin and other scientists of that era assumed that inheritable characteristics simply *blend* into subsequent generations. Through carefully managed experiments, Mendel demonstrated that inheritable traits *do not blend*, as a liquid might do, but are instead transmitted as if by means of insoluble "particles" that act in different ways under different circumstances. For instance, prior to Mendel's work it would naturally be assumed that a cross between a tall variety of pea plant and a dwarf variety of pea plant would result in only pea plants of medium height in subsequent generations. Mendel discovered that, instead, no medium plants were produced at all. In the first generation all of the offspring were tall, so it could easily have been assumed that the genetic material of the dwarf variety had been destroyed. In subsequent generations, however, the dwarf variety would reoccur in a clear ratio of one dwarf for every three tall plants, as seen in the illustration at right. Working with several distinct characteristics among separate varieties of pea plants, Mendel worked out the mathematics of how heritable factors are propagated throughout a population through generations. Mendel discovered what we now call *dominant* and *recessive genes*.

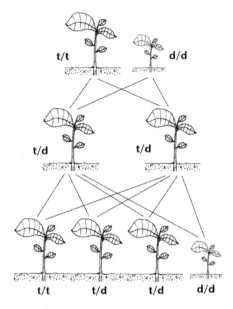

Mendel's discovery decimated Jenkin's assertion that genetic novelties would be diluted by interbreeding, and would eventually dissipate. Mendel's work also demonstrated that the outward appearance of an individual organism, is not necessarily a direct corollary guide to its genetic make-up. In other words, the *phenotype* (physical character) of an organism is not a complete indicator of its *genotype* (genetic structure).[13]

Charles Darwin was not the only scientist who did not notice Mendel's work. Mendel's findings went unnoticed in all of the scientific community until some thirty-five years later, when a group of biologists came across his paper in 1901 and realized that it contained the key to understanding heredity. Paradoxically, as the discovery of genetics eliminated one objection to Darwin's theory, it created a new one among the first geneticists who were conducting laboratory experiments with gene manipulation.

In his study of hereditary processes, biologist Hugo de Vries encountered striking variations in his primroses that had occurred in a single step through the alteration, or "mutation" as he called it, of genetic material. The differences were so pronounced that de Vries thought the resulting primrose represented an entirely new species.[14] In the following decades laboratory geneticists working with a variety of organisms discovered that small genetic changes could produce profound effects. In fruit flies, for example, gene mutations could result in flies with no wings or an extra set of wings or with curled instead of straight wings or with extra legs or with legs in place of antennae or with different shaped eyes or with white, purple or yellow instead of the normal red eyes.

As a result of such findings, most of the leading laboratory geneticists concluded that evolution was driven by abrupt and profound changes due only to genetic mutations, rather than by the very small incremental changes and natural selection that Darwin and Wallace had proposed. On the other hand, most naturalists, taxonomists, and breeders of domesticated plants and animals who could see evolution at work in the real world continued to believe in evolution by means of natural selection. This dispute persisted for about thirty years, until new findings and analysis in the 1930s and 1940s resulted in what came to be known as the "New Synthesis" or "Modern Synthesis"—so named because the findings of several scientific disciplines, most importantly genetics, were combined with a new appreciation of Darwinian evolutionary theory. Some have called the synthesis of Darwinian theory and genetics "Neo-Darwinism," but it is really just Darwinian evolution more fully explained and understood. While Charles Darwin had no idea about the underlying mechanism of heredity—genetics—he certainly understood the role of variation and heredity in the processes of natural selection and, thus, evolution.

Genetic scientists came to realize that large mutations are exceptions to the norm and are usually fatal. They also began to understand the significance of how even a small gene mutation can be advantageous, deleterious, or neutral to the welfare of its host. If the mutation enables its host to survive and/or to reproduce more effectively, then it will be preserved and passed on to subsequent generations, and if it is injurious to its host, it will be less apt to enhance survival and reproduction.

We also now know that "neutral" mutations often remain in a genotype for long periods until they may become either advantageous or disadvantageous as other genetic changes occur. Even more significantly, we now know that gene mutation is not the only source of variation in a species, and that genetic variation occurs much more frequently than anyone had previously imagined.

Most animals and many plants are sexually derived—they are formed as a result of the combination of genetic information received from each of two parents. Each of us receives half of our genes from our mother and half from our father, but we are nevertheless unlike our siblings. Indeed, our genetic make-up is unlike anything in human history. We are the product of what is referred to as the *recombination* of our parents' genetic material. Genes are not simply passed to descendents as whole particles. They are linked together as DNA along strands of chromosomes. Human beings, for instance, have 23 pairs of chromosomes. When germ cells (egg or sperms cells) are formed, the chromosome pairs split, resulting in 23 individual chromosomes. Then when egg and sperm cells are united in conception, the resulting zygote's cells will again have 23 pairs of chromosomes. The recombination occurs with the merger of the germ cells. When the pairs of chromosome strands merge, they do so in a somewhat random way, which affords the possibility of billions of different and novel gene sequences. In combination with gene mutation, the reconfiguration of the genetic make-up of organisms that takes place as a result of sexual reproduction provides an abundant and endless source of genetic novelty upon which natural selection can work.

It was once assumed that the particulate nature of genes would provide for the prediction of very specific characteristics with the known presence of identifiable genes. Scientists have discovered, however, that genes generally do not produce physical characteristics on a one-to-one basis. Instead they very often work in sequences, with the effects of a gene working in concert with other genes, or with the effects of a gene being altered or "turned on" or "off" by one or more other genes. Furthermore, genes do not even directly affect characteristics at all. Instead, they dictate the synthesis of proteins. It is the proteins produced according to the instructions of genes that determine the distinctive structures of organisms and their various properties and functions. For this reason, when mutation produces a new gene, its survival and its effect on the organism are contingent upon how well it harmonizes with the symphony of pre-existing genes.

Along with a better understanding of genetics came a better understanding of how natural selection produces evolutionary change. A central contention of Darwin's theory was that evolution takes place in populations, not in individuals. The Modern Synthesis merged Darwinian theory with a mathematical understanding of genetics that supported this idea. Much of modern evolutionary genetic research has moved beyond the genetic variability of individuals. It is focused more on understanding the genetic variability within the so-called *gene pool* of a given population of organisms, along with understanding the mechanisms that can induce evolutionary change in a gene pool.

New technologies in scientific research have enabled numerous discoveries that further support Charles Darwin and Alfred Russel Wallace's theory of natural selection, while those same technologies have also helped to facilitate the demise of competing theories that had been based on principles of *essentialism* and *finalism*. By the 1940s, the "Modern Synthesis," much like the original publication of *On the Origin of Species* in 1859, had marked a new era of thinking about all of creation.

Predominant Christian thinking has had to make numerous adjustments over the past several centuries. Perhaps none was more jolting than that which became necessary with the discovery of the true age of the Earth and the evolution of species. Christians may be comforted in knowing, however, that none of those adjustments have required a rewriting of Scripture. Scripture never really got it wrong. Instead, the errors were attributable to men's much too shallow understanding of Scripture. When properly understood, the Bible does not insist that the Earth is flat or that it is at the center of the solar system, and it does not declare that all living things are defined by an immutable essence.

As we learn more about the natural world, we need not struggle with any notion of compromising a personal understanding of the truth of Scripture. We can instead be open to the discovery of an even greater richness and depth of Scriptural truth, as it can be understood in conjunction with the natural and glorious world in which we live. An understanding of biological evolution can surely reveal just that—the natural glory of our world.

6

"Let the Land Produce Living Creatures"

W e live in a universe that is characterized by a great many immutable parameters that we recognize as the laws of physics or the laws of nature. One of these fundamental laws is the Second Law of Thermodynamics. Like all the laws of physics, it pertains to all things in the known universe. The Second Law of Thermodynamics dictates that all of the thermal energy in the universe is dissipating—that the entirety of the contents of the universe is moving toward a state of entropy. Entropy is the absence of usable thermal energy, often described as the degree of "disorder" or "randomness" in a system. It is primarily by this law that we know that the universe is not eternal—that, just as the Bible tells us, it had a beginning. In a closed system, such as the universe as a whole, energy and matter (ultimately the same thing) are constantly moving toward dispersal and disorder, indicating that they were originally in a purely organized state at a single point. We can also see this phenomenon locally as the heat of an object (a cup of coffee, for example) naturally dissipates until it is equal to its surroundings. What was originally separate and distinct (orderly) becomes the same and indistinct (disorderly or random). Without the intervention of an outside force, everything always progresses toward a state of decay, from the universe as a whole to the rusty hinges on an exterior gate.

Given this universal law of nature, we may wonder how it is possible that order can naturally emerge from disorder—how life might spontaneously emerge from inanimate chemistry—how a species of organisms can evolve into one of greater complexity and adaptability—how one species can evolve into two or more species—how those species further speciate to thrive in a diversity of ecosystems—and how a species can arise that is so intelligent and capable that it can build great cities and even machines that travel to other planets, as well as contemplate its own existence. The answer is that these things do not occur in a closed system. They occur in a system that receives a regular input of energy from the sun—energy that is the primary impetus of an evolving planet, as it acts in concert with other forces and the universal laws of nature.

We can see lots of examples of structures that emerge from the forces of nature. Of course a rainbow has already been mentioned as an example of how order is created (the separation of wavelengths) when sunlight is refracted as it passes through water droplets in the atmosphere. The Earth's irregular heating and cooling from intermittent exposure to the sun, as the planet rotates and orbits the sun on a tilted axis, creates weather and climatic patterns of great variation and complexity. As a result of the forces within these systems, rivers, canyons, ocean currents, both arid and tropical climates, and the polar ice caps have been created.

Gravity and the magnetic field of the Earth also play critical roles in creating and/or dictating the character of emerging structures. The Earth's magnetic field itself is the result of our planet's orderly, layered structure and its molten iron core, all of which were shaped by centrifugal and gravitational forces. The direction in which very large tropical storms rotate is of course dictated by the Earth's rotation and the opposing orientation of the so-called Coriolis effect in the northern and southern hemispheres.

Natural patterns and structures are usually the result of numerous forces, laws of physics, and unique properties of constituent materials. They are also usually the result of accumulative effects, with the structure's character evolving as the organization builds—as one thing leads to the next. The elegant patterns of undulating ripples in windblown sand dunes, for example, are the products of accumulative effects. The forces of wind, gravity, and friction act upon grains of sand as they move and collide with each other and fall to rest. As a grain comes to rest, it affects the forces acting on adjacent grains by occupying a space that contributes to the whole of a more wind-resistant structure. In the case of crystals, intermolecular forces induce the bonding of molecules in spite of other forces that tend to pull them apart. It is only after an accumulation of bonded molecules, to a point of a critical mass possessing enough attractive force, that crystals become stable enough to remain intact and then grow to their full potential. Sand dunes, river canyons, the orderly alignment of pebbles and sand along lakeshores and seashores, stalactites and stalagmites are all organized structures resulting from the cumulative effects of natural forces.

Despite the entropic trend of the universe as a whole, emerging complexity has been commonplace among its component parts. Since the initial point of creation, matter and energy within the universe have been continually evolving as they have been affected by momentum and by the forces and the laws of nature.

As understood by physicists and cosmologists, immediately after the so-called Big Bang the resulting energy and heat were so intense that only photons (particle-like units of light) could exist. Within only a fraction of the universe's first second of existence, as it expanded and began to cool, photons began to transmute their energy into the first particles of matter, including quarks and then the three-quark structures known as protons and neutrons. Within about a minute of further expansion and cooling, smaller particles emerged, including electrons. Only after about a million years of further cooling were the first stable atoms formed out of those elemental particles—atoms of hydrogen, containing a one proton and one neutron as its nucleus surrounded by a single electron, and smaller amounts of helium, with two protons and two neutrons in the nucleus surrounded by two electrons. (This initial "fireball" with which our universe began left a cosmic background radiation "signature" that is still detectable today.)[1]

Only the lightest elements existed for quite a long while after the Big Bang—mostly hydrogen, along with helium and trace amounts of lithium and beryllium. (Today, hydrogen still constitutes about 90 percent of the atoms and 75 percent of the mass in the visible universe. Almost all of the remaining 10 percent is helium, while all of the other known elements constitute only a minuscule portion.) After about a billion years, enormous clouds of hydrogen and helium had formed stars and galaxies as a result of gravitational and centrifugal forces. The heavier elements that make possible the formation of planets and living creatures then resulted from nuclear reactions that occurred within the explosions of massive stars (supernovas). After the heavier elements were created, gravitational and centrifugal forces collected them into solar systems with planets, moons and, in the case of our own solar system, a few remaining bits of debris in the form of comets and asteroids.

Soon after the atoms of the various elements were created, many bonded with different kinds of atoms to form molecules and compounds. These are, of course, the building blocks of life. Astronomers have identified many of the essential molecules of life in space, including methane, ammonia, formaldehyde, and water. Some scientists believe it is likely that other components of life, such as amino acids, purines, and pyrimidines, are also common in space, perhaps even among the components of those comets that occasionally sprinkle their ingredients onto the Earth. A meteorite that fell in September 1969 near Murchison, Australia was found to be "rich" in amino acids.

The ingredients for life on Earth may have come from meteorites, or they may have been present with the planet's formation, or they may have been later formed through natural events on the early Earth. In 1953, chemists Stanley Miller and Harold Urey, at the University of Chicago, conducted an experiment demonstrating that organic compounds could easily be created under conditions that they believed to have been present on the early Earth. In a closed system containing methane (CH_4), ammonia (NH_3), hydrogen (H_2), and water (H_2O) (all of which were believed to be major components of the

Earth's early atmosphere), they introduced a continuous electrical arc to simulate the lightning storms that were believed to be common at that time. After one week, 10 to 15 percent of the carbon had been converted to organic compounds, including some of the amino acids used in living cells to make proteins.

The Miller/Urey experiment has recently been criticized on two accounts. Many scientists are now doubtful that the Earth's early atmosphere contained the concentrations of ammonia and hydrogen that were used in the experiment. Also, though lightning was probably abundant, it would not have been continuous, as in the experiment. Even if the experiment was mistaken about the early Earth's atmosphere, however, it remains a valid demonstration of how volcanoes, which sometimes emit a similar chemistry and an abundance of lightning, could have been local centers for the synthesis of organic molecules.

In an even simpler experiment, University of Houston biochemist Juan Oro found in 1961 that an aqueous solution containing hydrogen cyanide (HCN) and ammonia (NH_3) could also produce amino acids. Just as importantly, Professor Oro's solution also produced a significant amount of adenine, one of the major component bases of nucleotides and the nucleic acids RNA and DNA. Subsequent experiments have shown that other RNA and DNA bases can also be produced through abiotic chemistry.

Though life might have begun before the advent of living cells—cells with an outer membrane capable of containing the components of life while allowing for an input of energy—no such life has been identified. (It was once thought that perhaps something akin to viruses might have arisen before the first living cells, but viruses are wholly dependent upon infected cells for their sustenance and their replication.) Some hydrocarbons have been identified that tend to assemble themselves into tiny membrane enclosures (called lipid vesicles) under experimental conditions, but it is not known how the first cells might specifically have been formed with the necessary ingredients for life.

117

Though we can see how the components of life could have emerged through natural processes, it is not known what event or process could have transformed inanimate compounds into the first autonomous, self-replicating biotic molecules—a process referred to as *abiogenesis*. It appears to have happened only once, and as far as we know, it might very well have been a miracle. But if what we have seen and understood about all of the other steps along the way of life's development is any indication, it probably was not. (Of course as we have seen, whether it was or was not a *direct*, miraculous act of God says little to nothing about what we need to know about God and His providence.)

The oldest and simplest forms of life that have been identified are tiny single-cell organisms called *prokaryotes*. These ancient microbes have been recovered from 3.5 to 3.6 billion year old geologic strata. Prokaryotic cells lack a number of the specialized structures (organelles) that are found in the much larger *eukaryotic* cells of other single-cell as well as all multi-cellular organisms. They have no distinct nucleus with a membrane—no mitochondria, chloroplasts, or paired chromosomes. The earliest of these types of organisms were believed to thrive around very hot, sulphurous seeps and volcanic vents on the ocean floor. Similar microbes can be found today around hot undersea volcanic vents, the geothermal vents in Yellowstone National Park, in similar geysers in New Zealand, or in the fuming vents of Italy's Mount Etna.[2]

Single-cell prokaryotic microbes represent two of the three phylogenetically distinct "domains" of all life on Earth—the countless species of *Archaea* and *Bacteria*. For about 2.4 billion years—some two-thirds of all the history of life on Earth—such simple single-cell microbes were the only living organisms in existence. Then about 1.4 billion years ago, a small population of these cells evolved into the more complex eukaryote cells. Eukaryotic cells are the building blocks of all of the many species of fungi, plants, and animals, including us, that have ever lived on Earth—constituting the third domain, *Eukaryota*.

The original chemical make-up of cells that were fossilized more than 3.5 billion years ago is too indistinguishable to determine whether the first cells were archaea or bacteria. But many scientists believe that there is enough evidence to suggest that the Archaea and Eukaryota domains share a common ancestor more recently than either do with Bacteria—that eukaryotic cells likely evolved from archaean type cells. This is believed to have occurred as a result of a symbiotic union of similar prokaryotic cells.

The mitochondria inside eukaryotic cells are believed to have originally been independent prokaryotic cells that were engulfed by the host cell. Mitochondria have there own cell membranes and their own genome (much like that of a prokaryote cell but much smaller) that is separate from its host cell's genome, which is contained in the nucleus. Furthermore, mitochondria reproduce in much the same way that prokaryotic cells do. It is believed that chloroplasts from cyanobacteria then entered eukaryotic cells in much the same way, creating the lineage that led to plants.

Of course mitochondria and chloroplasts are no longer independent entities. These organelles require proteins that are produced by the genes within the nucleus of their host cells. Scientists believe that the genetic code for those proteins was transferred from the organelle to the host cell at some point in evolutionary history, creating their interdependency and the eukaryotic cells that would go on to reproduce as such.[3]

A few hundred million years after the first appearance of eukaryotic cells, some of them began to band together to create the first multi-cellular organisms. In the approximately one billion years since then, life has undergone a great many transformative events, culminating in the diversity of life that we see around us today. (For a more complete account of the history of life on Earth, beginning with the first single-cell organisms, see in Chapter 8 what paleontologists have discovered through the systematic examination of fossils.)

The question of how life began can be puzzling and not really very interesting to many of us. The evolution of life through natural selection, on the other hand, is a fascinating and rather easily understood phenomenon of simple elegance. The origin of life and the evolution of life are, of course, two entirely separate matters of consideration. The cause or causes of abiogenesis were completely different than the causes of evolution. And while we do not know exactly how life began, we do know that, once begun, life has evolved and continues to evolve in a systematic and very logical way. Once organic molecules acquired the capacity to replicate themselves and to do it imperfectly, they became subject to the remarkable effects of natural selection. In arguing for the ultimate simplicity of the universe, Oxford University chemist Peter Atkins explained in his 1981 book, *The Creation*, that:

> A great deal of the universe does not need any explanation. Elephants, for instance. Once molecules have learnt to compete and to create other molecules in their own image, elephants, and things resembling elephants, will in due course be found roaming through the countryside.[4]

For most of us, elephants will likely need a great deal more explanation than Professor Atkins suggests, but he nevertheless makes a rather important point. The most remarkable thing about life is that molecules can replicate themselves in the first place. Given that they do, however, our understanding of natural selection renders the emergence of complex creatures, such as elephants, not really all that remarkable. Although, it did take quite a long time for elephants to eventually roam through the countryside.

Perhaps the greatest myth regarding Darwinian evolutionary theory is that it has something to do with the origin of life (abiogenesis). The second biggest myth about Darwinian theory is the idea that it proclaims the existence of complex organisms to be wholly accidental—that only blind chance has accounted for the complexity and the diversity of life on Earth. In his 1983 book *The Intelligent Universe*, astronomer Fred Hoyle compared the probability of abiogenesis to that of a whirlwind passing through a junkyard containing all the parts of a Boeing 747 resulting in the flawless assembly of the aircraft—a probability so remote as to be incalculable. Professor Hoyle's calculation was almost certainly an exaggeration of the actual improbability of natural abiogenesis, but his argument was nevertheless a reasonable one to make. So-called "young-Earth creationist" critics of Darwinian theory, however, have since used Professor Hoyle's analogy to profess the improbability of the development of complex organisms through Darwinian natural selection. They have evidently misunderstood the process of natural selection.

Accidents or chance occurrences are ubiquitous in our world. (As we saw in Chapter 3, the free will of human beings is contingent upon our living in a universe much like the one in which we find ourselves—one that is not bound by a determinism that would preclude accidents.) Evolution too is driven, in part, by chance events. There is the somewhat random and plentiful mutation of genetic information. There is the indeterminate recombination of genetic information during reproduction. There is also the possibility that a population of organisms could be decimated by microbial infection, or happen upon carcinogens, or be overrun by predators, or succumb to the effects of a large asteroid striking the Earth, or otherwise be impacted by chance occurrences that would affect its evolutionary path. Evolution by means of natural selection, however, is no accident. Complex living organisms do not simply materialize at random. Nor do they emerge in just a few steps as the result of any indiscriminate force resembling or analogous to a whirlwind.

Natural selection can be thought of as a sieve or a sorting process, whereby deleterious genetic characteristics and aberrations are purged from a population while beneficial aberrations are preserved. "Natural selection" could perhaps just as easily have been termed "natural elimination" because the failure of organisms to survive and pass along their genetic information is just as determinative of evolution as is successful propagation. Darwin called it "natural selection" simply because of its similarity to the "selection" involved with the domestication, by humans, of plants and animals.

In the process of domestication humans "select" those individuals that exhibit one or more desired characteristics and then breed them with similar individuals. At each successive generation, those individuals exhibiting the desired characteristics are preserved, while those that do not are removed from the population. Over multiple generations the genes that prescribe the desired characteristics will become more and more dominant in the population as those genes that would prescribe alternative characteristics are purged. The ultimate result is a unique new breed or variety.

With natural selection it is the natural environment that does the sorting. If a single-cell organism is more tolerant of temperature variations, it has a greater chance of survival and then passing its superior trait on to the next generation. Those antelope that can run fastest will be more likely to escape predators and then propagate their genetic information than a less capable antelope, ensuring that the general population of antelope can run at least fast enough to survive and prosper.

We can think of "natural elimination" as the sieve that guides evolutionary development and ensures, not necessarily the "survival of the fittest," as is often repeated, but certainly the *survival of the viable*. For example, an individual antelope born with a debilitating defect is much less likely to survive long enough to pass along its defective genes, thus ensuring the health of the greater population. Male giraffes are somewhat taller than females, and they are known to purposefully eat from the higher branches of trees and leave the lower leaves for the females. We may wonder how they learned to be so considerate. The answer is rather simple. Populations with males that did not exhibit such a propensity would have less well nourished females with which to propagate their genes. Similarly, we may wonder why all organisms possess a fierce instinctual determination for survival. Of course any organism that did not exhibit that trait would not be around to affect subsequent generations.

Indeed all organisms' first priority is survival. In order to survive they need nourishment. If it does not come to them, then they have to go and get it. It is this great instinct for survival and the necessary means of doing so that drives most evolutionary change. Organisms have to make a living, and as their environment changes, they have to find more efficient or alternative ways of making a living. As a result, they adapt and they evolve—not consciously, but through the sieve of natural selection working with the raw materials of a multitude of gene mutations and recombination.

Geneticists have discovered that genetic variation is abundant, giving the force of natural selection plenty of variation to work with. For a species that is in a stable and fruitful environment, genetic variation would only very rarely and perhaps only subtly offer any advantage for survival and fitness. In such cases variations would rarely take hold in the population. Evolution would move very slowly or not much at all. The American alligator and the various Western Hemisphere opossum species, for example, have changed very little over millions of years because they have been very successful at making a living in their environments and migrating to similar environments when needed.

For those species that experience environmental pressures, on the other hand, whether a lack of available food, a changing climate, or an introduction of predators, etc., genetic variation can occasionally provide some advantage for survival, and thus be incorporated into the population's gene pool. For example, if a group of lizards are separated from a larger group and then forced to move to a more arid environment in search of insects, or because of predators, or something else, any genetic variation that would allow the lizards to need less moisture would be beneficial to their survival and reproduction. Such a genetic change would, over many generations, be spread throughout the population. The separate population of lizards will then have evolved independently of the original group.

If the two populations are kept separated for an extended period, eventually enough genetic changes will have occurred in the gene pools of both populations so that they would no longer be able to successfully mate with each other. A new and separate species of lizards will have emerged.

Similarly, polar bears are known to have evolved from a population of brown bears that migrated north, eventually finding its way into the artic. As these bears spent more and more time in snowy conditions, the population's fur naturally turned white, since this mutation gave them better camouflage for hunting. As they began to prey on seals on arctic ice, they also grew in size, their claws grew into efficient meat hooks, and their necks and snouts grew longer and stronger so they could better snatch and extract seals from holes in the ice. At some point during the approximately 150,000 years since their separation from the ancestors that they share with today's brown bears (as measured by DNA analysis), the two population's genomes became dissimilar enough that they were no longer able to interbreed. They became separate and distinct species.

One of the more famous examples of natural selection actually being witnessed is that of the peppered moth of industrial England. Some two hundred years ago the peppered moth was white with small black speckles allowing it be camouflaged as it rested on woodland lichens. As a result of the industrial revolution, over time soot killed the lichens and turned the trees' bark black. The light colored moths then became more readily visible and therefore vulnerable to birds, while the occasional dark moth (as a result from gene mutation) became more camouflaged, increasing its odds of survival and the propagation of its genes. By the 1950s, the entire population of moths had become predominately black, with only an occasional light colored moth being observed. In 1956, Britain passed a "Clean Air Act" that reduced pollution, and eventually the trees returned to their natural color. As the tree color changed, so did the peppered moths. Today they have returned to their original ivory color with black speckles. A study determined that it only took some fifty generations for the genetic instructions for either a black or white color to become saturated in the gene pool of the population.

In the case of the peppered moth, the pressures that caused it to evolve were the changing color of the trees and the predation of birds. If the birds had not been there to prey more successfully on those moths with specific characteristics, then evolution would not have occurred.

Co-evolution

In many cases prey and predators evolve in tandem, as several species or individual species apply selective pressure to the others. For example, many newts can produce toxins in their skin secretions as a defense against predators. Some newts have toxins that are much more powerful than would ever be needed for most any predators except for a common garter snake. A half-pound garter snake can tolerate perhaps ten times the amount of newt toxicity than it would take to kill an adult human. Evidently, since some snakes could tolerate newt toxins, the newts evolved ever more powerful toxins. The snakes, in turn, then evolved more resistance to the toxins, and on and on, until both the newts' toxicity and certain snakes' resistance to it had become extremely powerful. Such a series of back and forth evolutionary responses has been called an "evolutionary arms race." When two types or two species of organisms both evolve in response to their interaction with each other, they undergo the process of *co-evolution*.

Co-evolution is commonplace in the world. The pollinators of flowering plants, whether bees and other insects, or birds, or bats have evolved a number of features to more efficiently extract nectar from flowers. Flowering plants, in turn, have evolved bright colors and nectar to attract pollinators, along with a variety of structures to more efficiently attach pollen to those pollinators so it can then be carried to nearby recipient flowers. Darwin wrote an entire book on the very many elegant ways in which orchids around the world have evolved elaborate structures for the transmission of their pollen onto a variety of pollinators.

An orchid in Madagascar named *Angraecum sesquipedale* sports a nectary inside an impressive sixteen-inch deep flower tube. Though one was not known at the time, Darwin boldly predicted that an insect would be discovered with an equally long tongue, as he was confident that some nectar-eating creature must have evolved along with the unusual flower. It wasn't until 1903, but entomologists did indeed discover just such a moth with a suitable tongue, which they named *Xanthropan morgani praedicta*, with the inclusion of *"praedicta"* in honor of Darwin's prediction.[5]

Sexual Selection

We often think of natural selection in terms of a species population's fitness or viability for survival within its environment—its ability to elude predators, its ability to cope with parasites or pathogens, or its success in competition for food and shelter, etc. But there is another way in which particular genetic qualities can be favored within a population. It involves what Darwin termed "sexual selection." Not all, but most organisms, both plant and animal, are sexual organisms. They reproduce by means of sexual intercourse. As a result, there are two important ways in which members of a species will often "select" which other individual members' genes will be consigned to subsequent generations. These are *intrasexual* and *intersexual* selection.

Intrasexual selection occurs when members of the same sex within a population compete for the privilege of propagating their genes. This usually involves males fighting with each other to establish the dominance of individuals and their right to mate with the females they choose. Northern elephant seals, for example, hurl their 3,000 to 5,000-pound bodies against each other, spewing blood and saliva, until they establish which male is the most powerful and determined, and thus, which will have the sole right to a harem of dozens of females. Naturally, this practice has resulted in a steady increase in the size of male elephant seals over generations. As a result, today male elephant seals are as much as four to five times larger than the females.

Lions behave in a similar way, with dominant males presiding over a number of females within a pride. If another male challenges and defeats the dominant male of a pride, the new leader will usually kill all of the cubs of his predecessor. After their cubs have been removed, the females will then go into heat and the newly dominant male can propagate his own genes and those traits that helped to establish his dominance.

Battles for dominance between the males of a great many species of ungulates have induced the evolution of ever more pronounced horns or antlers. In some of these cases, the mere presence of an impressive rack can prompt a different kind of sexual selection. The antlers of male moose, for example, which are made of bone and which can reach widths of up to six or seven feet, can directly attract females as a result of their size and their scent.

Intersexual selection occurs when one sex of a species (usually female) selects which individuals of the opposite sex they prefer to mate with. The most famous example of how this has guided evolutionary development is that of peahens' preference for those peacocks with elaborate tail displays. In mating season, peacocks gather into groups and call the females to them with their crows. As the females approach, the males will raise their tails and make them shiver. The peahens then choose mates that most appeal to them. Studies have shown that the peahens are attracted primarily to a large number of the "eye" designs on a peacock's elaborate tail feathers. This preference undoubtedly originated as a result of those peahens with a propensity for choosing more notable feathers choosing healthier mates for reproduction. As the traits of both the preference and the vivid tail feathers were passed along generation after generation, both traits naturally became more and more pronounced—in spite of the fact that

127

the larger tail feathers increase the vulnerability of the males to predators.

Similarly the big bright combs of roosters serve no purpose except for their attractiveness to hens. Other intersexual selection preferences include female crickets' preference for males with the most elaborate chirps; female swordtail fish's preference for males with longer tails; and female barn swallows' preference for males with long and symmetrical tail feathers.[6]

It is not difficult to see how characteristics or qualities that are favored by sexual selection for reproduction become more and more pronounced over multiple generations. Human intelligence is a good example. Intelligence is of course favored by plain old natural selection since cunning better enables any species to elude predators, capture prey, or otherwise cope with the trials of living in the natural world. But intelligence also plays a role in sexual selection since more cunning individuals will more successfully find ways to propagate their genes. In the case of humans, even after we had become successful enough to be somewhat immune to the forces of natural selection, sexual selection remained a powerful force in the amplification of intelligence over generations.[7]

Complex Structures

We can rather easily see how evolution can induce the development of structures such as peacock tails and rooster combs through small changes over generations, but many people are puzzled at how natural selection could possibly have resulted in such complex structures as eyes or wings by means of incremental steps. They tend to ask, "How could an organism benefit from half of an eye or any portion of a wing that is not well enough developed to be used for flying?" Unintelligent natural forces certainly cannot *foresee* the use of a wing for flight prior to its construction, nor can they have envisioned a fully functioning human eye prior to its evolutionary development. How then, could such complex and highly functioning organs have developed without forethought? It turns out that half an eye or half a wing might be much more useful than we tend to immediately imagine.

Eyes apparently first evolved in a creature that predates the emergence of many of the phyla that now inhabit the Earth. One indication is that similar genetic information is found across multiple phyla that appear to be instrumental in the construction of eyes, including genes that dictate their number and positioning on the body. Nevertheless, the complex structures that we know as eyes have evolved dozens of times independently and in many different ways. It is in fact rather easy to see how eyes have evolved since there are creatures alive today that possess varying stages of eye development. So-called "eyespots" (light-sensitive areas) are common among single-cell organisms. These eyespots enable an organism to detect light, often so that it can then reposition itself to enhance its photosynthesis. Some snails and flatworms have two primitive eyes positioned in slight depressions or "pits" that enable the vague detection of the direction of light. This configuration can probably only enable the creatures to tell whether or not they are in the safety of a cave or another dark protected area. Any genetic variation that results in the deepening of such an eye pit enables slightly more precise perception of the direction of light, since one side or another of the light-sensitive cells receives the light more indirectly. The more pronounced the deepening of the structure, the more precisely light direction can be detected—a trend easily produced as a result of genetic variation and natural selection.

As the pit deepens further into a concave and the size of its opening is reduced, an eye much like a pinhole camera is formed. Today's squid-like mollusk, the nautilus, possesses just such a pair of primitive pinhole eyes. The nautilus eye is shaped much like ours, but has no lens. Seawater can pass in and out of the pinhole opening. For such an eye, the genetic aberration of a tiny overgrowth of transparent cells could offer protection from parasitic infection along with the coincidental benefit of an improvement in the focus of images. It is believed that such a primitive lens of transparent cells probably developed layers with fluid between the layers, providing greater protection and gradually enabling wider angles of view and better focusing. Lenses, along with eye construction in general, have evolved in many different ways within different lineages, resulting in the wide variety of structures seen today. As Darwin noted, since the eye is imperfectly inherited—that is, inherited with variations, as it certainly is—any beneficial variations that provide some advantage in feeding or defense will naturally be incorporated into the gene pool of descendant populations. The development of complex and rather efficient eyes should be of no great surprise.

One of the most telling indicators of the evolutionary history of eyes is their imperfect construction. Because of its great complexity and efficiency of operation, the human eye is sometimes cited as evidence of God's *direct* participation in the creation of human beings. Yet the human eye (among other human anatomical features, as we will see in the following chapter) is rather inefficiently and imperfectly engineered.

When we consider its oddly contrived structure, it is evident that there was no preconception of an eye that managed its construction. It is the product of a multitude of tiny incremental changes that were adopted only by the requirement that each change would, in some way, offer an advantage over the preexisting structure. As a result, the human eye is not engineered in the best possible way. It appears as if it were jerry-rigged to a series of previous, ill-considered designs.

The retina of the human eye, as it is in all vertebrates, is inverted from what one would expect to be the ideal configuration. The all-important light-sensitive cells (rods) of the retina are located behind the nerves and blood vessels, and they are turned away from the incoming light. Before light hits the retina it must pass through a labyrinth of these nerves and blood vessels, as well as much of the structure of the rods until it reaches the light-catching layers that can "see" the light. The information is then passed through the nerves that run in front of the rods until they are gathered at a point where they pass through the retina to the optic nerve that leads to the brain. The nerves having to pass through the retina in this way results in our having a "blind spot."

The degradation of the light that reaches the light-sensitive layers of the rods is much less than we might imagine, but from an engineering standpoint, this arrangement seems quite less than perfect. We might be tempted to think that perhaps there is some reason that we do not comprehend for this odd construction of our eyes, but we can find other examples of eye construction that tell us otherwise. Cephalopod eyes (those of squid and octopuses, for example) are very similar to ours, except that the nerves carrying information from their photocells do not point forward like ours do. Instead, they lead directly out the back of the retina to the optic nerve and on to the brain, providing an unobstructed view of the world and an ability to see quite well in extremely low light conditions.

The structure of vertebrate eyes tells us a lot about how evolution works. There appears to have been no plan for the structure ahead of time—no end product in mind from the beginning. Instead, each step in the process of development was simply some slightly beneficial change from a previously existing structure. This is seen over and over again in the imperfections of biological structures, as we will see in the following chapter.

The wings of birds have also sometimes been cited as evidence of biological design with forethought, since incremental steps toward fully functional wings that would benefit their possessors each and every step of the way are, for some, difficult to imagine. Nevertheless, paleontologists have now unearthed numerous dinosaur specimens that not only establish evidence of their ancestry to birds, but also provide numerous examples of feathers that were not used for flight. Feathers evidently first evolved as a means of insulation for the benefit of warm-blooded theropod dinosaurs. As small tree-climbing dinosaurs leaped from branch to branch or from tree to tree, pronounced feather development likely enabled them to glide for a longer reach. Any genetic variation that would result in longer feathers would naturally enhance their gliding capability. Such a trend could easily lead to fully formed wings and flight capability over time. A number of fascinating examples of creatures that represent "intermediate species" between birds and theropod dinosaurs are described in Chapter 8.

Convergent Evolution

It is apparent that human and octopus eyes began from somewhat separate starting points, but have nevertheless resulted in very similar endpoints—similarly constructed eyes, except for that very telling difference noted above. The wings of birds and those of bats, too, obviously evolved from different starting points. They also took very different paths in their evolutionary progression. As mammals, bats have no feathers. Instead they evolved elongated fingers with a membrane of skin stretched between them and attached to the hind limbs. These two very different evolutionary paths have nevertheless resulted in very similar end products—wings for flying. Both of these cases are examples of what is called "convergent evolution."

There are many examples of convergent evolution that can be seen around the world. This phenomenon well illustrates the enormous power of natural selection and how it has shaped the diversity of life on Earth in concert with the Earth's environmental and ecological infrastructures. As we saw in Chapter 2, it was the ubiquity of convergent evolution around the world that induced Cambridge University paleobiologist Simon Conway Morris to conclude that the world's infrastructure may have been all that was required for the evolution of intelligent creatures.

As previously noted, all species' primary instincts are for survival and propagation. They have to make a living and they will do so in any manner that they find to be the most productive. They will exploit the resources available to them—mainly the food and shelter that has not been taken by a more capable species—while endeavoring to avoid predators. They will find and settle into a *niche* in which to thrive.

There are innumerable ecological niches in the world. In fact, each and every successful living organism thrives in its own niche—a physical location and/or a position in a predator-prey hierarchy where it can survive and prosper. Of course such niches, like the entire surface of the Earth, have changed many times over the course of the Earth's history, sometimes very dramatically and sometimes only subtly. That is why far more than 99.99 percent of all the species that have ever lived on Earth are now extinct. Those that do survive, do so because they adapt and evolve. They gradually evolve to exploit new niches or to address new challenges as they thrive in existing ones.

In addition to the cases, as noted above, of similar anatomical structures having evolved from different starting points, convergent evolution is a phenomenon where two species from wholly different evolutionary backgrounds evolve into very similar organisms as they come to exploit separate but similar ecological niches. Wholly different species of American cacti and African euphorbia, for example, have evolved into virtually identical forms as they have adapted to thrive in their separate arid environments. The independent evolution of nectar-feeding groups among four geographically separate songbird families is another example. The hummingbirds of North America, the honey-creepers of Hawaii, the honeyeaters of Australia, and the sunbirds of Africa have all evolved into very similar forms and behaviors as they have exploited similar but separate niches.[8]

The most famous examples of convergent evolution are the similarities between certain marsupial mammals, found in Australia and its surrounding islands, and certain placental mammals found in much of the rest of the world. The lineage that led to placental mammals is believed to have diverged from marsupial mammals some 140 million years ago. The continent of Australia became separated from other continents just as the dinosaurs became extinct, opening up a great many niches that could then be filled with the mammals that would evolve to exploit them. In much of the world, placental mammals proved more resilient and crowded out the marsupials. On the newly isolated island continent of Australia, however, marsupials had free rein to evolve into the available niches without competition from placentals. (This occurred in South America too, as we will see in the following chapter.) The effect of marsupial and placental mammals evolving independently of each other to exploit similar but geographically separate niches has produced some interesting and very telling results.

For instance, the common mouse is mimicked in Australia by a nearly identical creature, except for the telltale pouch in which it carries its tiny infant offspring. The mole also has a marsupial species counterpart. The ocelot is resembled by a marsupial species that has no genetic relationship to cats. The Tasmanian "tiger" similarly is not related to its bobcat equivalent. Nor is the Tasmanian wolf related to the *Canidae* family that includes the wolves of Europe, Asia, and North America. Even the flying squirrel has a marsupial counterpart—the flying phalanger. Marsupial equivalents of lemurs, anteaters, and many other groups prosper in Australia, New Guinea, and other nearby islands.

Excavations in South America have revealed a unique variety of large herbivores that evolved to exploit that continent's abundant grasslands millions of years ago. Fossils of huge rhino-like Leviathans that had no relation to the true rhinos of Africa have been recovered. As examples of convergent evolution, some of these herbivore species vaguely resembled modern animals such as elephants, camels, and horses, but were unrelated to those species. But others among these extinct herbivores looked like nothing on Earth that lives today. Despite a tendency of convergence, sometimes evolution takes a starkly different course.

In Australia, for example, the largest herbivores are very different from the grazing ungulates that exist today in most of the world, yet they evolved to possess some of the same necessary capabilities. Kangaroos have the same need to move rapidly in order to avoid predators, but they use a very different means of locomotion. Instead of the four-legged gait that horses, cattle, deer and antelope use, kangaroos use the two-legged hop. As the kangaroo developed the hop for its means of travel, it naturally evolved massive hind legs along with a large tail for balance. Kangaroos and ungulates had the same need for the capability of rapid flight, but since they began at different starting points and evolved independently, their adaptations to exploit similar environments resulted in very different characteristics that serve the same end.

As we can see, organisms evolve in any viable way that most efficiently utilizes the resources that are available to them. Populations adapt to the infrastructures and the competitive environments that they come to inhabit. And life tends to evolve toward a level of the full utilization of those infrastructures, whether local ecosystems or virtually our entire world. Through the amazing forces of nature that define our universe—natural selection being prominent among them— life, in a multitude of forms, has evolved to fully occupy the realm in which we live our lives. Just as the Bible tells us that God commanded, life has "filled the Earth."

Part 3

The Evidence of Evolution

7

Clues All Around

W hen Charles Darwin studied natural history and the processes of evolution there were five distinct areas of scientific exploration available to him — geology, biogeography, paleontology, embryology, and morphology (also known as comparative anatomy) — disciplines that were all still in their infancy at that time. Today, in addition to the great deal more that we have learned about those five categories, four additional areas of scientific inquiry have been added that are directly relevant to the study of biological evolution — molecular biology, biochemistry, population genetics, and the new and very illuminating science of genetic sequencing known as genomics. The systematic study of each of these nine areas of research, as well as the less directly relevant sciences of cosmology and quantum physics, and the integration of the findings of all of these disciplines have revealed an overwhelmingly compelling body of evidence that points to the emergence and the astonishing transformation of life on Earth over a span of about 3.6 billion years.

Newly discovered methods of testing and analysis have confirmed that the Earth is much older than anyone had suspected prior to the twentieth century. Techniques have been developed for reliably determining the age of rocks and geologic strata, fossil and organic remains, and even our solar system and the greater visible universe. We also now know that the Earth is not static. Its crust is continually moving and changing and is thereby inducing change in its living inhabitants. Scientists have discovered the fossil remains of many thousands of plants and animals that have long been extinct. Numerous evolutionary ancestors of a wide range of species that live today, including a number of our own recent ancestors, have been identified. This discovery of the rich history of the Earth and its living inhabitants has revealed a clear and logical pattern of evolutionary change.

New research capabilities have enabled scientists to discover a great deal about the inner workings of living cells. We have learned a lot about how DNA and the genes within it dictate the physical characteristics of all organisms. Scientists are even beginning to learn how instinctual and other behaviors may also be largely the product of an organism's genetic and biochemical configuration. Most relevant to the study of biological evolution, scientists have learned quite a lot about how genetic information, and therefore genetic variation, is propagated throughout the "gene pools" of organism populations. As we will see in Chapter 9, scientists have even discovered distinct genetic "markers" that have been passed down through generations of descendants, even dramatically evolved descendants, over many millions of years.

There is certainly a great deal more to learn about how evolution works and about how it has shaped the living world throughout history, but any doubts about whether biological evolution and speciation actually occur have long been dispelled. Indeed, today's biomedical, bioengineering, and other biotechnical research and innovation proceed with a firm understanding of the reality of biological evolutionary processes.

The very compelling body of evidence that has been discovered by geneticists and paleontologists will be discussed in the following chapters. But we need not rely solely on the opinions and the findings of scientists to reach our own conclusions about biological evolution. Nor do we need to have formally studied zoology, botany, paleontology, genomics, or any other field of biology to have a basic understanding of how evolution has shaped our world and to see that natural selection is the primary mechanism that guides evolutionary change. We can easily see evidence of evolution in the world around us and in the context of our own lives. The evidence is abundant enough and the logic is simple enough that evolution and natural selection can be readily understood and acknowledged by all who simply take the time to see for themselves.

Biological evolution is happening all of the time, all around us. We can see it in progress today, and we can see abundant evidence of its history. We can see it in the enterprises of horticulture and agriculture. We can see it in the distribution of plants and animals around the world. We can even see it in our domestic pets. We can also see the effects and the results of evolution in several issues concerning the practice of medicine and in our own human anatomy.

As we begin to notice many of the more easily perceptible indicators of evolution, and we then combine these observations with the enormous volume of evidence that has been gleaned from the systematic study of the fossil record, comparative anatomy, genetics, and several other related fields of scientific research, we find that an understanding of how the living world has been shaped by the natural processes of biological evolution becomes clear.

Upon reading *On the Origin of Species*, Darwin contemporary Thomas Henry Huxley reportedly remarked: "How extremely stupid not to have thought of that myself." As suggested by Huxley's comment, when the basic idea of natural selection is brought to our attention, it can seem very logical and its function in the world may even seem fairly obvious to many of us.

As we observe the world around us, we can see that almost all living organisms produce many more offspring than will survive and usually more than the local natural environment can sustain. We can see that those offspring are characterized by traits inherited from each of their parents, but they are nevertheless new and unique individuals. We can also see that those offspring that do survive do so as a result of sometimes good luck, but very often as a result of an ability to cope with the circumstances of their environment that is superior to their less fortunate siblings or other organisms that are competing for the same resources. These surviving offspring are better suited to cope with their environmental circumstances as a result of superior traits that they will, in turn, pass along to their own offspring. These simple observations along with a basic understanding of the Earth's evolving geology and a realistic conception of the enormity of geologic time, can, for many people, induce a rudimentary but nevertheless clear perception of how natural selection works to produce biological evolution.

For others, however, this organizing process may not be immediately apparent. Because we have long been accustomed to seeing the creation of life and individual organisms in a different way, the difficulty in immediately seeing and understanding the logic of natural selection can perhaps be somewhat like viewing one of those drawings that can be seen from a couple of different perspectives.* For

example, in the classic drawing seen here, people will usually see either a young woman or an old woman. Most people will not see both images until the alternative has been pointed out to them.[1] Once seen, however, the alternative perspective becomes perfectly obvious—perhaps eliciting a response somewhat similar to the one offered by Professor Huxley.

While the process of natural selection may not be immediately apparent to everyone, the fact that evolution occurs, the evidence of common decent, and even the mechanism of natural selection can be concretely demonstrated when we look at specific examples of evolution in progress and specific indicators of evolutionary history. Let us consider a few of those aspects of our world where the evidence of biological evolution and the processes by which it occurs are most apparent.

---

* In his charming and brief introduction to evolution entitled *Darwin for Beginners*, British author Jonathon Miller used the illustration of "puzzle picture[s]" in explaining how other scientists had not previously seen what Charles Darwin saw. The illustration can easily apply to us all.

Domesticated Animals

"Natural selection" is the term that Darwin chose to describe the process by which the evolution of plants and animals is guided by adaptation for survival because the process is very similar to the un-natural selection—the selective breeding, the grafting, and the controlled pollination—of plants and animals that has been undertaken by human beings for about the last ten thousand years. Human intervention has affected the evolution of a great many plants and animals, as species have been manipulated to serve both the critical needs and the simple pleasures of human beings. As a result, we can readily see the effects of evolutionary change in the animals that we consume for food, the animals whose fur or hair we use for clothing, the working animals that we use to perform utilitarian tasks or to provide entertainment, and even those animals that we keep as our personal pets.

Goldfish and koi, for example, do not occur naturally in the wild the way we find them today in pet stores. They have been altered by human intervention. There are at least twenty modern varieties of goldfish, all of which are the result of the selective breeding of lineages that originated with a single wild carp species—*Carassius auratus*. Although selective breeding of goldfish began in China around 300 A.D., most breeds have been developed within the last five hundred years or so. All of the morphological changes from the original wild carp are the result of naturally occurring genetic mutations that man has exploited by controlling the breeding of separate lineages over multiple generations. Through selective breeding, man has stabilized the various gene combinations that result in those characteristics favored by the breeders. The result is the wide variety of modern goldfish breeds that exhibit rather stark differences in physical characteristics.

Today's domestic cat breeds are the result of a similar history. Selective breeding of cats has been underway since the African Wildcat was first domesticated in Egypt about 5,000 years ago. At that time,

Egyptians stored much of their food in woven reed baskets and their storage areas were vulnerable to infestation by rodents that could eat through the storage containers. With no effective traps or chemical poisons, the spread of rats and mice could sometimes reach plague proportions. The abundance of rodents, however, attracted the African Wildcat into the cities. Since the cats were an effective solution to the rodent problem, people began to feed the animals in order to attract them to their homes. This symbiotic relationship resulted in the domestication of the African Wildcat (probably the sub-species *Felis silvestris lybica*), which over several centuries would become the sub-species *Felis silvestris catus*—that is, the modern domestic cat.

As cats were domesticated and their breeding could be controlled, humans began to selectively breed the animals to retain desired characteristics while eliminating others. This was done to create breeds with varying sizes, colors, and coats, ranging from the solid white, longhaired and flat-faced White Persian to the long-snouted and hairless Sphynx. While a few breeds like the Persian and the Siamese have been around for many centuries, most contemporary breeds have been developed only within the last 100 years.

With more than fifty domestic breeds, cats can vary widely, but they do not vary in shape and size nearly as much as dog breeds do. This is primarily because dogs have been bred to serve humans by performing a much wider variety of specific tasks, such as racing, herding, hunting, finding, fetching, pulling or guarding.

DNA analysis indicates that dogs diverged from wolves as a distinct species, *Canis familiaris*, about 135,000 years ago. Archeological evidence suggests that dogs were at least semi-domesticated by about 10,000 to 12,000 years ago in the Middle East. Fossil remains of five diverse types of dogs—wolf-like dogs, mastiffs, pointing dogs, shepherding dogs, and greyhounds—have been found that date back to the Bronze Age, about 4500 B.C. Cave drawings from that period show dogs working alongside human hunters. For thousands of years dogs were bred and selected for their abilities and propensities to perform specific tasks. Those that excelled at the desired trait were kept and bred with similar animals, while those that did not exhibit the desired traits would be separated or destroyed. This practice resulted in the great diversity of lineages that we find today, such as greyhounds (for running down prey and, later, racing), terriers (for hunting rodents in holes), pointers and retrievers (for flushing and fetching game), collies and shepherds (herding livestock), and malamutes and huskies (pulling sleds).[2]

Along with adaptations resulting from regional climatic conditions, many of the changes in physical appearance were simply natural side effects as the dogs were selected for their behavioral characteristics. As hereditary lines increasingly diverged, physical characteristics increasingly diverged as a natural result. It was not until the late nineteenth century, when kennel clubs were created, that dogs began to be bred more for their appearance than for their behavior, increasingly contributing to the distinctiveness of the many various breeds. The resulting Chihuahuas, Dachshunds, Beagles, Lhasa Apsos, Poodles, Bulldogs, Golden Retrievers, Dalmatians, Dobermans, German Shepherds, Great Danes, and as many as four hundred other distinct breeds that have all descended from a single ancient dog species, are clear examples of biological evolution.

Since the advent of agriculture, around ten thousand years ago, many breeds of domesticated animals have been developed in order to produce the highest quality and quantity of those commodities that we harvest from them—i.e. sheep (wool), goats (milk, wool, or mohair), pigs (meat and skin), chickens (meat and eggs), cows (labor, meat, hide, and milk), camels and llamas (meat, hide and transportation), and horses (meat, labor, transportation, and amusement). Separate breeds within each of these species have also been developed in order that the animals will be better suited to particular climates and/or so that they will thrive on the local grasses or grains.

The evolution of domesticated animals has thus far been confined to physical and behavioral changes within each of the affected species. Man has not witnessed the creation of any new species (by the modern definition of the term) through the use of selective breeding.

This limitation is simply a matter of time. Even though truly dramatic morphological changes have occurred, the six to ten thousand years since the domestication of animals began is too short a time period for the genetic make-up of diverging lineages to have reached a point of speciation. In the context of geologic time, of course, ten thousand years is a mere "blink of an eye." Evolution occurs over the course of several tens of thousands, hundreds of thousands, millions, tens of millions, hundreds of millions, and even billions of years.

Distinctions of species have historically been difficult to define. Even when the idea of species represented an "immutable essence" or a "natural kind," determining when variations constituted a different species was always unclear. For example, various ethnic races of human beings were once believed by some people to represent differing species, but determining how subtle ethnic variations were to be assigned could only be a subjective practice. The realization that species are continually subject to change blurred the distinctions even further. Charles Darwin and many other scientists, before and after his work, struggled with the task of defining a distinction of species. Darwin complained: "We shall have to treat species as ... merely artificial combinations made for convenience. This may not be a cheering prospect; but we shall at least be freed from the vain search for the undiscovered essence of the term species."[3]

Modern taxonomy roughly defines animal species according to an ability to procreate. By this definition, members of different species cannot, or otherwise will not, produce viable offspring. Members of closely related species, however, can sometimes produce sterile offspring, such as in the case of mules, which are the progeny of horses and donkeys. In addition to genetic incompatibility, behavioral differences and physical limitations can also preclude the mixing of genes between different lineages of animals, thereby constituting a distinction of species.

Chihuahuas and Great Danes, for example, could theoretically be classified as different species because of the obvious physical limitations to their mating. As it is, they are merely considered opposite ends of a spectrum of the many subspecies within a single species. In any case, if their gene pools were to be separated for a sufficient length of time, in addition to the physical limitation for procreation that they now have, they would eventually also become biochemically incapable of reproducing viable offspring. Their classification as separate species would then be assured. Whether separated by physical limitations, regional barriers, or behavioral barriers, when the gene pools of separate lineages of any animals do not mix, normal and regularly occurring genetic mutations in the separate gene pools assure that the separate lineages will become less and less similar and therefore less reproductively compatible over time.

The evolution of domesticated animals as a result of human intervention offers us a clear view of how evolution occurs when nature imposes its own requirements for survival upon the lineages of animals. It also provides us with a view of how several markedly different species can evolve from a single ancestral species population. Just as different breeds of domestic animals were created by different human demands, variant lineages of any group of animals can be created when different natural demands are placed on separate lineages that have been divided by any sort of barriers.

Horticulture and Agricultural Food Crops

Much like animals, plants can also undergo dramatic transformations and a divergence of lineages when either natural or human induced demands are placed on them. Archeological evidence indicates that, after a long history as nomadic "hunter-gatherers," humans first began to cultivate food crops a little more than 10,000 years ago in a region that would later become known as the Fertile Crescent—an area that today encompasses Lebanon and parts of Jordan, Israel, Syria, Iraq, Iran, and Turkey. A few centuries later, human populations in other parts of the world also began the practice of organized agriculture. These early farmers soon realized that they could increase their yields by selecting and crossing plants that exhibited desirable characteristics while eliminating those that did not. Over many centuries, this practice has transformed the low-yielding wild plants that were first cultivated into the high-yielding domesticated food crops that we enjoy today.

Wheat and other cereals were among the first crops to be domesticated. Modern wheat varieties were created through about 10,000 years of hybridization and selection, beginning with members of a tall, low-yielding wild wheat genus (*Triticum*) being crossed with members of another closely related grass genus (*Aegilops*). As a result, modern wheat varieties are generally shorter, husk free, usually without awns, and yielding large and abundant grains.[4]

Similarly, maize (or corn) was developed from a wild grass (*Teosinte*), beginning about 7,000 years ago in the region of present day Central America and southern Mexico. Through centuries of careful selection, the genetic code that produced the tiny seed kernels of *Teosinte* was altered to produce the succulent kernels found on the much larger cobs of today's corn.[5]

In addition to the dramatic evolution of staple food crops from their much less edible wild ancestors, man has used selective breeding to produce enormous varieties of fruits and vegetables as well as ornamental plants and flowers from individual species. For example, cabbage, collards, broccoli, cauliflower, kohlrabi, and brussel spouts all belong to a single species of wild cabbage (*Brassica oleracea*) that has been selectively bred to evolve the different lineages that exhibit the characteristics of those vegetables. The great many varieties of grapes, apples, tomatoes, roses, azaleas, orchids and other plants available today are the result of human intervention affecting the evolution of their respective lineages.

Sometimes human activity has caused the unintentional evolution of organisms. As a clear example of natural selection at work, the advent of mowed lawns has affected the character of some dandelions. The natural habitat of dandelions is usually fields of tall grasses where the dandelions grow tall to reach the sunlight. They do not produce flowers until the second year after germination in order to first reach their optimum height. "Lawn dandelions," on the other hand, bloom only four months after germination and produce three times as many seeds as field dandelions. Lawn dandelions also produce fewer and smaller leaves that lie flat, where they can escape the blades of a lawn mower.

The development of this new lawn dandelion variety has been the result of natural selection. As they grow in mowed fields or lawns, those dandelions that would normally grow tall before flowering are destroyed before they have a chance to flower, while those few odd ones that, because of gene mutation, grow shorter and flower earlier survive to produce seeds and propagate their lineage. In a more natural environment, the lawn dandelion type of mutation would not usually survive to produce seeds because it would be too short to get enough light, but in the new environment of mowed fields and lawns, a distinct new variety has evolved.[6]

One of the most pressing concerns of modern agricultural enterprise involves another instance of how human activity has caused the unintended evolution of organisms. Our efforts to control destructive insects and weeds have, in many cases, given rise to the recent evolution of a variety of species.

Ever since the domestication of food crops began, farmers have been pestered by the incursion of weeds and insect infestations. For many years, it was alternately believed that the insects were either the work of demons or the consequences of God's disapproving wrath. By around 2500 B.C., however, the Sumerians began to use sulfur as an insecticide. In addition to burning sulfur, the Romans used pitch and grease to repel insects and salt to control weeds. Organic solutions were also sometimes used. Greek farmers soaked seeds in a cucumber extract before planting. In the seventeenth century, Europeans would use extracts from plants like the newly discovered tobacco of the New World. In 1807, an extract of the pyrethrum daisy of Armenia was discovered to be an effective insecticide. Pyrethrin compounds are still used today by some farmers.[7] And home gardeners know that planting marigolds among their tomato plants will help to ward off some insects.

With a growing demand for higher yields, farmers simply wanted quick and efficient solutions and, during the twentieth century, they increasingly used man-made chemical pesticides. By the mid-1930s, American farmers were using as many as 30 million pounds of sulfur, 7 million pounds of arsenic-based compounds, and 4 million pounds of a compound consisting of copper and lime known as "Paris green." With the use of tractor-mounted sprayers and crop dusters, entire fields could easily be coated with pesticides.[8]

After World War II, the use of chemical pesticides in the United States increased dramatically. Several newly invented compounds that were inexpensive and initially very effective, such as the herbicide 2,4-D and the insecticide DDT, created the impression that farm habitats, as well as homes, parks, golf courses, schools, and other localities could be easily and safely "sterilized" of pests. However, it soon became apparent that tremendous harm to natural ecosystems and to human health could result from the use of these compounds. With the 1962 publication of Rachel Carson's book *Silent Spring*, the general public was made aware of the dangers and began to resist their use. Moreover, it eventually became apparent that such a wide use of pesticides could be counterproductive in the battle against pests.

There is little question that pesticides have benefited humankind enormously, but we now also know that both human health and the effectiveness of these compounds depend on limited and very careful management of their use, and on an understanding of biological evolution and the process of natural selection.

Though it has been more adequately appreciated only in recent decades, the tendency of insect and other pest populations to evolve and to acquire increasing resistance to pesticides has been known for quite a long while. For example, in 1914 an entomologist named A.L. Melander published an explanation of why the insecticide then being used along the northwest coast of the United States to eradicate a fruit-eating insect called San Jose scale was becoming less and less effective over time. Through his observations and testing, Melander deduced that the insect populations were evolving a resistance to the insecticide through the process of natural selection. When the trees were sprayed, most of the insects were killed. But the very few of them that did not receive enough poison to be killed and, more importantly, those that had a resistance to the poison as a result of a genetic mutation, would survive to reproduce. As the population rebounded, the genes that provided some resistance to the insecticide would then be propagated throughout the gene pool of the new population. After multiple generations of insects and many applications of insecticide, the result was a population of insects that had evolved a resistance to the insecticide.[9]

Since the 1960s, research has been directed at discovering methods of controlling pests that limit the use of pesticides. Certain crop rotation regimens and the introduction of beneficial predators are among the methods used today. Recent advances in genetic engineering have also enabled the development of plants that produce their own natural pesticides. With evolution in mind, the EPA is now mandating that at least 20 percent of fields be planted with ordinary crop varieties next to these genetically engineered crop varieties. The hope is that any resistant genes that may evolve in insects feeding on the genetically engineered crops will be diluted by the genes of insects that feed primarily on the unaltered crops.[10] There is also a chance that insects will learn to tell the difference and stay away from the engineered varieties when there is an unaltered variety available.

Medicine

Biological evolution that has been unintentionally prompted by human activity can also be seen in an area of even greater human concern. Among several other issues that provide illustrations of evolution in our world and in our history, the challenges associated with the evolution of microbial diseases represent a significant part of modern medical research.

In recent decades, most of us have become keenly aware that the use of antibiotics over the last half-century has affected the emergence of new strains of bacteria that are more resistant to antibiotics. This very simple and straightforward process by which the characteristics of a colony of organisms changes as a result of environmental changes is another example of biological evolution through natural selection. It does not matter whether the conditions that affect the change are imposed by man or by nature—the process is the same. In this case, those bacteria that cannot resist the antibiotic die out, leaving behind those very few bacteria that are strong enough to survive the drug. The surviving bacteria then reproduce and pass the trait of resistance on to their offspring. The eventual result is an entirely new colony of bacteria possessing the characteristic of resistance to the antibiotic.

This, of course, is one of the reasons why it is so important to consume the entirety of a prescription of antibiotics—to better ensure the likelihood that all of the bacteria will be destroyed. This is also why doctors are discouraged from prescribing antibiotics to treat an ailment that may be the result of a viral infection, rather than a bacterial infection. The overuse of antibiotics is believed to be a significant contributing factor in the recent evolution of many new strains of antibiotic-resistant bacteria.

One of the most urgent aspects of biomedical research has been the study of microbial diseases, and an understanding of biological evolution has been critical to that study. Penicillin first became available in 1943. It was extremely effective in fighting the *Staphylococcus aureus* bacteria that causes serious infections in hospitals. By 1947, however, the first penicillin-resistant strains of *Staphylococcus aureus* had emerged. When a newer staph-killing drug, methicillin, was introduced in the 1960s, it was not long before methicillin-resistant strains had evolved. By the 1980s, such new strains were widespread. Vancomycin became the next weapon for fighting staph, but a vancomycin-resistant strain of staph emerged in 2002. In describing the $30 billion cost of treating methicillin-resistant staph infections in the United States each year, biologist Stephen Palumbi has explained, "Antibiotics exert a powerful evolutionary force, driving infectious bacteria to evolve powerful defenses against all but the most recently invented drug."[11]

A similar battle has been raging against the evolution of various strains of viruses. Some viruses evolve quickly, some more slowly. Discovered in the 1980s, the HIV virus is among the fastest. HIV replicates itself with a high degree of mutation, allowing it to quickly assume new forms. Within just a few years of infection and drug treatment, each HIV patient comes to carry a unique version of the virus. As biologists and physicians have struggled to cope with the many strains of HIV, it has been an understanding of biological evolutionary processes that has allowed them to develop the drug "cocktails" that have greatly slowed the evolution of the virus within patients.[12]

Even without an exposure to suppressant drugs, colonies of bacteria and viruses can mutate and sometimes become significantly more dangerous. The avian flu or "bird flu" virus is a telling example. The avian flu, first identified in Italy more than a century ago, is caused by type A strains of the influenza virus. All type A influenza viruses, including those that often cause seasonal outbreaks of influenza in humans, are highly prone to genetic evolution.

The genetic composition of an influenza virus changes as the virus replicates in the body of its host. Strains are replaced by new "antigenic variant" strains as a result of the virus' rapidly varying replication and of the infected body's antibody response to the intruder. Much like the use of penicillin can cause the evolution of penicillin-resist strains of bacteria, the body's own immune system can facilitate the evolution of viral strains that can elude the body's natural defenses. The process that produces these small changes in the genetic composition of influenza viruses is called "antigenic drift."

A second characteristic of the type A influenza viruses that is of even greater concern, and which has been the recent focus of concern regard the avian flu viruses, is their propensity for "antigenic shift." Type A influenza viruses have the ability to rearrange their genetic make-up in the process of merging with another influenza virus, including subtypes that infect different species, such as birds and human beings. So, in addition to these viruses being able to evolve to better survive their hosts' natural defenses, sometimes into strains that are truly lethal, these viruses can also evolve into infectious and deadly strains that have "jumped" from one species to another.

In the case of the avian flu, there has been particular concern regarding a virus subtype called H5N1. This avian flu virus subtype evolves rapidly and also has a known propensity to acquire genes from the viruses infecting other host species. An epidemic of avian flu caused by H5N1 in bird populations began in late 2003 in Korea and has since spread to other Asian countries. Then in 2004, the H5N1 virus was found in humans exhibiting the symptoms of severe respiratory disease in northern Viet Nam. The greatest concern is that with the presence of the avian H5N1 virus in humans, when those humans come in contact with human strains of the influenza virus, the result will likely be the evolution of a new subtype of influenza. The new strain would be easily transmitted from person to person and, until one could be developed, no vaccine would exist.

The propensity of influenza viruses to undergo frequent antigenic evolution requires that annual revisions be made in the formulation of influenza vaccines. The World Health Organization has been monitoring the evolution of influenza viruses and working to develop effective vaccines in response to that evolution since the organization's founding in 1947.[13]

We can see the evolution of microbial diseases in real time because microbes have very short generational cycles. This allows us to observe significant evolutionary changes within a relatively short time frame.

Medical professionals not only have to deal with the encroachment of infectious microbial diseases, they must also contend with problems stemming from the way we are put together in the first place. When we read in Psalm 139:13 that God "knit[s]" a child in its mother's womb, we can assume that this must be another example of poetic symbolism and should not be taken literally. We can deduce that God does not *directly* create children in the wombs of their mothers and has not even *directly* created the process by which offspring are formed, because God is simply not prone to the kind of errors that are so often seen in reproduction.

When we see twins that are conjoined in sometimes very horrible ways, or when we see children born with genetic defects like Down's syndrome or cystic fibrosis, we know that such results cannot be the work of God. Such reproduction defects are clear indicators that human beings are the result of imperfect and varying natural processes.

Congenital defects result from a variety of causes. Some are caused by environmental contaminates or a combination of environmental factors and preexisting genetic factors that cause damage to the genes and their ability to replicate correctly. Most congenital defects are caused by mistakes in the replication process of genes during reproduction, or by faulty genes that are inherited from one or both parents.

Down's syndrome, for example, can occur in at least three different ways. The most common type is called "trisomy 21" because the patient's #21 chromosome has three units instead of the usual two. This occurs when one of the parent's germ cells (sperm or egg cells) has two chromosomes at location 21 rather than one. The child then gets one chromosome for location 21 from one parent and two from the other parent, leaving the child with an extra chromosome.

Another way that Down's syndrome occurs is when chromosome #21 is damaged during cell replication. In this case the chromosomes of the parents are normal, but an error occurs intermittently when new cells are reproduced. The inflicted person will then have some combination of normal chromosomes and faulty chromosomes, and may show varying degrees of symptoms. This type of Down's is called a "mosaic" disorder because of the mixture of normal and damaged cells.

In the case of cystic fibrosis (CF), faulty genes are inherited from both parents. Much like what determines our hair color and our eye color or the variations among Mendel's pea plants, as we saw in Chapter 5, cystic fibrosis is subject to the interplay of dominant and recessive genes.

The nucleus of most human cells contains 46 chromosomes—that is, 23 pairs of chromosomes. During reproduction, the sperm and the egg cells each carry 23 *single* chromosomes that are merged to again form 23 *pairs* of chromosomes in the resulting zygote. The chromosomes carry genes (a length of DNA) that are also paired as the chromosomes are paired—one from mom and one from dad. Variances of these genes are called "alleles," and so the appearance of certain characteristics in an organism is dependant on the types of alleles that are present. A person who has received the same allele from both parents is "homozygous" for that gene. A person who receives a different allele from each parent for a particular gene position is "heterozygous" for that gene. In a heterozygous gene pair, one allele will often be "dominant" while the other is "recessive," determining whether or not a particular trait will be expressed.

The CF gene is recessive, so it is expressed in a carrier only if it has been inherited from both parents. As the figure at right illustrates, the disease only occurs in about 1 out of every 4 children of those parents who are both carriers of the faulty gene. The same odds apply to these same parents having a child that does not carry the defective gene at all. But the chances that these parents will have a child that will carry the faulty gene to be passed on to subsequent generations is 1 out of only 2. Since historically those who have been afflicted by the disease have not lived long enough to reproduce, we can assume that 2 out of 3 surviving children born of parents who both carry the CF gene will also carry the gene and likely pass it to subsequent generations.

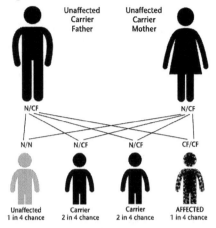

Genetic diseases and disorders are very often found to be more prominent in one section of the population or another. For instance, the incidence of hemophilia has been higher among European royalty than the wider population. The incidence of total color blindness is about 1 in 20 among the inhabitants of the island of Pingelap in Micronesia, while it is only about 1 in 20,000 worldwide. Higher rates of Tay-Sachs disease and cystic fibrosis are found among the Ashkenazi Jews of Central Europe. Understanding how genetic variations are propagated through and among various populations of humans makes it clear that we are not an immutable species. It helps us to understand one of the mechanisms by which we are constantly undergoing the process of evolution.

Cystic fibrosis is the most common genetic disorder among people of Northern-European descent. It is not known what caused the high incidence of CF in that population but our understanding of genetics and evolution can offer a few clues. We know that genes usually work in tandem with other genes, so the CF mutation may have been beneficial in the past as it worked with another mutation that has since been purged from the population. More likely perhaps, is that the CF mutation could have offered a degree of protection from the encroachment of a severe outbreak of a microbial disease, such as the

Black Plague that began in Western Asia and swept across Europe, killing about half of the population of Europe in the fourteenth century. It could also have been the result of an earlier outbreak, or it could have resulted from the effects of several such events. CF carriers do benefit from an increased resistance to cholera, suggesting some likelihood to such a scenario. The idea that the forces of natural selection may have played a role in the spread of the CF gene is further supported by what we know about a very similarly transmitted congenital genetic disease—sickle-cell anemia.

There is little question that sickle-cell anemia has resulted from circumstances surrounding the presence of a gene mutation that has been instilled in several populations through the force of natural selection. These populations are comprised of people with recent ancestry in sub-Saharan Africa, South America, Cuba, Saudi Arabia, India, and several Mediterranean countries such as Italy, Greece, and Turkey, where mosquito-borne malaria has been endemic for many centuries.

The sickle-cell gene is inherited in much the same way that the Cystic Fibrosis gene is. When both parents are unaffected carriers, their descendants have a 1 in 4 chance of inheriting the gene from both of them and then being inflicted with the disease's debilitating effects. The descendants also have a 1 in 4 chance of not inheriting the sickle-cell gene at all. The remarkable thing about sickle-cell genetics, however, is that there is a 1 in 2 chance that the descendants will inherit the sickle cell gene from only one parent and, with it, a resistance to malaria. The sickle-cell gene is not completely recessive, so carriers can often have a few "sickle" red blood cells mixed in with normal red blood cells. This condition is called "sickle-cell trait." Those with sickle-cell trait show little or no deleterious symptoms of the disease, while benefiting from a heightened resistance to malaria. The condition disrupts the malaria parasite's ability to digest hemoglobin, thereby increasing resistance to the parasitic infection.

Carriers of the sickle-cell trait have a higher fitness for survival in malaria prone regions than do people without the disease. As a result, natural selection has worked to instill sickle cell trait into the populations of such regions. Scientists have concluded from the analysis of chromosome structures that the sickle-cell mutations found in modern populations are the result of at least four separate mutation events that occurred in Africa and Southwest Asia between 3,000 and 6,000 generations ago.[14]

While sickle-cell disease is the most common genetic disorder among African-Americans—about 1 in 12 carries the gene—the rate is nevertheless much lower than it is in West Africa where the ancestors of most African-Americans once lived. The frequency of the gene is dropping in the United States where there is no problem with malaria largely because of the mortality of homozygous carriers (those who carry two copies of the gene) without any corresponding advantage for heterozygous carriers (those with only one copy of the gene and a resistance to malaria). In other words, the sickle-cell gene is slowly being purged from the African-American population through natural selection.

Our understanding of how errors occur in the reproduction processes of organisms does not merely inform us that God does not have a *direct* role in these processes—it also enables our understanding of an important component in the process of evolutionary change. It is the errors that occur in the replication of DNA, and therefore genes, that produce the variation and novelty upon which natural selection can work. Most such errors have no immediate consequence for an organism and they lie dormant until, in concert with other genetic variations, they become either injurious or beneficial to the organism. If a genetic anomaly becomes sufficiently injurious, it will either be eliminated through natural selection or it will result in the demise of the affected population. If, on the other hand, a genetic anomaly becomes beneficial to the organism, it will be propagated throughout the population, and the species will then be strengthened through change—the species will have evolved.

Sometimes congenital defects can exhibit quite dramatic anomalies. For instance, polydactylism, a condition in which a person has extra fingers and/or toes is pretty common among the Amish people of Pennsylvania. People are also sometimes born with extra nipples, as with other mammals, running along the so-called milk line of the torso. Less common cases of deformity involve people who have been born with excessive body hair and even a monkey-like tail. These kinds of phenomena, along with genetic laboratory experiments such as those with fruit flies that have produced flies with legs growing out of where antennae should be and other monstrous anomalies, tell us a couple of important things about how evolution works.

First, it is apparent that the genetic information for whole structures are embedded in our DNA, sort of in the form of parcels, and that even a single gene mutation or a short series of mutations can sometimes cause these larger parcels of instructions to be misapplied—to be applied slightly or dramatically differently from the norm. This is important because it explains how significant novelties can arise in an organism to then be subjected to the force of natural selection. Such monstrous deformities are often either directly fatal or otherwise injurious to an organism. In these cases, the genetic mutation will, either never enter the gene pool of the wider population, or its carriers will be so weakened that they will eventually be eliminated by competition. But occasionally, such an anomaly will be beneficial to the organism and will then be propagated throughout the gene pool of a wider population—thereby contributing to the evolution of the species.

Second, the occasional appearance of those rare anomalies like extra nipples, animal-like fur, or a tail suggests something more about the information that is contained in our DNA. Our DNA apparently contains the remnants of instructions for the production of structures that were used by our ancestors but have since been overwritten. The rare reappearance of these structures as a result of genetic aberration is called "atavism."

Perhaps the most striking occurrence of this phenomenon in humans is the appearance of a tail, alternately known as a "coccygeal process," "coccygeal projection," or "caudal appendage." In newborns, these tails range from about one to five inches. Most lack skeletal structures, but some tails contain cartilage and as many as five well-developed, articulating vertebrae. Some very subtle musculature for these tails has also been observed.

Of course, atavistic structures occur in other animals too. Both whales and dolphins have occasionally been seen with hind legs, indicating the atavistic reappearance of the limbs of their terrestrial ancestors. Horses are rarely but sometimes born with extra toes that are similar to those that are seen in the fossils of their ancient *Mesohippus* and *Merychippus* ancestors. Other examples include: wings on normally wingless earwigs and extra toes on guinea pigs and salamanders.

The presence of DNA instructions for ancestral physiology is also apparent in the appearance and subsequent fading of ancestral structures in developing embryos. An example is the formation of gill slits in the embryos of reptiles, birds, and mammals. Another example is found in the embryos of some whales that develop teeth in early stages of development only to be reabsorbed and dissipated before birth. The appearance and subsequent disappearance of ancestral characteristics in succeeding embryonic stages is so striking that in the nineteenth century it led to the "theory of recapitulation," which asserted that embryonic development involves a recapitulation of an organism's entire evolutionary history. Recapitulation theory has now been thoroughly discredited, but it is nevertheless quite well known that occasional obsolete ancestral structures do appear and then recede. It is now understood that these ancestral structures serve as embryonic "organizers" in the ensuing steps of the development of evolved structures.[15] Discoveries in biochemistry research have revealed that various proteins and enzymes, directed by increasingly evolved genetic codes, serve to block or facilitate the development of these structures.

Vestigial Structures

In addition to the very rare appearances of atavistic structures in mature organisms and the short-lived appearances of such structures during fetal development, we can also see the physical vestiges of ancestral structures in the normal physiology of a great many fully developed organisms.

Did you ever wonder why humans have an appendix that serves no significant beneficial function, wisdom teeth that give us so many difficulties, and a tailbone but no tail? Or why your dog has a largely useless thumb, high on his foot? These are the remnants of previously functioning anatomical structures of ancient ancestors. A so-called "vestigial structure" or a "vestigial organ" is usually one that offers little or no function for the benefit of an organism. Some anatomists' lists of vestigial structures in humans have exceeded eighty. (The vestigial nature of some of the structures listed is uncertain, however. Such lists also usually include a number of the vestigial structures that appear and then dissipate during embryonic development, as noted above.)

The best-known vestigial structure in humans is the vermiform appendix. (In addition to humans, the vestigial vermiform appendix is found in all hominoid apes, including chimpanzees, orangutans, gorillas, and gibbons.) In humans, its length can vary from an inch to more than a foot. The organ normally shrinks with age and its small opening to the intestinal tract usually closes by middle age. Some people are born without one at all.[16]

While the appendix may continue to serve some minor function, perhaps in connection with our immune system, it is nevertheless a vestige of the much more prominent cecum that, in herbivorous mammals, is used for the digestion of the cellulose in plant material. It is undoubtedly a remnant of our herbivorous ancestors.

Our herbivorous ancestors also had a longer jaw than we do, along with a third set of molars for chewing and grinding plant material. As we evolved into the omnivorous creatures with the much larger brains and craniums that we have today, not only did we lose much of our ability to digest cellulose, we also experienced a shortening of our jaws, leaving little room for the third set of molars that give us so much trouble. Our so-called wisdom teeth are of little use to us today and often become trapped within the jawbone and inflamed. A few people do not even develop wisdom teeth, further indicating the vestigial nature of this extra set of molars.

The small bit of flesh on the inside corner of our eyes, called the "plica semilunaris," is believed by some to be a remnant of a nictitating membrane—the "third eyelid" that is found in many reptiles, birds, and a few mammals. We also have underdeveloped muscles in our ears that are likely remnants of muscles that, just as we can see in many other animals, enabled our ancestors to quickly move their ears toward the source of a sound. Our fingernails and toenails are, of course, the vestiges of more utilitarian claws that were once used for digging, for traction when running, and as defensive and offensive weapons.

Our tailbone is a vestigial structure. The coccyx consists of three to five (usually four) vestigial vertebrae at the base of the spine that are fused together. These vertebrae are not part of the structural support of our spine and they no longer serve any significant function. The coccyx is sometimes surgically removed in patients that suffer chronic pain from a condition called coccydynia, and the removal of the coccyx generally causes no debilitating effects. In those rare cases where human beings are born with external tails, the tail (coccygeal projection) is an extension, sometimes with the addition of even more vertebrae, of those vertebrae that normally form the coccyx. Some people also have subtle remnants of tail-extending muscles.

Vestigial structures can be found in a great many species of animals all around the world. The so-called "dewclaw" is a vestigial appendage exhibited by many birds, reptiles and mammals. Many of us are familiar with the dewclaws found on dogs, as mentioned above. Most dogs have the extra digits on their front legs and a few also have them on their hind legs. The dewclaw is found on the leg above the paw, and therefore does not touch the ground when the animal is standing. In some cases, dewclaws can have some utility in self-grooming, but in many other cases these extra digits serve no function at all.

Small leg bones can be found floating inside the smooth bodies of whales and other marine mammals, providing compelling evidence of their descent from terrestrial mammals. Some whales also have vestigial pelvic bones that, like the leg bones, serve no function. In addition to an unused pelvic bone, the manatee, an aquatic mammal sometimes referred to as a "sea cow," has fingernails on the end of its front flippers. These flippers evolved from the legs of the manatee's terrestrial ancestors. Manatees also have hyoid bones (a bone that supports the tongue in other animals) that no longer serve any function.

Most pythons have the remnants of a pelvis and tiny leg bones within their bodies. Like those of whales, python pelvis and leg bones are not attached to any vertebrae. They are simply suspended in the flesh under the smooth skin of the snake. Undoubtedly these bones are vestiges of the skeletal structure of the four-legged reptiles from which these snakes evolved. There are also several species of lizards that could perhaps be considered "transitional species," since they have tiny vestigial legs that they do not use.

There are numerous examples of flightless beetles that still have well developed, but useless wings enclosed beneath fused wing covers. Others have the encasement for wings, but no wings. Evolutionary pressures have caused most of these beetles, which are found in arid regions, to lose their ability to open their wing encasements because of issues concerning the conservation of body moisture. Darwin also noticed that many species of flightless beetles reside in coastal areas where flight would subject them to the risk of being blown out to sea.

The eyes of moles and other burrowing rodents that mostly live in darkness are usually rudimentary in size, and in some species such as the mole rat *Spalax typhlus*, the eyes are completely covered by skin and fur. There is a wide variety of blind, cave-dwelling species with various stages of vestigial eyes. As adults, many North American blind salamanders have non-functioning eyes that are covered by skin. The endangered blind salamander, *Eurycea rathbuni*, found in the water-filled caves of the Edwards Aquifer in central Texas has only two small black dots under the skin where its ancestors' eyes once were. There are also blind, cave-dwelling fish that have rudimentary eyes covered by skin. Some cave-dwelling crayfish have eyestalks, but no longer have any eyes on them.

It is not surprising that these animals, which have migrated into dark cave environments, are slowly losing their eyes. (An indication that these species have migrated into the caves is their close relatedness to nearby species outside the caves.) Since eyes are no longer of any use to them, they cannot offer any selective advantage. In fact, since eyes can be prone to injury or infection, in the case of these creatures that do use them, eyes are a selective disadvantage. As a result, the eyes of these creatures are slowly disappearing through many generations of gene mutation and natural selection.

A structure that functions differently than is usually seen among related species can also be considered a vestigial structure. The wings of flightless birds, for example, are often used for courtship or defensive displays, as well as for balance when running, or in the case of penguins, as fins. But these structures are nevertheless vestiges of the wings that the birds' ancestors used for flight. This is clearly the case since these wings are usually far more complex than needed for the functions that they are currently being used for. In addition, most of the bones of these birds are hollow—a condition that is disadvantageous for an earthbound creature because they are weaker, but advantageous for a flying creature because they are lighter.

There are also a great many plants that retain vestigial structures. For example, dandelions have evolved to reproduce without the use of pollinating sexual reproduction (a process called apomixes), yet they still have the pollen producing stamen and the pistil necessary for sexual reproduction, along with the flower petals that would be necessary to attract pollinating insects. Many grasses and other nonflowering plants have vestigial structures that resemble the functioning components of closely related flowering plants.

We can also see vestigial reflexes or impulses and even vestigial complex behaviors in some organisms. For instance, our own experience with "goose bumps" can be caused by fear or stress or by a reaction to a cold environment. Not only are the muscles that enable this response vestigial, the reflex that activates these muscles is a vestigial reflex. They are holdovers from our furry ancestors who could erect their coat in order to look larger in the face of a predator and for better insulation against the cold.

Several species of whiptail lizards belonging to the genus *Cnemidophous* consist of only females. By means of a process called parthenogenesis, the females are able to reproduce without the fertilization of their eggs by males. Occasionally, a female will assume the role of a male and try to copulate with another female. Since it is believed that these lizards descended from a species that required copulation for reproduction, this attempted copulation is considered a vestigial behavior.

A vestigial behavior with which many of us are more familiar is a dog's tendency to paw at and circle his bedding material, even if it is a hardwood floor. This is an instinct that is a vestige of when, in the wild, the dog's wolf-like ancestors would make their beds by clearing a place among the leaves and debris. Today's wolves exhibit the same behavior.

When we consider those vestigial structures in our own bodies that give us so much trouble, such as our appendix, our coccyx, or our wisdom teeth, we might be tempted to think that we are simply the product of shoddy workmanship or of poor design. Of course the presence and the character of these structures serve as pretty clear indicators that we were not designed from the top down at all. Instead, we are the product of natural processes that have created us from the bottom up.

Imperfection of Design

While the creation of all the laws of nature and the ultimate results of that creation can reasonably be attributable to God and His intent, as we saw in Chapters 2 and 3, Christianity tells us that things can happen within that creation that are apart from the direct Hand of God. Therefore we can understand the possibility that God has not *directly* and supernaturally created human beings and the other organisms that exist on Earth. Furthermore, we can know with reasonable confidence that He has not *directly* created the world's organisms because, just as He is not prone to error, God is not prone to inadequate or imperfect design either. While God's plan, as a whole, may be perfect, we can easily see that many things in nature are not.

The efficiency of natural selection as a steering mechanism in the evolution of complex organisms is truly astounding. The enormous complexity and elegance that it produces on a cellular level surely probes the limits of human comprehension. But it is not perfect. The evolution of living organisms is not driven toward a goal of perfection by a teleological force—it is a natural process that results from haphazard and indeterminate events that are prescribed and limited by the laws of nature.

Natural selection cannot, unlike God, make something from nothing—it can only act on that which already exists. The evolution of a species can only proceed in small incremental steps because each step is constrained by the necessity that, at each step, a population of organisms must continue to survive and compete for its livelihood. All organisms, and all of the component parts of complex organisms, are always merely altered forms of previously existing structures—the latest in a long line of usually tiny incremental steps. Therefore, we find that organisms and many of the parts of organisms are very often not constructed in a way that they might have been if they had been preconceived, planned, and constructed for maximum utility, efficiency, and durability. Instead, they are very often (at least from our perspective) quite imperfect.

Let us consider our own human anatomy. We saw the imperfect structure of the human eye described in Chapter 6. We can see other imperfections too. In addition to the vestigial structures with which we sometimes have difficulties, as noted above (and aside from our susceptibility to starvation, physical injury, infection, addiction and disease), there are a few other aspects of our body structure that perhaps could have been designed and constructed differently for better performance and reliability.

For example, our mouths and interconnected sinus passages are used in the operation of as many as six separate functions that can sometimes get in the way of each other—respiration, taste, smell, food mastication, food ingestion, and speech. As a result of this configuration, we are susceptible to infections that can affect multiple systems within the body. A mistiming of the swallowing mechanism can cause potentially fatal choking, a hazard made even more likely as a result of an elongated larynx—an adaptation that facilitated the development of speech. We can also sometimes have difficulty hearing while chewing because of the proximity of the jawbone and the structures of the inner ear.

At the other end of the facilities, we find a similar circumstance of problems arising because of structural passages that are shared by separate functions or which occupy a close proximity. In men, the urethra is used to convey both urine and semen. This arrangement tends to facilitate the exchange of infections from one system to the other. In women, the urethra, the vagina, and the anus are separate structures, but their close proximity also tends to promote the exchange of infectious microbes between the three orifices.

Perhaps the most profound design flaw in the opinion of many women concerns the system by which infants are expelled from the womb. The evolution of human beings through numerous species over several million years resulted in an increasingly large brain size and, with it, an increasingly large cranium, culminating with the rather large craniums of *Homo sapiens* that exist today. Unfortunately for women, the evolution of such a large cranium size in fetuses occurred so rapidly that an adequately corresponding evolutionary change in the birth canal has not yet had time to occur. (As an alternative, natural selection is probably responsible for the fact that our infants are born earlier and less developed in comparison to most other placental mammals.) Of course, along with the larger brain size came the ability for others to assist in the birthing process, thereby reducing the effects of natural selection. Indeed, today's cesarean sections and other advanced medical capabilities have essentially eliminated those effects entirely.

In human beings, the primary function of the lumbar (lower) spine is to act as a support column for carrying our vertical upper torso, arms, and head. If we were to design a column for such a purpose, it would probably be straight, but the one that we have is rather sharply curved at the base, leaving the lower discs that separate the vertebrae significantly wedge-shaped. As a result, ruptured or herniated disks tend to occur more frequently in the lumbar region of the spine. Some advantages of such a curved spine have been cited, but many more disadvantages tend to arise, suggesting an inefficient or imperfect design.

The primary reason we have such a curved spine is that it is the result of raising the upper body to a vertical position with straight knees for bipedal locomotion, while the pelvis retains much the same orientation of our quadrupedal ancestors—the same orientation that continues to be exhibited in modern apes. Similarly, the fascial support for the abdominal viscera in humans appears to be more suited to a quadrupedal posture than to our bipedal habit.[17]

We have two lungs and two kidneys that provide us with some degree of security against the failure of one of these organs. In a sense, we have a couple of back-up components. If we were to design and build our own ideal human being, however, we would likely install back-up components for all of its vital functions—the heart, the liver, the brain, or the entire head, for example. But since we are not constructed with that kind of forethought, we lack back-up components for most of our vital organs.

Numerous other examples of imperfect design can be found throughout nature. For example, very often the stinger of some bees cannot be withdrawn from its victim. Instead, the bees die as their viscera are torn from their bodies. While this circumstance can benefit an entire colony, and thus be the result of natural selection, from the individual bee's point of view, it is rather an imperfect design. It appears that the stinger is an adaptation of an instrument that continues to be used for boring holes in other members of the same order of bees. It has been adapted as a stinger, but not perfected.[18]

Relatives of sharks, the various rays and skates have evolved very flat bodies to hug the ocean floor as they lie in wait for prey. As they stealthily settle into the mud and sediments of the ocean bottom, their slightly raised two eyes remain uncovered so they can see their surroundings. They appear well designed for how they make their living. There are other bottom-dwelling flatfish, however, that exhibit one of the oddities of nature. Halibut, sole, and plaice are bony fishes that, like their relatives trout and herring, are designed to be vertically slim for swimming with the usual side-to-side waving of the body and tail fin. Despite their body design, however, these fishes have taken to the habit of lying flat on their sides on the ocean floor for stealth. As a result, evolution has produced a rather bizarre contrivance.

These flatfish begin their lives swimming near the surface with symmetrical and vertical bodies much like those of herring and trout. As they mature, however, their skulls begin to grow asymmetrically until both eyes eventually end up on one side of the head. With some species it is the right side, some species the left side, and with other species it can be either. These fishes have evolved their contorted bodies as a result of a multitude of slight advantages that were bestowed on those fishes whose genetic variation had moved their downward facing eyes toward a more useful position. The contortion is not present at birth because there is no advantage then. Only those genes that instructed the contortion upon maturity offered enough advantage to have become dominant in the gene pool over many millions of generations.

Perhaps the most often cited example of imperfect design in the natural world is that of the giant panda's so-called thumb. The panda's thumb not only illustrates an imperfect organic design, it also shows us how a species' evolution can diverge from its closest relatives' when their respective environments diverge. Native to the dense bamboo forests in the higher elevations of western China, pandas are members of the order *Carnivora*, which includes a wide array of mammals, such as cats, wolves, hyenas, weasels, raccoons, and bears. Carnivores are distinguished for having powerful jaws and teeth that have been adapted for piercing, tearing, and eating flesh. Most of these animals eat only meat or a combination of meat and vegetation. Pandas, on the other hand, have adapted to eating bamboo, almost exclusively.

Pandas spend almost all of their waking hours consuming bamboo. In doing so, they sit upright and grasp the stalks while stripping the leaves and stems with their forepaws and eating only the shoots. The remarkable thing about pandas is that they are able to firmly grasp the bamboo without the kind of opposable thumb that human beings and apes have. Like other bears, pandas have five short digits with claws that face forward at the end of their paws. What pandas use as a thumb is actually a dramatically enlarged radial sesamoid bone, along with an extensive rearrangement of muscles in the paw. The radial sesamoid is usually a very small wrist bone that is common to most mammals. On pandas the bone underlies the round pad on the forepaw. The usual five digits connect to an elongated pad called the palmar. A shallow trough runs between the two foremost pads and provides a channel for grasping bamboo stalks.

It is believed that relatively little genetic variation was required for the panda's pseudo thumb to evolve—perhaps primarily a single mutation affecting the timing and rate of growth of the radial sesamoid bone. All of the basic components are found in all bears, and many bears already have a slightly enlarged radial sesamoid. Natural selection favored the genetic variations that produced pandas with larger and larger radial sesamoids because those animals could more successfully manipulate their indigenous food source. The surrounding muscles, which previously extended past the sesamoid to the "true" thumb, were only slightly modified as a result of the same process. The result is an extra digit that has only limited muscle control, but serves as a sort of backstop for grasping bamboo—an imperfect but nevertheless highly useful evolutionary adaptation.

Darwin observed that species tend to only reach the degree of perfection that is required for survival in the environment in which those species reside. This has been most clearly revealed as humans have transported various species from their native environments and placed them into new regions of the world. In the new region, the introduced species will sometimes not be able to compete in the natural environment and therefore will not take hold beyond a limited domestic use. Very often, however, the species that are transported are thought to be desirable because of their heartiness, and as a result, the introduction of some species into new regions can disrupt the existing ecological order or "ecological balance" of that region. For example, Darwin remarked that many of the native plants and animals of New Zealand were being crowded out and destroyed by "the advancing legions of plants and animals introduced from Europe."

In the United States, the federal and state agricultural departments must regularly contend with disruptive species that have been brought from other parts of the world. One example is *Hydrilla verticillata*, a rooted submerged aquatic plant that has recently become a nuisance in many of the fresh water lakes of North America. DNA analysis has determined that *Hydrilla* likely originated in the warmer waters of Asia before it spread to Africa and Europe long ago. Two separate *Hydrilla* strains have recently arrived in the United States, one from South Korea and the other from India. The first of these *Hydrilla* strains arrived in Florida in the early 1950s and quickly spread across the southeastern United States. The other strain arrived in the late 1970s and has also spread rapidly since its arrival.

Hydrilla has displaced several native species of aquatic plants and the thick mats that form at the water's surface facilitate the breeding of mosquitoes and inhibit recreational boating and sport fishing. *Hydrilla* is difficult to prevent or control. Numerous man-made and natural remedies are being used to combat it, including a natural enemy that has also recently immigrated to North America—the Asian moth, *Parapoynx diminutalis*.

Another recent arrival in the United States is the Asian Longhorned Beetle. Believed to have hitched a ride on wooden pallets and shipping crates from China, the beetles arrived in New York City and in Chicago in the mid-1990s. With no natural enemies in North America, the beetles quickly multiplied and began destroying large numbers of native trees (primarily elms, maples, and willows). To combat the beetles in heavily infested trees, the trees must be completely removed and destroyed. In Chicago, three separate heavy infestations occurred in 1998, and a great many trees were destroyed, either by the insects or in the efforts to control their spread.

An even more destructive beetle—another immigrant from Asia—was first found in Detroit in 2002. Since its discovery in the United States, the Emerald Ash Borer has spread throughout Michigan and beyond, and it has reportedly destroyed more than 15 million ash trees. These destructive invaders strikingly illustrate the vulnerability (the imperfection) of entire ecosystems.

Imperfections in the physiology of individual organisms tell us a lot about how species evolve as a result of incremental steps toward adaptation to the challenges of the species' changing environmental circumstances. The fragility of entire ecosystems in the face of frequent changes, such as the migration and introduction of new and competing species, a change in the climate, or a dramatic change in the geology of a region, explains why numerous species have such a frequent need to adapt.

The vulnerability of regional ecosystems to the encroachment of species from other regional ecosystems also tells us a lot about how ecosystems that are separated by geologic or climatic barriers evolve independently of each other, and as a result, often evolve differently. The study of these regional differences in ecosystems and the differing organisms that reside in them, along with the study of the historical migration of various organisms is the subject of biogeography.

Biogeography

Scientists whose work involve biogeography study a great variety of often complex issues concerning the historic and the contemporary habitats and migration of various species. But we need not immerse ourselves in the complexities of complicated scientific studies to appreciate the evidence of evolution that can be readily seen in the biogeography of our world.

Did you ever wonder why penguins are only found in the southern hemisphere around the icy waters of the Antarctic, and not in the very similar waters of the Artic? Or why hippopotamuses, zebras, lions, and giraffes are only native to Africa? Or why, of the two species of elephants, one is native to Africa and one is native to India while none are found in the western hemisphere? Or why there are large flightless birds that are quite similar, yet of different families, living in Africa (ostrich), Australia (emu), and South America (two species of rhea)? Or why Australia, Tasmania, and the Galapagos Islands all have such seemingly exotic animals that are not found in nature anywhere else in the world?

The exclusivity of the territories of these various animals cannot simply be the result of climatic or other environmental conditions, because comparable habitat conditions do not correlate with the distribution of species. There is no environmental reason why penguins could not live in the Artic. The American bison could certainly have grazed the grasslands of the Serengeti Plain just as they once did the great plains of North America. We find unique species in so many places around the world because those habitats in which they evolved are separated by barriers, such as vast oceans, mountain ranges, or climatic conditions. These species and the entire ecosystems in which they reside have evolved independently of the rest of the world and, as a result, they have evolved in different ways.

For example, there are dozens of species of honeycreepers in Hawaii that are found nowhere else in the world. Similarly, thirteen different finch species on the Galapagos Islands fill various niches that are usually dominated by wholly different kinds of birds in other parts of the world. Both the Hawaiian and Galapagos Islands are volcanic islands that rose up out of the sea without ever being connected to mainland continents. As a result, the lineages of those few animal species that did make it to the islands were able to evolve to exploit the available ecological niches without the usual competition found on the mainland. (The only mammals found on some of these kind of remote and newly formed islands are bats, because they are the only mammals with a means to get there.)

We can also see that when members of the same species become separated by barriers their descendents will evolve in different ways. Ostriches, emus, rheas and kiwis are very similar to each other because they share an ancient common ancestor and they continue to live in relatively comparable habitats. Yet they are different from each other because each has evolved independently of the others—residing on different continents or oceanic islands, separated by the sea.

These birds are known as "ratites," meaning flightless birds having flat breastbones absent a keel. There are six known families of ratites. Two of the families are now extinct—the "elephant bird" of Madagascar, the largest bird ever discovered, and the Moa of New Zealand. There were at least ten Moa species, ranging in size from slightly larger than a turkey to the Giant Moa that was about nine feet tall, until human beings hunted the last of them to extinction by around 1500 A.D.

The ancestors that were common to these ratites lived on a "supercontinent," referred to today as Gondwana, that once existed in the southern hemisphere. The various populations of these ancestral birds that eventually evolved into the six distinct families known today were separated when Gondwana broke apart as a result of plate tectonics (continental drift). Beginning about 160 million years ago, large sections of this giant continent gradually separated to form the land masses found today in the southern hemisphere, including South America, Africa, Madagascar, Antarctica, Australia, and New Zealand.

Some of the most interesting evidence of Gondwana's existence, its relative movement across the surface of the Earth, and its eventual breakup are the fossils that are being found on the continent of Antarctica. These fossils include dozens of plant species, such as giant ferns, that indicate the landmass of Antarctica was once a warm and wet tropical forest environment. Since 1986, scientists have also discovered the fossils of giant aquatic reptiles that have been extinct for about 65 million years and more than a half-dozen species of dinosaurs. The dinosaurs include both carnivorous and very large herbivorous species. An abundance of vegetation would have been required to support these large herbivores. A few of the dinosaur species found in Antarctica had also been found in North and South America, while others are newly discovered species.

The tropical forests of Antarctica were likely the result of two separate factors. First, there are indications that the Antarctic landmass was once much closer to the equator when it was a part of the Gondwana supercontinent. Secondly, even after the landmass had migrated to the region of the South Pole, the climate may have remained much warmer than it is today for an extended period. Some indications suggest that during the Cretaceous period, which ended with the extinction of the dinosaurs about 65 million years ago, the entire Earth was subject to what we today call a "greenhouse" climate, with much higher levels of CO_2 in the atmosphere. During this period, even the Earth's polar regions may have been warm enough to support forests.

One of the most pressing issues of modern human society very clearly illustrates that our planet and the life it sustains have a history of dramatic change. That is, our insatiable appetite for oil—our extraction and consumption of the petroleum that is the product of the decay of algae and zooplankton beds from ancient seas that were once where we now find dry inland areas of the continents, including the barren deserts of Africa and the Middle East.

The previous connectedness of the world's continents and their subsequent isolation from each other has dictated the distribution and the character of life on Earth, as life has adapted in different ways to similar and to variant environments. The distribution of mammals is a good example. Mammals are distinguished from other vertebrates in part by the presence of fur (or hair), mammary glands with which the females nurse offspring, and the control of internal body temperature (warm-bloodedness). There are three types of mammals in the world today—categorized according to how their offspring develop from fertilized eggs. The vast majority of mammals fall into two groups, marsupials and placentals. A less familiar group of mammals are the monotremes.

Monotremes are the most primitive in that they most closely resemble the early mammals that evolved from reptiles. They reproduce by laying soft leathery-shelled, pea-sized eggs with large yolks which they carry in a slit on their belly for incubation. When the eggs are hatched, the infants nurse from mammary glands that ooze through pores in the skin. Monotremes have not evolved well-defined nipples. They get their name because, like birds and reptiles, they have a common opening for the genital, urinary, and defecatory tracts. There are only three monotreme species that still survive—the duck-billed platypus and two species of echidnas ("spiny anteaters") that are found in Australia and New Guinea.

Marsupials are distinguished by their offspring being born incompletely developed and then carried and nursed in a pouch on the mother's belly. The immune system of all animals serves to expel foreign objects or substances. Even though a fetus carries half the DNA of its mother, it is still somewhat of a foreign object. Without a placenta to act as a go-between, the mother's immune system would soon attack the fetus as an intruder. Therefore, after a brief gestation period, the forelimbs of the tiny embryo are developed well enough for it to crawl out of the uterus and make its way to the pouch on the mother's belly where it then attaches itself to a nipple. (Male marsupials have a forked penis that is used to fertilize twin uteruses in the females.)

Placental mammals, by contrast, are born more fully developed because the presence of a placenta enables more complete fetal development. The placenta acts as a sort of storage unit for the oxygen and nutrition that is provided to the fetus by its mother. This enables the fetus' needs to be met more independently of the mother's metabolic system. Most of the mammals that we are familiar with, including humans, are placental mammals.

Marsupials are less familiar to most of us because they are found almost exclusively on the isolated islands of Australia and New Guinea. Though three families of marsupials, including the opossums, are found in the Americas. The existence of such a wide range of both marsupial and placental mammals, and their separated distribution around the world, resulted primarily, much like the differing ratites, from plate tectonics.

Mammals have been around for a very long time—about 200 million years. The lineage of placental mammals is believed to have split from marsupials about 140 million years ago. Until the extinction of dinosaurs, however, there were relatively few mammal species. They were small in stature and probably mostly nocturnal. It was the extinction of the dinosaurs that opened up ecosystem resources for exploitation by mammals, allowing for the diversification of species and for the growth in size of many of those species.

At the end of the Cretaceous period, about 65 million years ago, an asteroid is believed to have caused the conditions that resulted in the extinction of the dinosaurs. This marked the beginning of the Cenozoic era, which saw the rise of mammals as a more dominant class of animals on Earth. This same time period also coincided with the break-up of the Pangaea supercontinent that once comprised all of the landmass of the world. As the Pangaea continent broke up—first into the two supercontinents of Laurasia in the north and Gondwana in the south, and then into the continents that we see today—the mammals were dispersed and isolated on the various continents. As the dinosaurs died out and resources became available for exploitation by mammals, it was marsupials that thrived and diversified on the isolated island continents of Australia and South America, while placentals thrived and diversified in what would become Africa, Europe, Asia, and North America.

Alternate hypotheses suggest that marsupials may have flourished first on either Australia or South America before migrating to the other by way of a land bridge through Antarctica before that continent became impassible due to separation and climatic conditions. The fossil record shows that South America once contained a much wider range and variety of marsupials, including some very large herbivores and carnivores. This suggests that South America may very well have been the ecosystem within which a great diversity of marsupials first evolved.

Today when we think of marsupials, however, we usually think of koalas, kangaroos, or the numerous other marsupials that are found in Australia. This is because most of the marsupials that once lived in South America are now extinct. Their extinction was the result of the Isthmus of Panama that rose to connect North and South America only two or three million years ago. South America had been an isolated island continent for sixty-to-seventy million years, allowing for the evolution of many unique species, including a wide diversity of marsupials.

When North and South America were connected with the formation of what we now call Central America, the separate eco-systems of the two continents were also joined, allowing for the migration of species from one continent to the other. As we saw earlier, the introduction of new species into an ecosystem can often dramatically change the "balance" and then the character of that ecosystem. In this case, the placental mammals of North America proved to be generally more resilient than the marsupials of South America. As a result, in the competition for territory and resources, most of the marsupials lost to the placentals. Although, a number of marsupials do continue to thrive in South America, including as many as sixty-five species of opossum. One species of opossum has even successfully migrated as far north as Canada. The so-called Virginia opossum found today throughout much of the United States, along with the armadillo, an ancient placental mammal found in and around the state of Texas, are both visible migrant representatives of that ancient South American ecosystem.

We and All Other Living Things Are Made of the Same Stuff

If all of the species in the world are indeed evolutionary descendants of a single ancestral species, then we might expect to find that all living organisms would share some fundamental, common properties. They do. If we set aside viruses (which some scientists have argued are not really "life" at all), all living things, including humans, are made of the same basic biochemical molecules, including DNA, and all species use the same genetic code in which the same nucleotide sequences produce the same amino acids—the very building blocks of all life on Earth.

In addition to these fundamental building blocks, biologists have found that many of the genes that dictate the organization of living things are common to all organisms—from ferns to bacteria to worms to iguanas to humans. Furthermore, we can easily see the correlation between our own outward physical anatomy and many of the other animals that we see in the world, especially vertebrates. The four appendages that are common to most vertebrates (which can be manifested as legs, arms, fins or wings), the single head, the two eyes, the sexual nature, all represent a familiar configuration that suggests kinship. Just a superficial look at many of the plants and animals that we see around us offers numerous clues of relatedness.

Since the emergence of very simple single-celled organisms some four billion years ago, populations of such reproducing organisms have had an immense amount of time to evolve into increasingly complex forms along a variety of avenues. The mere fact that we and all other organisms are made of the same basic stuff and that we share a lot of the same genetic information and physical characteristics provides compelling evidence of the hereditary relatedness of all life on Earth.

The Evolution of Languages (As an Analogy)

Regardless of what may have actually happened concerning the Tower of Babel, we have ample evidence that all modern languages are evolutionary descendants of previous languages, and that most of today's languages share common ancestors called "parent languages" with other languages. For these reasons, the evolution of languages can serve as a useful analogy that may help us to visualize biological evolution and speciation.

The evolution of languages and biological evolution are two different things. Languages do not undergo gene mutations and recombination from which natural selection can work. Languages evolve as a result of both inadvertent and deliberate cultural selections that are made by human beings. But the evolution of languages provides us with a clear demonstration of how our world is constantly evolving, and how several different and complex languages (or "species," so to speak) can naturally evolve from a single ancestral language (or "species"). In a sense, languages are living things, and like all other living things, languages undergo evolution and speciation.

Consider how the ancient Hebrew, Aramaic, and Greek languages in which the Bible was written have changed. Today, Aramaic is nearly extinct while Hebrew and Greek have evolved so dramatically that translation and interpretation are required to understand ancient scriptural texts. Indeed, we need only read or attend a Shakespearian play or read the King James Bible to see just how dramatically the English language has changed in a mere four hundred years.

Because of the nearly world wide conquest of the British Empire only a few centuries ago, the evolution of the English language around the world presents an opportunity for us to see how, when similar populations are separated, evolution can take different paths. Consider the very wide range of English language dialects and accents that can be found around the world—from upper class society to cockney; from London to Liverpool; from England to Wales, Scotland, and Northern Ireland; from Great Britain to Hong Kong, Australia,

New Zealand, South Africa, Canada, and the United States; from Manhattan to Brooklyn, the Bronx, Boston, Appalachia, Georgia, Minnesota, and even East or West Texas. As these various populations have been somewhat separated for a couple of centuries, each of their cultures and languages have evolved independently and differently.*

Much like the separate lineages that produce different breeds of domestic animals, the common language of separated populations will naturally diverge and become less and less similar over time. Given enough time, separated "lineages" of languages have commonly become distinct new languages.

Like living organisms, languages can be grouped into families and groups of related languages that have all evolved from a common ancestor. For example, the Indo-European language family includes Albanian, Celtic, and the Germanic languages (which include Dutch, English, German and others). Also falling under the Indo-European family are Greek, Indo-Iranian, and the Romance languages (which include Spanish, French, Italian and others). Other language families include: the Sino-Tibetan family that encompasses Chinese, Thai, Burmese, and Tibetan; the Afro-Asian family that includes Arabic, Hebrew, the Berber tongues of North Africa, and Amharic of Ethiopia; the Uralic or Altaic family that includes Finnish, Estonian, Hungarian, Turkish, and many other languages in northern and central Asia. The Japanese and Korean languages, in turn, constitute another family.[19]

In many cases, we have at least some written evidence of ancestral languages that have split and diverged to become multiple descendant languages. Just as has been the case with the speciation of living organisms, however, no one could directly "see" the evolution of Latin into the languages of French, Italian, Spanish, Portuguese,

---

* In the last half-century or so these trends have begun to reverse as advances in trade, travel, and communications have fostered more of a "global community." In fact, quite different languages can even merge to result in a "Creole" language or a new language. In this way the evolution of languages is different from the evolution of living organisms. Whenever the lineages of living organisms become chromosomally incompatible, they can never again mix their genetic material.

Romanian, and Albanian, and historical texts are inadequate to fully explain these transitions. But there is little doubt that these modern languages evolved from ancient Latin. Direct observation, of course, is not the only source of knowledge. Systematic comparative analysis can tell us a lot about languages and their origins, and it can tell us a great deal about living organisms and their ancestral origins too.

We find indications of an evolving world all around us. The geology of the Earth is pretty well understood by most of us today, and we can see that it is in a constant state of flux. We know about earthquakes, volcanoes, and most of us have a reasonable understanding of the concepts and the histories of continental drift and recurring ice ages.

We can also readily see that large-scale changes in the character of life on Earth have occurred over the course of many millions of years, as well as in our own lifetimes. A trip to most any museum of natural history reminds us of the do-do birds, the wooly mammoths and the many more commonly known species of dinosaurs that have all gone extinct. During our lifetimes, we have seen the extinction or dramatic reductions in hundreds of species. This is usually due to natural environmental changes, but it is also increasingly due to the dramatic expansion of human civilization, undoubtedly the most significant change in the character of life on Earth since the extinction of the dinosaurs. Indeed, for those of us who have reached the age of fifty, we have seen the world's population of human beings more than double in size during our short lifetime.

The regional nature of the world's races and ethnicities suggests that separate populations of humans have evolved in separate ways. Not only have each of the many various ethnicities in the world evolved their own language and culture, they frequently exhibit their own distinct physical characteristics too. And these characteristics naturally resemble those of closely related ethnicities in adjacent regions. We need only consider the transition in human appearance and culture as we move from the indigenous population of Alaska to China

183

to Nepal to Bangladesh to India to Pakistan to Iran to Iraq to Turkey to Greece to Italy to France to Germany to Sweden and Norway.

We can even see subtle indications of evolution and evolutionary principles in our own families and short-term heritage. Each of us tends to resemble one or both of our parents, but we are nevertheless unique individuals. As we trace our heritage through just the very few generations since the advent of photography, we can see the subtle evolution of family resemblances—we can see how heritable traits evolve over successive generations.

Unquestionably, we live in an evolving world. This is apparent in the history of languages, in political and cultural history, in Jewish, Christian and other religious histories, and in the history of the plants and animals that we see around us and at our local museums. As we have seen, biological evolution is utilized in our propagation of domestic plants and animals, and it is a key consideration in our fight against heritable and microbial diseases. Evolutionary history is evident in atavism, in vestigial organs and other structures, in the imperfections of anatomical designs, in physiological and biochemical similarities between species, and in the geographic distribution of species.

In addition to the subtle (and not so subtle) indicators noted above that we see all around us and in our own lives, our understanding of evolution is bolstered by scientific evidence that has been gathered and tested for more than a century and a half. The systematic scientific study of biological evolution has revealed dramatic evolutionary changes over millions, tens of millions, hundreds of millions, and even billions of years, as we will see in the following chapters. The discoveries that have been realized by modern science have not only helped to more thoroughly explain what we see around us, such discoveries have also revealed that in many ways our universe is far more complex than is first apparent, and even more glorious than we had imagined before.

8

The History of Life

W hen we think of paleontology, most of us probably think of those few large dinosaurs that can be seen in museums and that are often represented by children's action-figures. The findings of paleontologists are of course much more extensive than merely an account of those large animals that are so well suited to youthful imaginations. The science of paleontology encompasses the study of fossilized remnants of everything from the tiniest and oldest of organisms found on Earth to the most modern and complex of organisms. A couple of centuries of such study has resulted in a fossil record that has revealed an astounding transformation of life on Earth, from the very simple single-cell organisms that first appeared in geologic strata that is now 3.6 billion year old, to the more complex single-cell organisms that emerged some 1.4 billion years ago, to the very first multi-cellular organisms that arrived about 1.2 billion years ago, to the more familiar phyla of complex multi-cellular plants and animals beginning about 600 million years ago, and finally to the great complexity and diversity of life that we see around us today.

Uncovering the fossils that illustrate these transitions has not been easy and the fossil record is certainly very far from a complete chronicle of the tens of millions of species that have ever lived. In fact, the fossil record represents only a very tiny sampling of the history of life on Earth.

For this reason, detractors of evolutionary science will often cite what is *not* found in the fossil record as evidence that evolution has not occurred. The familiar refrain is, "Where are all of the transitional forms?" or "intermediate types"? (fossils representing intermediate, transitional forms between known species) Darwin himself cited the scarcity of fossils representing intermediate forms as the most troubling hurdle in gaining general acceptance of his theory of *gradualism*. Today we have many more examples of fossils representing "transitional species," but there are two very important considerations that help us to better understand why they are so uncommon. Modern scientists have modified Darwin's idea of gradualism by varying degrees and, just as importantly, we must consider how fossils are made in the first place.

Darwin's theory of gradualism postulates that evolution takes place through a multitude of tiny incremental steps and, therefore, the process occurs very gradually over a long period of time and through a great many generations. He was right for the most part. But what Darwin did not fully appreciate is the irregular pace or the "starts and stops" that very often occur in the evolutionary process. Scientists now have a better understanding of how a species population can undergo relatively rapid evolutionary change as a result of any number of environmental pressures and can then reach a point of greater stability—a point of stasis, where very little change occurs over a long period. (As mentioned in Chapter 6, alligators and crocodiles are both somewhat ancient species that have been in relative stasis for a long period of time because they have been so successful in their current forms. Opossums, armadillos, cockroaches, horseshoe crabs, nautiluses, and dragonflies are other examples.) The fossils of a very successful species that has been in stasis for some time will naturally be much more abundant than the fossils of much smaller populations of relatively rapidly changing transitional species. (Of course the smaller a population, the faster genetic changes arising in individuals can be propagated throughout its gene pool.) In fact, the existence of any fossilized remains at all of such small and fleeting populations is rendered unlikely by the extreme rarity of fossilization.

In his book, *A Short History of Nearly Everything,* the popular science writer Bill Bryson eloquently described how unlikely it is that we will ever find many of the fossils that we may be looking for:

In order to become a fossil, several things must happen. First, you must die in the right place. Only about 15 percent of rocks can preserve fossils, so it's no good keeling over on a future site of granite. In practical terms the deceased must become buried in sediment, where it can leave an impression, like a leaf in wet mud, or decompose without exposure to oxygen, permitting the molecules in its bones and hard parts (and very occasionally softer parts) to be replaced by dissolved minerals, creating a petrified copy of the original. Then as the sediments in which the fossil lies are carelessly pressed and folded and pushed about by Earth's processes, the fossil must somehow maintain an identifiable shape. Finally, but above all, after tens of millions or perhaps hundreds of millions of years hidden away, it must be found and recognized as something worth keeping.

Only about one bone in a billion, it is thought, ever becomes fossilized. If that is so, it means that the complete fossil legacy of all Americans alive today—that's 270 million people with 206 bones each—will only be about fifty bones, one quarter of a complete skeleton. ... Most of what has lived on Earth has left behind no record at all. It has been estimated that one species in ten thousand has made it into the fossil record.

Others have estimated that perhaps only one in over a hundred thousand species has been found. And yet, enough fossils have been found to provide us with a lot of information about how life has evolved, including the fossils of numerous so-called transitional species.

We have all likely noticed that on the sheer walls on the side of roadways where they have been cut through hills or mountains, clearly visible layers of geologic strata can often be seen. Layers of strata are also often exposed in the erosion of seaside cliffs and where rivers have cut deep canyons into the landscape. These layers are sediments that have accumulated over various time periods, but usually on a scale of many millions of years as rocks were eroded to sediment and the sediment then hardened to form new rock. Naturally, the top layers are younger than those below, with each successive layer having been laid upon the previous one. The distinction of one layer from another is indicative of the varying conditions that were present at the time of each sedimentary accumulation, as our ever-restless planet has dictated. The Earth's processes have also pushed, pulled, sunken, raised, folded, and moved the Earth's crust so that these strata are hidden or exposed in various ways all around the globe. As a result, we can find evidence, for example, of an ancient sea in the arid mountains of West Texas, or

of great forests of fern trees in Antarctica. This process has enabled scientists to find ancient strata that have been pushed to the surface in various places all around the Earth, and to find fossils within the strata of the many eras of our world's history. These exposed geologic strata provide numerous opportunities for paleontologists to do the work of systematically unearthing the history of life on Earth.

Strata revealed by erosion in Texas

As fossils have been found in geologic strata of various ages, a distinct pattern has been revealed—from a lifeless planet found in the oldest strata, to very simple single-cell organisms found in subsequent strata, to more complex single-cell organisms, and then to multi-cellular organisms found only in much younger strata. Among complex organisms, an unmistakable chronology can be observed as they first developed in the sea and then only much later migrated to land, with some species eventually taking flight in the air. Paleontologists have discovered that the historic proliferation of life on Earth was punctuated by numerous mass extinctions, with each episode of devastating extinction being eventually followed by a diversification of new species and, among many lineages, a trend toward greater complexity and adaptability.

The Earth (along with the rest of our solar system) is about 4.6 billion years old. For much of the first 700,000 years or so, the Earth was an inhospitable boiling mass. Found in West Greenland, the oldest sedimentary rocks are about 3.75 billion years old, suggesting a time when the Earth's crust was first becoming stable enough to support life. Though chemical traces in older geologic strata suggest earlier life, the oldest fossils that have actually been found are those of simple single-celled organisms that can be found in strata about 3.5 to 3.6 billion years old.

As we saw in Chapter 6, these first single-celled organisms, called *prokaryotes*, lack a number of the specialized structures (organelles) that are found in the much larger *eukaryotic* cells of other single-celled and all multi-celled organisms. Prokaryotic cells have no distinct nucleus with a membrane—no mitochondria, chloroplasts, or paired chromosomes. These single-celled organisms have taken the form of countless species of cyanobacteria (blue-green algae). The fossil record clearly illustrates that for some 2.4 billion years—about two-thirds of all the history of life on Earth—blue-green algae were the only living organisms in existence.[1]

Then about 1.4 billion years ago, the simple prokaryote cell evolved into the more complex eukaryotic cell, which would become the building block of almost all of the many species of life with which we are most familiar. Relatively soon after their initial appearance, eukaryotic cells evolved into a diversity of forms—first into single-celled amoebas, diatoms, and dinoflagellates, and then eventually into multi-cellular animals, plants, and fungi.

In geologic strata 542 to 530 million years old—the early part of what is known as the Cambrian period of geologic time—the fossils of animals representing almost all of today's known phyla have been found. The term "phyla" is used to classify animal groups according to their basic body construction—i.e., *Arthropods*, with jointed legs and external skeletons (later to include crabs, scorpions, spiders, and insects) and *Annelids*, with repeating segmented bodies (like earthworms, lugworms, and leeches). There are also *Nematodes* (worms with un-segmented bodies) and *Chordata*, with nerve cords that run down their bodies and with notochords (a cartilaginous skeletal rod) and gill pouches during embryonic development (later to include all vertebrates, including humans, along with sea squirts and lancelets).

The seemingly sudden appearance and diversification of these complex animals has prompted the event to be called the "Cambrian explosion." (In terms of geologic time, a period of 15 to 40 million years is quite brief.) The puzzling circumstances surrounding these discoveries have been the subject of controversy and wide ranging speculation ever since the mid-nineteenth century.

Some Christian commentators have even suggested that the sudden appearance of these animals is persuasive evidence of God's creative activity. In considering such a view however, we must be mindful of the hazard of, once again, invoking God as nothing more than a "God of the gaps." The existence of God and our connection to Him are certainly not dependent on the *direct, supernatural* creation of these strange animals some 550 million years ago.

Hypotheses for the cause of such an "explosion" include the possibility that a threshold was reached in the development of the genetic code, and thus the expression of so-called Hox genes triggered new arrangements in the development and organization of bodily structures. On the other hand, several other plausible explanations and a few new discoveries tend to support those paleontologists who believe that there was not really any "explosion" at all.

The general conception among scientists is that complex animals had indeed evolved over a great span of time prior to the Cambrian period, but for one or more of several possible reasons, they were not preserved as fossils that can be easily found. One of the most important reasons that fossils of multi-cellular organisms are more readily found in strata no older than the Cambrian period is that only soft-bodied animals existed prior to that time. As sea life diversified, predators evolved that could live by consuming other animals. Through natural selection, many animals evolved protective shells (a process called "biomineralization") to shield themselves from these predators. Shells, exoskeletons, or other hard parts increased the likelihood of creatures possessing them being preserved as fossils.

Other factors contributing to the scarcity of pre-Cambrian fossils and their sudden appearance over just a few million years include the possibility that climatic conditions and/or changes in the Earth's chemistry (something that has happened numerous times in the Earth's history), or even a threshold in DNA development could have induced previously very tiny organisms to suddenly grow much larger, increasing their likelihood of being fossilized and later discovered. Indeed, there are very abundant but tiny arthropods in existence today that, because of their diminutive nature, have left no fossil record.[2] Similarly, changes in the Earth's chemistry could have facilitated the very process of fossilization.

Though the fossils of complex animals older than the Cambrian period are rare, a few have been discovered in recent decades. Named for the Ediacara Hills of South Australia where one of the first discoveries of pre-Cambrian multi-cellular animals was found, organisms that correspond to this period are referred to as "Ediacaran biota" or "Ediacaran fauna." As a result, a newly designated geologic time period that immediately precedes the Cambrian has been named the Ediacaran period. A few similar and some of the same Ediacaran multi-cellular organisms have also been discovered in Siberia, Newfoundland, California, China, and West Africa.

One of the most important of these finds was made in 2002. Genetic analysis had suggested that bilateral symmetry in animals probably arose around 575 million to 650 million years ago. However, no fossils of bilateral animals had yet been found that were older than the Cambrian fauna until a team of Chinese and American scientists made the discovery of a microscopic bilateral creature in 580 million to 600 million year old strata in southern China. Their discovery demonstrated that the genetics of complex bilateral creatures had evolved some 50 million years before the Cambrian explosion—that the necessary genetic ingredients had evolved well before their manifestation in the larger sizes of the Cambrian fauna.[3]

Though a few of the pre-Cambrian creatures appear to be ancestors of Cambrian fauna, many others seem to be unrelated to any organisms found in strata younger than the Ediacaran period. These creatures encompassed a wide range of shapes and sizes. The specimens include jellyfish-like creatures with radial spokes or concentric ridges, and many that resemble flat disks, fronds, upright pens, or segmented worms. Aside from some of the jellyfish, most Ediacaran organisms were quite unlike anything that exists today. Evidence suggests that a mass extinction occurred at the end of the Ediacaran period, and therefore, the creatures that are found in strata corresponding to the Cambrian are the descendants of just those few organisms that survived that extinction.

Even among the Cambrian fauna where the body types largely corresponded to recognizable phyla, most of the creatures were unlike anything with which most of us are familiar. Classified as an arthropod, a creature named *Opabinia* had five eyes and a nozzle-like snout with claws on its end. Most Cambrian fauna were quite mysterious and some appear to represent phyla that did not survive beyond that period. A group of animals that sported protective plates can be classified as neither worm nor sponge and appears to fall outside of any phyla existing today.[4]

A particularly noteworthy group of animals that flourished during the Cambrian period and beyond were the trilobites. These were a class of marine arthropods that included many thousands of widely varied species over numerous orders, families, and genera. These strange and magnificent animals ranged from about the size of a peppercorn to the size of a dinner plate. Most species were about the size of beetles. So far, more than 1,500 genera and 17,000 species of trilobites have been identified. Just as the Triassic, Jurassic, and Cretaceous periods lasting about 160 million years are often referred to as the "Age of the Dinosaurs," and the Paleogene and Neogene periods encompassing the last 65 million years are referred to as the "Age of Mammals," an era spanning more than four geologic time periods and lasting some 290 million years can easily be considered the "Age of the Trilobites."* A diversity of these creatures was so ubiquitous for such a long time on Earth that trilobite experts can date strata by noting which trilobite species are found within them. The historic movement of tectonic plates can sometimes be tracked in much the same way. Even after being decimated by several mass extinction events, the trilobites survived through the ages, living on Earth for nearly twice the length of time as the dinosaurs' reign. Despite their resilience, however, the last of the trilobites eventually perished some 245 million years ago.

Among several of their peculiar characteristics, trilobites had crystal eye lenses. Most animals have lived in environments where sight offers numerous advantages, so the occurrence of light-sensitive cells has provided a foundation for the evolution of eyes. Geneticists believe that they have identified a set of genes that trigger the production of various bodily structures, including eyes, which are so ancient that they predate the divergence of the various known phyla. So eyes have developed a number of different ways in various animals throughout history. In the case of trilobites, the lenses of their eyes were constructed of clear calcite crystals. Among many thousands of trilobite species, the number of these lenses in each of the creature's eyes ranged from a mere one to several thousand. Remarkably,

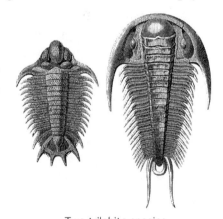

Two trilobite species

---

* Entomologists may well assert that since shortly after their first appearance, insects have been the dominant class of animals on Earth ever since, both in numbers and in activity. On the other hand, biologists and perhaps physicians could argue that from nearly the very first appearance of life on Earth until today, it is bacteria that have truly reigned supreme.

with their multi-crystal and dome-shaped eye lenses, one group of trilobites' field of vision was apparently as wide as 360 degrees on all axes.[5]

From the Endiacaran period through the Cambrian and Ordovician periods (a span of 210 million years from about 650 million years ago until about 440 million years ago), the seas of the Earth underwent a tremendous growth and transformation of multi-cellular life. But this great proliferation of living organisms was confined to the sea. Aside from a few strains of bacteria around springs or regularly moistened shores, the land was barren and lifeless. There were no trees, shrubs, or grasses. No amphibians, reptiles, mammals, birds, or insects. There were no calls or cries of living creatures and no shades of green in the landscape, only the unheard whistling of wind among mountains and cliffs and unseen shades of yellow, red, brown and gray.

Geologic strata have revealed that it was not until about 470 million years ago that plants first began to move ashore. That is about 10 percent of the current age of the Earth. This was made possible only as the result of a change that had occurred in the chemistry of the Earth's atmosphere.

When life began on Earth there was virtually no oxygen in the atmosphere. The first bacteria species thrived in extremely hot, acidic and sulfuric environments. Many could not even survive significant exposure to oxygen. Such bacteria can still be found on Earth in the high temperatures of hot springs and under-sea volcanic vents. These first single-cell organisms that used the Earth's heat to synthesize nutrients soon evolved into cells that could process light with chlorophyll to synthesize foods. Photosynthesis, of course, is the process that converts gaseous carbon dioxide into carbon for the nourishment of cells while releasing oxygen into the atmosphere as a by-product. It was the great volume of these photosynthesizing cyano-bacteria (blue-green algae) around the world that produced the oxygen that animals would later evolve to utilize. After about 3 billion years of photosynthesis, enough oxygen had been produced to form a layer of O_3 (ozone) in the upper atmosphere. Prior to the development of this protective ozone layer, the sun's ultraviolet radiation prohibited the development of land-dwelling organisms. It was only after the ozone layer had gained sufficient protective capability that life's colonization of land became possible.

Some of the first plants to encroach landward were creeping moss-like plants that would send up very small shoots that bifurcated only once or twice. Leaves clung to the shoots like scales. There is nothing quite like them alive today. Many of these early plants are believed to have migrated from fresh water lakes and rivers where both plants and animals had previously migrated from the sea.

Over the next 20 million years or so, plants spread inland and diversified to include numerous species the size of small shrubs. It was then that animals too began to come ashore.

Once the landward migration of vascular plants had begun, each step along the way led to new opportunities. As plant life covered the land, animals that could feed on the vegetation eventually followed. Then as plants and animals lived and died, their decomposed carcasses created humus to further enrich the soil, leading to even more varieties of plant life and, in turn, providing even more opportunities for exploitation by a greater variety of animals.

The lineages of several animal phyla made the transition from the sea to land. For example, the *Arthropod* lineage produced mites, millipedes, centipedes, scorpions, spiders, and eventually insects; the *Annelid* lineage produced earthworms; the *Nematode* lineage produced roundworms and threadworms; and the *Chordata* lineage produced all of the vertebrates—amphibians, reptiles, dinosaurs, birds, and mammals (including us, of course). Interestingly, genetic similarities among all terrestrial vertebrates suggest that the Chordata transition to land occurred only once, as a single lineage of fish evolved into the first tetrapods some 380 to 360 million years ago.

Fish first appeared during the Ordovician Period about 475 million years ago. These first fishes were jawless, with just a simple opening for a mouth. Hinged jawed fishes are found in younger strata, beginning about 430 to 400 million years ago. Jawed fish fall into two groups, those with a cartilage skeleton (like sharks, rays, and skates) and those with a bony skeleton. It was during the Devonian Period, between 400 and 360 million years ago, that the jawed fishes greatly diversified and grew to dominate the seas. Among these ancient fishes were rather strange looking giant predators that sported protective armor composed of external bone. These strange creatures, along with many thousands of other species, have long been extinct.

During this time, fishes also evolved to cope with the brackish waters of estuaries, and then moved upstream into freshwater rivers and lakes feeding on algae, aquatic plants, and the arthropods that preceded them. The first tetrapods, it is believed, evolved from bony fishes in swampy brackish or freshwater habitats around 380 million years ago. These increasingly amphibious creatures were probably predators that sought to exploit the opportunities found near the waters edge in swampy habitats. Perhaps not coincidentally, insects were becoming increasingly abundant during this period.

A number of the earliest tetrapods were found to have seven toes. Found in 365 million year old sandstones and siltstones of East Greenland, these "ichthyostegids" have been described as little more than "walking fish." In addition to primitive legs with seven toes, they had "a fish-like tail and long jaws with rather undifferentiated teeth."[6] It was discovered that at least one species of these so-called walking fish had eight toes. Not surprisingly, these eight-toed creatures are just what we might expect as fish fins containing eight skeletal digits evolved to become appendages for walking.

Whether it was one species of these creatures that soon evolved to possess only five toes or whether it was an altogether different lineage whose progeny would carry on, we know that all terrestrial vertebrates after that time in history either had five toes, or were descended from ancestors with five toes. Even those vertebrates that no longer have five toes, such as the ungulates that now possess only one, two, or three toes, are all descendants of five-toed ancestors, as we will see a little later.

By the time of what is called the Carboniferous geologic time period, from 286 to 360 million years ago, large swaths of land were covered with the great swampy forests—locales that would eventually produce the coal deposits that we use today. (Coal is the high-density remains of ancient trees and other organic material that were partially preserved as they fell into the boggy, oxygen-deprived soils of these forest floors.) With giant trees and a humid atmosphere, these forests somewhat resembled today's tropical rain forests, but there were some significant differences. For example, there was little variety in color since flowering plants had not yet evolved. And there was no sound of the calls of mammals or the songs of birds. Paleontologist Richard Fortey has called them the "silent forests."

In addition to giant club moss trees and a plethora of ferns, the moist oxygen-rich atmosphere of these forests produced some rather large amphibians, insects, and other arthropods. Dragonflies were bigger than hawks (the largest insect ever known), and there was a plant-eating amphibian that grew to twenty feet in length. There were six-foot millipedes. Just imagine stepping across one of those fellows, or encountering one of the giant scorpions that were there. Cockroaches were there too of course—about twice the size of those that we see today.

The Carboniferous forests contained an enormous variety of amphibians, including some that roughly resembled today's alligators and another group that resembled snakes. Amphibian species filled the ecological niches of predators and herbivores that we usually associate with faster or more cunning reptilian or mammalian species. Since reptiles and mammals had not yet evolved to compete with them, amphibians were able to prosper by freely exploiting the available resources. As a result of this great diversity and abundance of amphibians, the Carboniferous period is often described as the "Age of the Amphibians."

Though amphibians were clearly dominant, evidence of the first reptiles has also been found in Carboniferous strata. Discovered in 1987, an eight-inch specimen given the name *Westlothiana Lizzae* (affectionately called "Lizzie") is the oldest reptile fossil ever found. It was discovered in Scotland among sediments that were dated at about 340 million years.

Just as has happened so many times throughout its history, it was a change in the Earth's climate that brought about a change in its living inhabitants during the Permian period, between 285 and 245 million years ago. Colder and dryer weather brought an end to the Carboniferous forests and, with it, an end to the reign of amphibians among vertebrates. With their scaly skin and shelled eggs that they incubated on dry land, reptiles were better suited to this new climate and they began to spread and diversify. Many new reptilian species evolved to exploit newly available ecological niches.

The entire Permian period witnessed a gradual decline of life all around the world. By its end, an apparent ice age and other unknown circumstances had conspired to produce one of the several great mass extinctions of life on Earth. Sea life was most affected. After having flourished for more than 200 million years, the trilobites were lost forever. All the reef corals were destroyed. (The corals that replaced them and those that live today are wholly different varieties.) The brachiopods, echinoderms, mollusks, clams, and snails were all decimated. The descendents of these animals that live today are all the progeny of just those few species that survived the extinction, while many thousands of other species met the end of their lineages.

Though sea life was most affected by the mass extinction of the Permian period, land-based vertebrates did not escape the carnage. Amphibians had been in decline throughout the period, but events toward the end also wiped out many of those reptilian species that had only recently taken the place of amphibians.

For those reptiles that did survive, however, new opportunities arose when conditions improved. A great divergence of reptilian species soon emerged as they exploited new ecological niches and successfully competed for many of those that had previously been dominated by other animals. By the Jurassic period, beginning about

200 million years ago, reptiles had come to dominate the landmasses of the world.

There were flying reptiles called pterosaurs (also called pterodactyls), the first vertebrates to evolve an ability to fly. These reptiles had wings that consisted of a skin membrane and muscles that stretched from the thorax to an extremely elongated fourth finger. Like the feathered birds that evolved later, these reptiles had hollow bones that reduced their weight and facilitated flight. Various species ranged in size from that of a woodpecker to the largest flying creature that has ever been discovered. Found in the Big Bend area of West Texas, the *Quetzalcoatlus* species (named for an Aztec God) had a wingspan of nearly fifty feet. This giant was also among the last of the flying reptiles. Pterosaurs thrived for more than 160 million years before they went extinct, along with the dinosaurs, some 65 million years ago.

Similarly, a few of the marine reptiles of the Jurassic and Cretaceous periods first discovered in the nineteenth century seemed perfectly akin to the menacing dragons of legend. Like today's marine mammals, these reptiles were descendants of predatory terrestrial ancestors that had returned to the sea in search of food. Two different orders of these animals and dozens of species have been uncovered. Those that fall under the order Ichthyosauria mostly resembled fish except with long toothy snouts, though some of the earlier species looked more like giant lizards with fins. Most ichthyosaurs were about six to twelve-feet in length, but their sizes varied widely and the largest species, discovered in British Columbia in the mid-1990s, grew to an enormous seventy feet.

One group of ichthyosaurs that lived around 190 million years ago, the genus *Temnodontosaurus* found in England and Germany, had eyes that were as much as 10 inches across—the largest eyes of any creature ever known. Its large eyes enabled this fierce predator to see in near total darkness at great ocean depths.

Another order of marine reptiles had an even more unusual anatomy. Unlike any other aquatic animals, plesiosaurs sported four paddle-shaped limbs for propulsion and a reptilian tail rather than a tail fin. Most plesiosaur species had proportionally small heads and very long necks. (The so-called Loch Ness Monster has sometimes been speculated to be an individual from the last surviving population of these unusual animals.) The *Thalassomedon* genus of plesiosaurs had a 20-foot neck that comprised half of its body length, while each of its four flippers was the size of a grown man. These animals carried stones in their stomachs for ballast and/or to aid in food digestion. Six specimens within the *Thalassomedon* genus have been recovered in the state of Colorado where these creatures roamed a sea that was there some 95 million years ago. An even larger group of plesiosaurs have been found in New Zealand. Some species of the *Mauisaurus* genus grew to lengths as much as sixty-five feet.

The fossils of marine reptiles are usually preserved in shale that was once dark ocean mud. Such formations can preserve the animals in remarkable detail, including their smooth skin and sometimes even the contents of their stomachs, revealing their predatory habits. The Natural History Museum in London has a sizable collection of ichthyosaurs and plesiosaurs, mostly discovered in the nineteenth century. The collection even includes an ichthyosaur with several tiny ichthyosaurs in its womb and birth canal. The creature evidently died while in the process of giving birth. It appears that these animals bore live offspring rather than laying eggs, something uncommon among today's reptiles.[7]

Both the flying pterosaurs (pterodactyls) and the marine reptiles, ichthyosaurs and plesiosaurs are sometimes thought of as dinosaurs by popular culture, but they were not. Though they lived during the same time period as these unusual reptiles, dinosaurs were exclusively terrestrial animals and they exhibited specific character-istics that are easily distinguishable from other reptiles. In fact, dino-saurs were so distinctive that some taxonomists suggest that they should not be considered reptiles at all, but should be regarded as an entirely separate class of animals.

Dinosaurs stood more erect than other reptiles with their limbs positioned more directly under their bodies. This difference in structural anatomy is evident in several of the animals' skeletal components, making a number of their bones easily identifiable as dinosaur. It is believed that this more erect posture enabled the dinosaur respiratory system to function more efficiently under exertion, and thus enhanced the animals' quickness and stamina. Furthermore, it is now widely believed that, unlike reptiles, dinosaurs were warm-blooded (or most were at least somewhat warm-blooded). If so, this would have provided them with still another advantage in respiratory function. The dinosaurs' advantages among terrestrial vertebrates are evidenced by their great success in dominating a wide variety of the terrestrial habitats on Earth for more than 160 million years—from around 225 million years ago until 65 million years ago.

Dinosaurs were first discovered and identified as distinctive in the early part of the nineteenth century. The name "dinosaur," a combination of Greek words meaning "terrible lizard," was assigned by the English biologist and paleontologist Sir Richard Owen in 1842. In the more than a century and a half since then, many hundreds of species have been found and classified. Recent years have been very productive, with dozens of new species being identified each year. Many of the latest and most dramatic finds have been in China and in Argentina, though discoveries continue to be made throughout much of the world. The various dinosaur species exhibited an enormous array of unique anatomical characteristics, including some that can seem truly bizarre by comparison to modern animals. They included both herbivores and carnivores. Sizes ranged from very small and delicate (about the size of a sparrow) to the largest and fiercest looking terrestrial vertebrates that ever walked the Earth.

Many people are most familiar with the largest dinosaur species and genera. Drawings and scale models of the herbivorous *Brachiosaurus*, for example, have donned the walls and bookshelves of many young dinosaur enthusiasts. Weighing in at perhaps as much as 50 to 60 tons and reaching lengths of 90 feet, *Brachiosaurus* was once believed to be the largest dinosaur genus. New discoveries of partial skeletons, however, indicate that there were other genera that were even larger. *Brachiosaurus* fossils were first discovered in 1900, in western Colorado. Additional specimens dated at 145 to 150 million years old have since been found in both Colorado and Utah, while similar finds have also been made in East Africa.

Perhaps the favorite among many young dinosaur fans is the *Tyrannosaurus rex*. As one of the largest—over forty feet long and weighing six to seven tons—and one of the fiercest looking terrestrial predators to ever live on Earth, *T. rex* readily excites the imagination. With their ten-foot high bipedal legs and their powerful four-foot jaws with six-inch serrated teeth, these predators could likely move very fast and easily snatch and kill large prey. Barnum Brown, who discovered one of the first specimens of *T. rex* in the badlands of eastern Montana in 1902, described the beast as "the very embodiment of dynamic animal force." Numerous fossils of these creatures (including a few complete skeletons and, in one case, some soft tissue) have been found in the western United States and Canada within 68 to 65 million year old rock formations. Five other *Tyrannosaurus* species are also well known, and several additional species are thought to be either closely related or belonging to the *Tyrannosaurus* genus.

With the observation of fossil evidence (as scant as it may be in places) along with a little deductive reasoning, we can rather easily infer how a single linage of ancient reptiles evolved into a linage of dinosaurs over many generations. That lineage of dinosaurs then split into separate lineages that eventually became multiple lineages of omnivores on the one hand and multiple lineages of carnivores on the other. From there, we now know that one of the lineages on the carnivore side of the dinosaur family eventually led to modern feathered birds—and for this transition in particular, we have a great deal of fossil evidence. (Genetic evidence also points to birds as the descendants of these dinosaurs, as we will see in the next chapter.)

To begin with, we can pretty easily observe that the very-often bipedal means of locomotion and the warm-bloodedness of dinosaurs made them quite a bit more similar to modern birds than any other reptiles—in fact, any other vertebrates. A closer look at the fossil record reveals that some dinosaurs exhibited even more traits, both physical and behavioral, that are also seen in modern birds.

New discoveries suggest that even the fearsome *Tyrannosaurus rex*, along with other members of the *Tyrannosaurus* genus had a primitive type of feathers as juveniles. For warm-blooded creatures, feathers would have acted to insulate their immature bodies from the cold just as they do for modern birds. As the animals grew larger the feathers would probably have been shed in most cases, as they would be no longer needed. (The larger an animal, the more heat its body generates in proportion to its surface area. That is one reason why large mammals like elephants, rhinoceroses, and hippopotamuses do not need fur for insulation.) *Tyrannosaurs* shared other characteristics with birds too. Their feet had three primary toes that all pointed forward. Similarities in their skeletal structures also included hollow bones, a joint in the lower jaw, large eye orbits, and a fused clavicle (a so-called wishbone).

Feathered dinosaurs were first discovered in the late 1990s. Since then, it has become well established that many of the theropod dinosaurs had feathers. The theropods are a large group of carnivorous dinosaurs whose members, including *Tyrannosaurus*, were typically bipedal and ranged in size from rather small and delicate to very large. Many of the most important finds of these feathered dinosaurs has been in the 130-million-year-old Yixian geologic formation in northeastern China. Because of unusually fine-grained and oxygen-deprived sediment deposits on the ancient lake bottoms there, the resulting shale uniquely preserved impressions of ancient plant and animal soft tissues. Delicate features such as flowers, insect wings, scales, hair, and feathers can be observed in the paper-thin layers of what are called "paper shales."[8]

The dinosaur feathers that have been found range from very simple structures to some that more closely resemble the feathers of modern birds. The feathers of some species appear to have been used primarily for display, just as we see in some of today's birds. Feathers could also have facilitated the incubation of eggs long before they were ever put to use in flight.

Perhaps one of the most famous fossils in history, aside from *Tyrannosaurus rex*, is that of *Archaeopteryx*, an apparent transitional genus between dinosaurs and modern birds. The first complete specimen was discovered in 1861 within a quarry of 150-million-year-old lithographic limestone in Bavaria. The fossilized specimen was controversial for many years because *Archaeopteryx* was the only known example of a dinosaur-like creature that sported feathers—fully formed and flight-capable feathers at that. Sir Richard Owen, who first described the genus in 1863, was even accused of fakery before additional specimens were brought to light. So far, a total of nine *Archaeopteryx* specimens have been discovered in that same limestone formation over the last 150 years or so. All of the Bavarian specimens are generally thought to be examples of the same species.

Averaging about eighteen inches in length, the *Archaeopteryx* specimens exhibit characteristics that were once thought to be exclusive to birds while, at the same time, exhibiting other characteristics that were once thought to be exclusive to dinosaurs. These creatures had feathered wings, and they also had a reptilian tail. They had an opposable toe as seen in birds (though less developed than in modern birds), and they also had teeth as seen in dinosaurs.

With the recent discovery of other dinosaurs that exhibited various stages of feather development, *Archaeopteryx* now seems much less remarkable. Among the more notable of these discoveries are six specimens of a species of feathered-winged dinosaurs named *Microraptor gui* that were discovered in 125-million-year-old fossil beds of Liaoning Province in northeastern China. Described as "four winged dinosaurs," these specimens, along with more than a dozen others described under the genus *Microraptor*, had long feathers on their hind limbs as well as on their forelimb wings. It is believed that these animals were unable to fly very well, if at all. With sharp claws on both their front and hind limbs, however, they could probably climb trees and then easily glide to lower branches or to the ground. *Microraptors*

were more primitive in their development of flight than the *Archaeopteryx* genus, even though their fossils are about 25 million years
younger. This suggests that they are not descendants of the *Archaeopteryx* genus, but apparently evolved separately.

In addition to so many shared physical characteristics, scientists
have also discovered evidence of behavioral characteristics in some
dinosaurs that we usually associate with birds. Dinosaurs, like birds,
were evidently very attentive to their young hatchlings. At least some
dinosaurs would not completely bury their eggs like reptiles do, but
would leave them partially exposed and would incubate them by sitting
on them. A dinosaur was even found to have been sleeping with its
head tucked under a forelimb. These activities further suggest the
warm-bloodedness of dinosaurs and their similarity to birds. The
consensus among scientists today supports the belief that dinosaurs did
not entirely disappear 65 million years ago as once thought. Rather,
dinosaurs are flying all around us in the form of modern birds.

Mammals first appeared at around the same time as dinosaurs,
during the Triassic period (in rock formations about 230 million years
old). They were almost certainly descendants of a suborder of therapsid
reptiles called cynodonts, also known as "mammal-like" reptiles.
Cynodonts lived from about 260 million years ago until about 185
million years ago. These little animals shared a remarkable number of
anatomical traits with the mammals that appeared only after cynodonts
had been around for about 30 million years. They were given the name
"cynodont," meaning "dog teeth," because their teeth—which were
fully differentiated and included molars—looked more like those of a
dog than a reptile. Their skulls were also shaped more like a mammal
skull with its characteristic braincase bulge in the back, and, like
dinosaurs and mammals, some of them walked in a more upright
manner with their legs set under the torso. They had more expansive rib
cages that could house a diaphragm, allowing them to breath more
deeply for enhanced stamina. And many of them also had a bony palate
that caused airflow from the nostrils to enter at the back of the mouth,
allowing them to, like mammals, breath while chewing food. Though

they laid eggs, cynodonts are also thought to have been warm-blooded, or at least partially warm-blooded, and were probably covered with fur.

The evolutionary transition from reptile to mammal is perhaps most clearly illustrated by the changing structure seen in the cynodont's jawbones. The earliest cynodonts exhibited a jaw that was rather similar to other reptiles. Cynodont species that have been found in younger strata, however, exhibited changes that increasingly resembled the jaws of mammals. These animals had a reduced number of bones in their lower jaw, as their previously reptilian jawbones migrated toward the ear.

All mammals (including humans) have three little bones in our ears—the malleus, the incus, and the stapes (or hammer, anvil, and stirrup)—while reptiles have only one, the stapes. As a lineage of reptiles evolved into mammals, it was a couple of jawbones that evidently migrated to the ear to become a part of the function of the mammalian ear.

Whether it is legs and feet used for walking that evolved from fins that were used for swimming, or feathers that facilitate flight that evolved from feathers that first served as insulation, or ear bones that evolved from ancient jawbones, we can see time and time again how anatomical structures are very often evolutionary derivatives of previously existing structures once serving either partially or wholly different functions. Scientists often draw such conclusions by means of deductive reasoning that may invoke skepticism in many of us. We are naturally anxious to see some tangible evidence of such a transition. We want to see an "intermediate type" or one or more "transitional species." Fortunately, several such transitional species have been found among the cynodonts.

A subgroup of cynodont species that are found in strata only slightly older than strata in which mammals are first found exhibit an intermediate stage between a reptilian jaw and ear structure and a mammalian jaw and ear structure. These animals had a double-hinged jaw. The prominent hinge was like that of a mammal while the other structure—the previously reptilian hinge structure—was further back and reduced in size. Furthermore, the bones of the second hinge abutted the eardrum, probably already serving to enhance the function of the ear.[9]

As cynodonts evolved into the first mammals they acquired certain advantages that enabled them to exploit niches that were not so easily available to dinosaurs or reptiles. Their warm-bloodedness and higher metabolic rate enabled them to evolve into smaller sizes and to hunt or scavenge at night when cold-blooded reptiles were less active. A higher metabolic rate requires more food as fuel, but these little animals also evolved keener senses and improved cognitive abilities that made them more effective at exploiting the available resources. Their skeletal structure indicates that, in addition to their improved hearing abilities, they also had a greater sense of smell. Their larger brain size suggests the first development of a cerebral cortex, which would have enabled them to make good use of their heightened senses and to exercise cunning in their activities.

These first mammals were mostly shrew-like creatures, probably insectivores or scavengers. Their accelerated metabolic rate would have required that they be quite efficient hunters or scavengers, as they scurried inconspicuously under the detection of the many larger predatory dinosaurs and other reptiles that occupied the top of the Mesozoic era food chain.*

It is apparent that for well over 100 million years mammals remained quite diminutive in the animal kingdom. The fossil record shows us that it was only after the demise of non-avian dinosaurs and many other terrestrial vertebrates, as the result of a catastrophic mass extinction event that occurred 65 million years ago, that mammals began to grow larger, diversify and exploit many of the ecological niches that had previously been dominated by dinosaurs and reptiles.

Widely believed to have been the result of a meteor impact, the so-called "K-T event" or "K-T boundary" (for Cretaceous-Tertiary

---

* Although, at least one recently discovered mammal of that era was opossum-sized. Remarkably, this animal's last meal, a small dinosaur, was still visible in its belly.

mass extinction) wiped out about 70 percent of the Earth's species of plants and animals, in the seas and across all of the continents. Most plankton, corals, and tropical invertebrates became extinct. Ammonites disappeared completely. Large vertebrates were especially vulnerable. The plesiosaurs, mosasaurs, pterosaurs, and non-avian dinosaurs were all lost forever. The K-T extinction event, just like several other mass extinctions that had come before it, initiated a reshuffling of the deck of life on Earth, so to speak, and presented another occasion for a new world order. As so many species were lost, new opportunities arose for the survivors to exploit newly available ecological niches, and this time, it was mammals that gained the upper hand among terrestrial vertebrates.

After the end of the Cretaceous period and the K-T extinction event, fishes, corals and invertebrates in the sea and flowering plants, insects, birds, and mammals on land soon began to prosper and diversify. Perhaps because the climate had become more seasonal, the protection of feathers for birds and fur for mammals may have offered a distinct advantage for those warm-blooded creatures—that is, in addition to the greater quickness and stamina usually associated with the higher rates of metabolism in warm-blooded animals. Whatever the causes, geologic strata clearly reveal that both birds and mammals underwent a great acceleration in diversity and abundance. Within only about three million years, those few small mammals that had been seen in geologic strata of the Cretaceous Period were accompanied by a much wider variety of mammalian shapes and sizes.

Over the course of the last 65 million years, mammals have become the dominant class of terrestrial vertebrates on Earth. Some have even moved beyond their strictly terrestrial roots to exploit other niches, such as the marine mammals that have (like the marine reptiles before them) returned to the seas, or the great variety of bats that have taken flight. But of course not all species have succeeded. Long lists of extinct mammals, along with other classes of plants and animals, can be found in paleontological literature. As we tend to favor the biggest or the fiercest of animals, some of the most notable among extinct mammals are the mastodons, woolly mammoths, saber-toothed cats, or the less commonly known giant sloth and giant armadillos of South America.

Today we can see a wide variety of mammalian herbivores, ranging from mice, squirrels, rabbits, armadillos, and kangaroos to the many ungulates, like horses, cows, sheep, goats, camels, elk, llamas, gazelles, elephants, rhinoceroses, and hippopotamuses, among many others. Given the great variety of prey for the taking, there are also a lot of carnivorous mammals around, such as weasels, otters, sea lions, hyenas, wolves, foxes, some bears, and a wondrous array of large and small cats. Mammalian insectivores include hedgehogs, aardvarks, anteaters, shrews, moles, and a tremendous diversity of bat species. Omnivores include some rats, raccoons, opossums, pigs, most bears, and primates (including us). In all, there are many hundreds of mammalian species around the world today, each exploiting their own ecological niche and each with their own evolutionary history. The fossil record is far too sparse to account for the evolutionary lineages of most of these species, but we do have a fairly complete record of a few.

Perhaps the most commonly cited comprehensive fossil record of an ancestral lineage is that of *Equus*, the genus that includes the modern domestic horse along with six other species. Hundreds of ancient species of horse-like creatures, representing dozens of genera, have been found in strata that span some 50 million years. Among these finds, scientists have observed a gradual anatomical evolution of species over time. Most of the evolutionary branches that were produced eventually came to a dead-end, as those species simply died out without leaving any descendant species. But the lineage that continued and resulted in the genus *Equus* that we see today can be traced all the way back to an ancestor that lived more than 50 million years ago.

Our knowledge of the evolution of horses begins with a genus of animals that had four toes on their front legs and three toes on their hind legs. About the size of small dogs, these *Hyracotheriums* exhibited numerous ungulate-like characteristics. Especially notable were ridges on their molars like those found in modern horses. These herbivores would have browsed the low hanging vegetation of ancient forests. In addition to being linked to the ancestral lineage of the *Equus* genus (horses, zebras, and asses), some scientists believe the lineage that led to rhinoceroses and tapirs can also be traced back to the *Hyracotherium* genus.

Over the course of about 20 million years, descendents of the *Hyracotherium* genus evolved to exhibit only three toes on their front legs instead of four. This transition can be seen to have occurred gradually as the previously functional digit can be seen as a vestigial structure that becomes smaller and smaller over successive generations. Slightly leggier and taller (about 24 inches at the shoulder), these animals also showed signs of adapting to a grazing lifestyle. They had a longer head and neck, and their teeth even more closely resembled those of modern horses, including the familiar gap between their front and back teeth within which a bit can be fitted.

By around 35 million years ago, the *Miohippus* genus exhibited a significant increase in size and further changes in its head shape and ankle structure. The *Miohippus* genus also began a period of greater diversification of species, with some species adapted for scavenging forests and others for grazing the prairies. (Grasses had first appeared only about 20 million years earlier and were becoming more abundant and widespread.)

The open prairie dwellers prospered by evolving greater attributes for speed and quickness to elude predators, all the while growing larger and more efficient at grazing. In achieving greater speed, the middle of these animals' three toes became stronger and more dominant. By about 15 million years ago, the three toes had become three small hooves. Over time, the middle toe grew larger while the other two toes grew smaller, eventually becoming merely vestigial in nature. Through millions of years and many tens of thousands of generations, these vestigial toes grew higher and smaller on the skeletal structure until only the slightest traces can be detected on the bones of today's one-toed (hoofed) *Equus* genus.

The range of species included in the *Equus* genus declined significantly over the last two million years, with their complete extinction in the Western Hemisphere. (European horses were, of course, first brought into the Western Hemisphere by Spanish conquistadors in the late fifteenth century.) Today's surviving members of the genus include the modern domestic horse, *Equus caballus*, plus three species of zebras and three species of asses.

Another interesting case of evolutionary transition can be seen in the fossils of whales (cetaceans), a diverse and wide-ranging group of aquatic mammals that includes dolphins and porpoises. Since we already know that mammals evolved from reptiles, reptiles from amphibians, amphibians from fishes, and since no whale fossils have ever been found in strata older than the advent of other mammals, we can logically reason that whales must be the evolutionary descendents of terrestrial mammals that have returned to the sea. Fortunately, however, we need not solely rely on deductive reasoning in this case. We have enough fossils of transitional species to understand how terrestrial mammals evolved into the marine mammals that we see today.

One of the earliest believed ancestors of whales was a carnivorous mammal found in 52 million year old strata in Pakistan and was thus named *Pakicetus*. This somewhat dog-like creature had hoofed toes and a long, thick tail, but it also had serrated triangular teeth like those of whales and ears with a bone structure that appears to be transitional between terrestrial mammals and fully aquatic whales. It is thought that these animals may have been semi-aquatic—hunting for food mostly in rivers while resting, mating, and giving birth on land, somewhat like sea lions or alligators do today.

A slightly more aquatic and alligator-like animal found in 49-50 million year old Pakistani strata has been named *Ambulocetus*, or "walking whale." These creatures still exhibited small hooves on their forelimbs, allowing them to walk or run easily on land, but their hind feet were clearly adapted for swimming in much the same way otters use their back feet and undulating tails today. Like most terrestrial mammals, these animals had a long snout with nostrils on the end. Within a couple of million years, however, the nostrils of whales had begun to move back along the top of the snout toward the position seen in modern whales.

Also first found in Pakistan, this time in 47 million-year-old strata, several species classified under two genera, *Rodhocetus* and *Artiocetus,* had nostrils that had begun to move back along the top of the snout, among other features suggesting that these animals were transitional between terrestrial mammals and fully aquatic mammals. Still possessing small hooves on the fingers of their forelimbs, these creatures had powerful tails and webbed feet for propulsion in water. Their ears were much more like those of modern whales, their neck vertebrae were shorter, their sacra were divided into several loose vertebrae while their pelvises were only fused to a single vertebrae and disengaged from the legs, suggesting limited terrestrial mobility.

Several nearly complete skeletons of both *Rodhocetus* and *Artiocetus* along with one fully complete skeleton of *Rodhocetus* have helped to more clearly establish the link between whales and artiodactyls, an order of mammals comprised of even-toed ungulates, including cattle, goats, sheep, pigs, camels, giraffes, antelope, and hippopotamuses. The ankle bones of these early whales exhibited several key skeletal characteristics that are otherwise found only in artiodactyls. (Recent biochemical studies, including DNA analysis, indicate that hippopotamuses are the closest living terrestrial relatives of whales—having shared a common ancestor more recently than other artiodactyls.)

By around 35 to 40 million years ago, several varieties of whales had become fully adapted to life in the sea and roughly resembled the whales that we see today. Though their nostrils had still only moved about halfway back along the top of the snout, the tails of both the *Basilosaurus* and the *Durudon* genera had fully developed horizontal flukes for propulsion. These animals also continued to exhibit anatomical structures that were mere vestiges of ancestral appendages. Though they could certainly not walk on land, the very slim fifty-foot *Basilosaurus* whales had tiny hind legs complete with toes. They had flippers where front legs had been on their ancestors and their tails now had powerful flukes, leaving these diminutive hind limbs with no apparent purpose.

As we saw in Chapter 7, the vestigial remnants of pelvises and leg bones can still be found inside the smooth bodies of some whales even today. And occasional genetic anomalies have been known to cause the deformational appearance of hind legs in dolphins and other whales in the process of atavism, where normally over-written ancestral genetic instructions erroneously re-emerge. Among the many other hints at the ancestry of modern whales and other marine mammals is the skeletal anatomy of their front flippers, where the standard configuration of mammalian wrist and finger bones continue to provide the basic infrastructure.

Ancestral evolutionary lineages of many other types of animals can be seen in the fossil record with varying degrees of completeness or shortcomings. But many readers are perhaps most interested in what has been discovered among the fossils of our human ancestors. In the case of our human and pre-human ancestors, in addition to tracking the evolution of their anatomical characteristics, we can also learn a lot about the evolution of their cognitive skills—that attribute most closely associated with being human—by the tools, weapons, and other artifacts that have been found alongside their fossilized or soft-tissue remains.

An examination of human evolution that reaches all the way back to the time when our ancestral line split from that of other modern animals—namely chimpanzees and bonobos—necessarily begins with our "common ancestor." We have no fossil remains of this species that we are aware of. (We may have fragmented remains of the creature without them having been identified as such.) Thus it has no scientific name and is sometimes referred to as the "missing link." This title tends to be somewhat misleading, however. Many people assume that the so-called "missing link" would be a direct link between humans and chimpanzees. But of course both lineages have evolved through a great many species since their divergence.

The time of this common ancestor's existence can be calculated by measuring the differences in the genetic makeup of chimpanzees and humans, and by estimating the rate at which genetic mutations occur.[10] (Chimpanzees and bonobos are known to be our closest living relatives through DNA analysis. The genetic makeup of humans and these apes are about 97 percent identical.* In fact, chimpanzees and bonobos are more closely related to humans than they are to gorillas.) This common ancestor has been estimated to have lived around 5 to 7 million years ago. It is not surprising that no fossil remains have been determined to be those of this creature. There may have been only a small number of them and they may have only existed for a relatively short period of time. Since natural fossil preservation is the exception, not the rule, such a species that lived so long ago may well never be found. The difficulty is not merely finding a specimen, but also being able to confidently identify the specimen as the last common ancestor.

Even though we have no identified fossil remains of this creature, we do have the fossilized or soft-tissue remains of between 19 and 23 (depending on how they are classified) different species of our ancestors and their relatives that lived between the time of this common ancestor and ourselves. Though not a complete picture, the fossils of these nearly two-dozen ancestral species provide a pretty clear illustration of human evolution. Let's take a look at just a few of them.

Hominidae is the family classification that includes modern human beings along with all of our ancestors and relatives that lived

---

* Of the 3 billion base pairs that make up the human genome, only about 3 percent are different in chimpanzees (there is a 0.1 percent variance among humans), and yet, we do not seem to be all that similar to chimpanzees. This offers another illustration of how relatively modest variations in genetics can result in rather significant differences in the characteristics of organisms—how pronounced changes in a *phenotype* (the physical character of an organism) can result from relatively subtle changes in a *genotype* (the genetic makeup of an organism).

after our lineage split from the lineages of other modern primates.** The oldest find that appears to have been hominid is a 6 to 7 million-year-old skull (minus the lower jaw) found in the African nation of Chad in 2001. (Though a complete skeleton is obviously preferable, a skull can generally tell us more about an animal than any other part of the anatomy.) Given the name *Sahelanthropus tchadensis*, this creature possessed two key features that suggest its hominid status. Like humans, it had small canine (or "eye") teeth that did not project in a fang-like manner, as they do in modern apes. Secondly, the hole at the base of the skull through which the spinal cord connects to the vertebral column (the foramen magnum) was significantly forward of the position found in apes. This suggests that the creature stood upright and was bipedal. The creature also had a rather flat face, but its brain size was even smaller than that of a chimpanzee.

With *Sahelanthropus tchadensis*, as well as all of the hominids described here (with the exception of Neanderthals), we have no way of knowing for sure if they are our direct ancestors, or if they are close relatives of our ancestors, or, in the case of these very early hominids, if they descended from a completely different lineage than the one that we share with chimpanzees. Given the more ape-like characteristics of some of the hominid candidate specimens that are much younger than *Sahelanthropus tchadensis*, the latter possibility seems quite plausible.

It is entirely possible that the transition from tree-dwelling primates to bipedalism may have occurred more than once, just as we saw with the evolution of dinosaurs to birds. When we come to the *Homo* genus, however, it becomes rather clear that we are looking at our ancestral family. As we saw with the ancestors of the *Equus* genus above, and as has been the case throughout the history of life, a great many more lineages have come to an end than have survived to this

---

** The increasing use of genetics (rather than morphology) in taxonomic classification has prompted some scientists in recent decades to include the "great apes" in this family classification. Here, however, the "hominid" classification is intended to include only humans and our direct human and pre-human bipedal ancestors and their cousins.

day. Some of the hominid species that have been found are undoubtedly not our ancestors, but are likely to have been cousins of our ancestors whose lineages came to an end. On the other hand, at least some of the species that have been uncovered are undoubtedly the evolutionary ancestors of *Homo sapiens*.

Among the recovered fossil specimens that are younger than the *Sahelanthropus tchadensis* species but older than about 3.8 million years, five separate species of hominids have been named. Very little is known about four of them. Of those four, none are represented by a complete skull, which makes their classification less certain than later finds. Nevertheless, the recovered partial skulls, jaws, teeth, leg and knee bones suggest their dietary habits and/or their bipedalism, and thus, their hominid status. The fifth fossil specimen, however, has recently become rather famous. That is *Ardipithecus ramidus*—more popularly known as "Ardi."

In 1992 the first fossils of Ardi were recovered from 4.4 million-year-old sediments in the Afar Depression area of the Middle Awash River in Ethiopia by a team from the University of California at Berkeley. These included skull fragments, a mandible, several teeth, and arm bones. When additional specimens were unearthed in 1994, about 45 percent of a complete skeleton had been recovered, including most of the hands, feet, pelvis, and cranium. The skeleton represented a 110-pound female that would become the now famous "Ardi." Between 1999 and 2003 a team from Indiana University discovered the fragmentary remains of an additional nine *Ardipithecus ramidus* individuals a few miles away.

Ardipithecus would probably have appeared more ape-like than human at first glance, but the species exhibited a number of distinctively non-apelike characteristics. Like modern apes, Ardi had opposable big toes for grasping, but in all other respects, the feet exhibited the characteristics of a creature with the habit of bipedal walking. The upper portion of the pelvis also showed signs of bipedalism, while the lower pelvis was more ape-like. *Ardipithecus* exhibited monkey-like characteristics, as well as ape-like features, but according to Owen Lovejoy, a comparative anatomist at Kent State University in Ohio who has studied the skeletal remains, Ardi possesses some two-dozen distinct traits that link the species to later hominids.[11]

Perhaps the *most* famous pre-human hominid find is the nearly half of a complete skeleton that was found in 3.2 million-year-old sediments in a gully near the Awash River in the Hadar region of Ethiopia in 1974. As the team of American and French paleontologists who found the fossils celebrated on the evening of their discovery, a tape that included the Beatles' song "Lucy In The Sky With Diamonds" played several times. As a result, the skeleton was affectionately given the nickname "Lucy." Though the original *Australopithecus afarensis* skeleton did not include a complete skull, additional fossils of the species, including several skulls, skull fragments, and a nearly comp- lete skeleton of a three-year-old child, have since been found at various nearby sites in Ethiopia and Tanzania.

Like *Ardipithecus Ramidus*, *Australopithecus afarensis* would likely have appeared more chimpanzee-like than human at first sight, but exhibited even more significant human-like traits. They had small jaws and reduced canine teeth. Their ribcages and arms were also more human-like than are found in apes. Their skeletal anatomy indicates that these animals were bipedal, though they lacked the hip joint extension that is seen in the gait of humans. They may have often used their forelimbs for additional weight support as well as when running or moving quickly. Their relatively short toes and fingers suggest that tree climbing was secondary to their activities on the ground. Lucy's halluces (big toes), unlike Ardi's, pointed forward, much as they do in humans, further indicating a bipedal nature.

Slightly younger than Lucy, the *Australopithecus africanus* species lived from perhaps as long ago as 3.5 million years until around 2.5 million years ago. Calculating the age of the *africanus* fossil sites, however, has been less precise than the *afarensis* fossil sites. No complete skeleton has yet been found, but numerous skeletal compo- nents have been unearthed at two locations in South Africa. The resulting collection of fossils has enabled scientists to assemble composite reconstructions of the skeleton. While largely resembling chimpanzees, *Australopithecus africanus* also exhibited remarkably human-like characteristics. Their face was relatively flat and more vertical than in modern apes. Their jaws were shorter than apes and included somewhat human-like teeth. The neck musculature apparently attached low on the skull and the foramen magnum (the hole at the base of the skull for the spinal column) was located more forward than in modern apes, indicating an upright posture and bipedal habits. On the other hand, the configuration of the lower back and pelvis suggest that these animals were not fully bipedal, but likely often used their forelimbs for locomotion. The ratio of arm to leg length of the *Australopithecus africanus* species was about halfway between those of humans and chimpanzees. Their hands were also very human-like, but proportionally larger than those of modern humans.

The *Australopithecus afarensis* and *Australopithecus africanus* species are jointly referred to as "gracile australopithecines" because of their light and slender build. By contrast, three (or possibly four) generally younger species are sometimes referred to as "robust australopithecines" because of their powerful ("robust") teeth and skulls. Because of significant anatomical differences, however, most scientists have placed these species in a separate genus called *Parathropus*. The use of the Greek root "para" reflects the belief that these animals were a side-branch of our human ancestors that ultimately came to an end. Despite the robust nature of their teeth and jaws, the *Paranthropus robustus* species, possibly a similar species named *Paranthropus crassidens*, the *Paranthropus aethiopicus* species, and the *Paranthropus boisei* species all exhibited significant anatomical similarities to humans. In fact, some skeletal characteristics are so similar that occasionally *Paranthropus* bones have been mistakenly attributed to the *Homo* genus. Primitive tools made of stone and/or bone have been found at most *Paranthropus* recovery sites. Bone tools found alongside *robustus* fossils that had been burned at temperatures higher than would have been caused by a grass fire suggests that at least some of these creatures may have intentionally used fire.[12]

All of the hominid genera and species described above have been classified as our "pre-human" ancestors or their relatives. Our "early human" ancestors and relatives are currently represented by eleven known species that have been classified within the genus *Homo*. *Homo* is of course the genus within which we, *Homo sapiens*, are classified. We are definitely not the only humans to have lived on Earth. We are merely the last surviving species.

Among the oldest of our "human" ancestors was a species found in 1.88 to 1.9 million-year-old strata in northeastern Kenya that has been named *Homo rudolfensis*. Represented by only a skull without teeth and without its lower jaw, a separate lower jaw with a few teeth, another partial skull, and a few small bone fragments, little is known about *H. rudolfensis*. One of the more notable characteristics, however, is that its brain case size was larger than is seen in the older hominids.

The fossils of a slightly younger human species given the name *Homo habilis* have been uncovered in 1.53 to 1.83 million-year-old strata at several sites in Tanzania and northwestern Kenya. Though no intact skeleton has yet been found, enough skeletal components have been recovered to enable scientists to reconstruct a complete skull and much of the *Homo habilis* skeletal frame. Like *H. rudolfensis* and all other members of the *Homo* genus, the *H. habilis* species exhibited a significantly larger brain case volume than the various *Australopithecus* species or any of the other pre-human hominids. The skull appears more human-like than ape-like and, like *H. rudolfensis*, exhibits the bony brow ridge above the eye sockets that will become even more pronounced in later *Homo* species. The *H. habilis* species had human-like hands that were wide with a large thumb. But the fingers were also relatively large with a chimpanzee-like curvature, and the thumb was more rotated from the other fingers than is seen in modern humans.

Several tools have been found alongside the remains of *Homo habilis*. One site was found to include simple hammer stones and stone flakes, while at another site, stones that had been worked on both sides were found. Rather than just banging on a stone until it was more useful for scraping, poking, chopping, or cutting, the deliberate shaping of a stone by flaking or knocking chips off of two sides in order to form a point indicates that its maker could foresee how the tool would be used. The sites also contained animal bones from which meat had apparently been cut and scraped off.

A species given the name *Homo ergaster* has been found at sites in South Africa and northern Kenya. These fossils are found in strata spanning a period from about 1.9 million years ago until about 1.49 million years ago. In addition to several individual skulls and numerous skeletal fragments, a nearly complete skeleton of an approximately nine-year-old child has been uncovered. *H. ergaster* is in many ways similar to *Homo habilis*. The head size and brain case volume, however, appear to be greater in H. *ergaster*. In the adults, the brow ridge protrusion is also more pronounced. The species was given the name "*ergaster*" (Greek for "workman") because of stone tools that were found near the first of these fossil discoveries.

In 2002 a newly described hominid species was given the name *Homo georgicus*. As the name suggests, all of the specimens associated with the species were found in the central Asian nation of Georgia within 1.77 to 1.81 million-year-old sediments. Three skulls with jawbones, one skull without a lower jaw, and a large lower jaw are believed to represent five individuals—probably a large male, a smaller adult male, a young adult female, an adolescent male, and a toothless old female. A number of other skeletal components have also been unearthed, but they have yet to be formally analyzed and described. Simple flaked stone tools that had been worked only on one side have also been found at *H. georgicus* sites.[13]

As we can see with *Homo georgicus*, hominids had migrated out of Africa by at least 1.8 million years ago. The first and perhaps most famous discovery of a hominid species outside of Africa was that of the so-called "Java man," later to be assigned the name *Homo erectus*. Found on the Indonesian island of Java where volcanic activity had raised the landscape and a river and its tributaries had cut through to expose ancient sediments, the species was originally described on the sketchy basis of a partial skullcap, a molar, and a thighbone discovered in 1891. In the more than 100 years since that first discovery, however, additional skulls and skeletal components attributed to *Homo erectus* have been unearthed. Disparate ranges in age—from about 1.5 million to only 700,000 years old—and slight physical variations have induced some scientists to suggest that, while all of these specimens are clearly hominid, they should not all be attributed to the same species.

Hominid remains found in China, once dubbed "Peking man," were also initially thought to be those of *Homo erectus*. Significant differences in the skulls, teeth and thigh-bones, however, have prompted the designation of a different species with the name *Homo pekinensis*. Both species have very prominent brow ridges, but the *H. pekinensis* forehead rises more vertically than the *H. erectus* forehead, producing a sort of gutter where the brow ridge meets the braincase. The *H. pekinensis* braincase may also have been slightly larger than that of *H. erectus*.

A great many stone artifacts have been found in conjunction with *Homo pekinensis* fossils. Most are simple flakes and chopping tools, with a few having been worked on both sides. Some evidence suggests the use of fire, but it is inadequate for a firm conclusion.

As a result of the Japanese occupation of China, most *Homo pekinensis* fossils were tragically lost in 1941 when an attempt was made to ship them to the United States. Fortunately, casts of the pre-war fossils had been made and those continue to be housed at the American Museum of Natural History. After the war, a few additional fragmentary specimens were discovered in 1951, 1955, and 1966. All of the *Homo pekinensis* fossils were found in sediments that have been dated at between 420,000 and 600,000 years old.[14]

Also in Asia, a much younger species was discovered on the Indonesian island of Flores that lived from about 400,000 years ago until only about 12,000 years ago. Excavated in 2003 and 2005, the *Homo floresiensis* species is represented by the fragmentary skeletal remnants of at least eight individuals, plus a fairly complete skeleton that includes the skull with an intact mandible. The *H. floresiensis* species was quite small in stature, with the height of an average adult estimated to have been around 36 inches.

The small stature of the *H. floresiensis* species may have been the result of what is called "island dwarfism." As explained by biogeographer Mark Lomolino, "We know that when evolutionary pressures change, some species respond by shrinking." The only land mammals on the island of Flores were rats, stegodonts (an extinct ancestor to modern elephants) and the *Homo floresiensis* people. Without competitors, the rats and lizards on the island grew to enormous sizes, but with the absence of predators and with the availability of limited resources, the stegodonts and the people shrank in size. Dwarf stegodonts have also been found on the islands of Sicily, Crete, and Malta. Elephants are strong swimmers, and it is believed that large ancestors of these animals swam to the islands from the mainland. Once there, the absence of predators and limited food supplies prompted them to evolve to sizes as much as only twenty percent of the size of the mainland animals. Some scientists have speculated that perhaps *Homo floresiensis* are the descendants of a small group of *Homo erectus* that had made it to the island many thousands of years earlier. Although, no *Homo erectus* remains have yet been found on the island.[15]

The *Homo floresiensis* arm to leg length ratio was between the range of apes and modern humans. Although the skull is human-like in many ways, there are also some significant differences. The braincase is comparable in size to that of a chimpanzee, and the bone separating the mouth from the nose opening is very narrow in comparison to modern humans. Unlike earlier hominids that had very pronounced brow ridges that extended across the entire brow, the *H. floresiensis* species had arched brow ridges above each of their large and very round eye sockets.

The tools that have been found in connection with *Homo floresiensis* fossils are more advanced than those found alongside earlier hominids. In addition to an abundance of simple stone flakes that had been worked on both sides, there was "a 'big game' tool kit that included points, blades, punches, and micro-blades."[16]

Back in North Africa and at a site in Spain, hominid fossil fragments that predate both *H. pekinensis* and *H. floriensis* have prompted the name *Homo antecessor*. Found in sediments dated at a little older than 780,000 years, the fossils were given the name *"antecessor"* (Spanish for "ancestor") because they were the oldest hominid fossil remains that had been found in Europe and were believed likely to have been ancestors to *Homo neanderthalensis* (Neanderthals) and *Homo sapiens*. The basis for such a conclusion is rather sparse, however, and as we will see momentarily, other evidence suggests otherwise.

Tools associated with *Homo antecessor* include hammer-stones and stone flakes that had been worked on a single side. Microscopic analysis and tool wear indicate that these implements were probably used for shaping or cutting wood, scraping and cutting meat, and perhaps animal skin preparation.

A younger hominid (around 600,000 years old) has been found at three widely separated locations in Ethiopia, Zambia, and South Africa. *Homo rhodesiensis* is known from three skulls and most other skeletal components. The skulls and skeletal features of *H. rhodesiensis* mostly resemble those of modern humans, with only a few indicators of a different species. Among the notable differences are more sloping foreheads as they relate to somewhat smaller braincases and the very prominent brow ridges that are seen among most of the early human species.

Homo rhodesiensis is the oldest human species known to have used tools other than those made of stone. In addition to chert and quartz tools that had been shaped on two sides, bone, horn, and ivory tools have been found in connection with *H. rhodesiensis*. A granite sphere that may have been used for grinding grain was also found.

Aside from the *Homo floresiensis* species, which was found in southern Asia and lived as late as 12,000 years ago, the two youngest human species that preceded our own—*Homo heidelbergensis* and *Homo neanderthalensis*—have been found principally in Europe.

Homo heidelbergensis fossil specimens, found in sediments that range in age from 190,000 to 350,000 years old, have been unearthed in Germany (hence the name), France, England, Spain, Italy, Greece, Hungary, Morocco, and Israel. It has been suggested by some scientists that specimens found in India and China may also be the *H. heidelbergensis* species. Some scientists have hypothesized that perhaps *Homo rhodesiensis* and *Homo heidelbergensis* could have been the same species, but the long distance between their respective fossil sites and their age difference are thought to be reason enough for a separate classification.

The similarities among many of the various hominid species occasionally prompt disagreement among scientists when it comes to the classification of some specimens. For example, specimens that are dated between or slightly overlapping the known time spans of *Homo heidelbergensis* and *Homo neanderthalensis* can be difficult to identify as one or the other because they exhibit features that are ambiguous to either classification. Of course, this is just what we might expect as one species evolves into another.

Until the recent discovery of the *Homo floresiensis* species that lived until only 12,000 years ago, the *Homo neanderthalensis* species (Neanderthals) was long thought to have been the last surviving human species other than our own. They lived from about 200,000 years ago until only 28,000 years ago, overlapping the time span of our own species by 70,000 years or more. In fact, it is generally believed that Neanderthals and modern humans lived in close proximity and probably competed for resources in Europe and in western Asia for about 15,000 years until the Neanderthals' extinction. Though numerous circumstances likely contributed, it is not difficult to imagine that modern humans may have played a significant role in the ultimate demise of Neanderthals, whether by means of direct conflict or by simply dominating in the competition for resources. While Neanderthals evidently continued to simply charge their prey with wooden spears, *Homo sapiens* invented spear-throwers and specialized heads for the tips of their spears, allowing them to hunt game more efficiently and at less risk to themselves. In addition to their likely inferior intellect, the Neanderthal physique would have required that they consume many more calories than do modern humans, making daily life much more taxing for them.

Neanderthals are the best-known extinct human species because their fossilized and organic remains are relatively abundant and easily recognizable. Dozens of skulls and numerous specimens of all the other Neanderthal skeletal components have been recovered. Specimen sites are most abundant in Europe, but others have been found in Israel, Iraq, Georgia, and as far to the east as Uzbekistan and southern Siberia.

The Neanderthal skull differs from that of modern humans in a number of ways. Their brain volume was on average slightly larger than ours, but the braincase was more elongated from front to back and much lower than ours with a sort of "bun" at the back of the skull. Below their low forehead, each of the Neanderthal eye sockets had its own separate but very pronounced brow ridge. The opening for their nose was also larger and broader than ours. Both their upper and lower jaws were larger, but they had what we sometimes call a weak chin, with less protrusion than is generally seen in modern humans.[17]

The Neanderthal skeletal structure differs from modern humans primarily in its proportions. They had stocky, robust bodies with wider and sturdier pelvises, much more spacious ribcages, and shorter, heavier lower limbs. Their sturdy limb bones indicate a rather heavy, muscular physique. The average male was about five feet, five inches tall and likely weighed around 185 pounds.

Tools associated with Neanderthals are more diverse and more refined than those of earlier hominids. They included spear points and scrapers that were manufactured in a way that indicates skill and forethought. Neanderthals also used bone and ivory. These materials are easier to shape and they are of course lighter than stone, making them useful for more specialized and finely crafted weaponry and for the more delicate tools, such as fishhooks made of antler. Wooden tools were also used alongside the stone, bone, and other tools, but very few specimens have survived the ravages of decay. In one location, apparent ornamental objects such as pierced animal teeth and ivory rings were found in association with Neanderthal remains. In another location, hundreds of "crayon-like blocks of manganese dioxide" that produce a black pigment were found. It has been suggested that perhaps these "crayons" were used for body decoration.[18]

Evidence suggests that Neanderthals cared for their sick and wounded and that, on occasion, they ceremonially buried their dead. It has also been suggested that, because of their material culture, they were likely capable of speech. In fact, newly completed analysis of Neanderthal DNA has provided evidence of language capability, although whether they were capable of using a sophisticated language or just simplistic verbalizations is unclear. Paleontologist Steven Mithen and others have written that Neanderthals, as well as earlier hominids, might well have had a propensity to sing.

Neanderthal DNA has yielded a great deal of information about Neanderthals and, perhaps most interestingly, their relationship to modern humans. In 1995 scientists were surprised to discover that the first Neanderthal fossil ever found—recovered in 1856—still contained usable DNA. The initial analysis was conducted with different samples by teams in Germany, where that first discovery was made and where it continues to be housed, and at Penn State University in the United States. Newly discovered Neanderthal remains are now extracted with the greatest of care to guard against contamination of any recoverable Neanderthal DNA. As a result, good samples have been recovered from a number of sites. Much like the human (*Homo sapiens*) genome project undertaken a few years ago, Neanderthal genome sequencing has been underway for several years at both the Max Planck Institute for Evolutionary Biology in Leipzig, Germany and at 454 Life Sciences, a private biotechnology firm and subsidiary of Roche Diagnostics Corporation in the United States.

It was long thought that, because of climactic conditions in the generally higher latitudinal range of many Neanderthal populations, pale skin, blonde or red hair, and light eyes would likely have been be common. DNA analysis supports this conjecture. In 2007, German scientists announced that they had isolated a pigment gene in two separate samples—one from northern Spain and one from Italy—that indicated "red hair, pale skin, and possibly freckles." Interestingly, the gene is different than what is found in the modern redheaded peoples of northern Europe. Evidently, the gene developed in each of the two species independently.[19]

In fact, DNA analysis has confirmed that we, *Homo sapiens,* are not descendants of *Homo neanderthalensis.* Neanderthals are not our ancestors—they are our cousins. This is not especially surprising given the geographic ranges and the time spans of the two species. DNA analysis gives us reliable confirmation, however, and it informs us that *Homo sapiens* and *Homo neanderthalensis* share a common ancestor from which the two lineages diverged about 370,000 years ago.* Opinions vary as to who that common ancestor might have been, and which other species may be included in each of the two lineages. Without DNA from the various other, older hominid species, we may well never be able to solve that puzzle.

We do have, however, a pretty good idea of where *Homo sapiens* originated, and how our species eventually radiated throughout the Earth. Though alternative evolutionary hypotheses persist, most scientists have concluded that "anatomically modern humans"—*Homo sapiens*—originated with a very small population in sub-Saharan Africa sometime between 200,000 and 100,000 years ago.

The paleontological evidence for the "out of Africa" theory is inconclusive for a couple of reasons. Firstly, as mentioned above, species classification can be difficult with specimens that exhibit ambiguous characteristics. Specimens that resemble more than one named species may be transitional or they may simply be examples of the kind of variation that can sometimes be seen within a population. (Such specimens that are more than 100,000 years old are often described with the unofficial classification of "archaic *Homo sapiens.*")

---

* It should not go unnoted that the findings of a recent study suggested that some interbreeding may have occurred between Neanderthals and *Homo sapiens.* The authors of the study purportedly found a genetic link between Neanderthals and some present-day European populations, but not other populations around the world. Further testing is needed, however, to confirm the reliability of this conclusion.

Secondly, those ancient specimens that *can* be clearly identified as anatomically modern humans are found throughout much of Africa with no readily apparent point of origin. Therefore, the best evidence of modern human origins is not paleontological or archeological—it is genetic.

In the last twenty years or so population geneticists have been able to supplement the paleontological and archeological evidence of modern human origins and migration patterns. Genetic "markers" in the human genome enable scientists to determine ancestral relationships between ethnic populations around the world and, thus, provide a virtual roadmap of initial (as well as subsequent) human migrations. Furthermore, by calculating the rate of gene mutations, scientists are increasingly supplementing the archeological evidence of when those migrations occurred.

Such analysis has indicated that today's population of nearly seven billion humans is descended from a small original population of *Homo sapiens* in sub-Saharan East Africa. Modern man then migrated further south in Africa about 60,000 years ago; across southern Asia to East Asia, the northwestern edge of North America and Australia about 50,000 years ago; to southern Europe some 30,000 years ago; and to the northern reaches of Europe and deep into the Western Hemisphere only about 10,000 years ago.[20] As *Homo sapiens* spread and settled across the Earth, the various populations were effectively isolated from each other for thousands of years and thus evolved into the many various races and ethnicities that exist within our species today.

A realistic understanding of the history of life on Earth necessarily includes an understanding of the enormity of geologic time. Analogies can sometimes be helpful in effectively illustrating the timeline. John McPhee offered such an analogy in his book *Basin and Range*, emphasizing the lateness of modern human arrival in the history of life on Earth. He suggested that if we imagine the entirety of the Earth's history as the length of our arms stretched out to their fullest extent, then the distance from the fingertips of one hand to the wrist of the other is representative of the pre-Cambrian period. The remaining hand would then represent the entire time period within which complex life evolved. Most startling is his suggestion that, "in a single stroke with a medium-grained nail file you could eradicate human history."[21]

Such a realization, along with much of what else has been discovered about the natural world, might prompt many of us to feel rather insignificant. We do well to keep in mind, however, as we saw in the beginning of this book, that a God that transcends space and time would surely witness the entire history of the universe, not even within the same instant, but within a single conception. The fact that humanity takes up so little of the Earth's history certainly cannot preclude the possibility that the universe was created with human beings in mind.

Over the past two centuries paleontologists have uncovered a vast fossil record of the history of life on Earth. This collection of fossils is certainly far from representative of a comprehensive history, but it nevertheless provides a clear illustration of how life began with the simplest of organisms and evolved over a period of some three and a half billion years to become the multitude of very complex organisms that we see around us today. Uncertainties about the history of life are not found in the general concept of evolutionary history, but in its details—how certain mechanisms affect the processes of natural selection, or how certain lineages may be specifically related to each other, for instance. As we have seen with the example of early *Homo sapiens* migrations and as will be further explored in the following chapter, progress in the science of genetics is increasingly enabling scientists to resolve many of those uncertainties. As more fossils are found and scientific technology continues to advance, we will undoubtedly continue to be delighted in our discovery of the amazing and magnificent history of life on Earth.

9

The Tree of Life

I t is apparent from what we can see in the fossil record that life began at a single point—a "first cause," if you will—a single species which then evolved into two species, which then evolved into three or four species, and then five, six, or eight species, and then... The fossil record strongly suggests that all of life on Earth is the result of one common ancestor that began it all. So do the genes and the biochemistry contained in each and every organism that lives today. All organisms are composed of the same basic chemistry and live, reproduce, grow old and die by means of the same basic principles. Genes can also tell us a lot about historic lineages and about the more recent relatedness of various organisms—about the many branches that comprise the so-called "tree of life."

It was long before the advent of the sciences of paleontology, genetics and genomics, however, that naturalists first began to see patterns of order among living things. Aristotle is often cited as one of the first persons known to have attempted to categorize organisms in a systematic way. He grouped plants and animals according to their physical characteristics and their habitats or their mode of locomotion (i.e. walking, swimming, or flying). He introduced the idea of a "binomial" (two named) description, with the first name describing a group or family of similar organisms and the second name describing the uniqueness of an individual species. While a few of his classifications have endured, such as his correctly grouping sea mammals with terrestrial mammals, his findings were too often based on vague or overly subjective criteria and inconsistent physiological analysis.

By the early part of the eighteenth century several different methods of nomenclature were in use. As a result, many plants and animals had a number of different names, each designated by a different system of classification. As noted in Chapter 5, it was the eighteenth-century Swedish physician, botanist, and zoologist, Carl (Carolus) Linnaeus who developed the nomenclature that became the standard that has endured to this day. That is, the Latin binomial system for naming individual species. Somewhat like Aristotle's method, species are described by their genus (a grouping that includes other, similar species) and a specific name. For example, the name chosen by Linnaeus for our own species, *Homo sapiens*, consists of the genus "*Homo*" (the Latin word for man or human) and the species "*sapiens*" (the Latin word for wise). Just as importantly, Linnaeus' classification of all organisms into groups within larger groups within even larger groups according to their physiology provided the first tangible framework for understanding the relatedness of organisms around the world.

Though it may not have been his intent, Linnaeus' grouping of very similar individual species of plants and animals into genera, similar genera into families, similar families into orders, orders into classes, classes into phylum (later changed to "divisions" to describe plants), and phylum into kingdoms, implied a hereditary link among species and a pattern of evolutionary descent. Therefore, when the work of Charles Darwin invigorated thought and discussion of biological evolution, the Linnaeus system was seen as a very logical construct in support of the idea.

Building on Linnaeus' work, as well as a small branching sketch that had appeared in Darwin's *Origin of Species*, German biologist Ernst Haeckel in 1879 published the first diagram of a "tree of life" illustrating the genealogical descent of species. With the publication of Haeckel's tree, which was even so bold as to depict humans and other animals evolving from single-cell organisms, the image of evolutionary speciation as a branching tree soon became well established.

The criteria for determining species assignment to large groups or to more specific lineages—determining the configuration of "phylogenic trees"—has long been based on the science of morphology. That is, the study of the physical anatomy of species as compared to other species. For example, based on their physical characteristics, vertebrates (which fall under the phylum *Chordata* along with a few invertebrates) are divided into a number of classes, such as: bony fishes, distinguished by cold-bloodedness with gills for respiration and living wholly in water; cartilaginous fishes, distinguished by cartilage skeletons instead of bones (sharks, rays, and skates); amphibians, distinguished by being cold-blooded and having an aquatic gill-breathing larval stage and a lung-breathing adult stage; reptiles, distinguished by being cold-blooded with dry scaly skin and by laying soft-shelled eggs on land; birds, distinguished by being warm-blooded with feathers and beaks and laying and then nurturing eggs; and mammals, distinguished by being warm-blooded with the presence of fur or hair and by the nursing of infants with lactation.

Similarly, the phylum *Arthropoda* (a group characterized by exoskeletons, segmented bodies, and the presence of more than four jointed legs) includes crabs, centipedes and their relatives, spiders, insects, and eight additional classes of animals—each with distinguishing characteristics. Most animals belong to just nine of the thirty-eight known phyla.

In recent decades a method of taxonomic analysis called cladistics has gained favor among many scientists. Cladistics strives to classify organisms according to their evolutionary descent through a strictly methodical analysis of morphological and genetic characteristics. Rather than referring to hierarchal groups of classification as Linnaean taxonomy does, the cladistic method holds that the evolutionary tree of life is so complex and continuous that the use of distinct hierarchal categories can be misleading.

We can rather easily see evidence of the relatedness of species—evidence of their common ancestry—by looking at specific similarities in their anatomy, as well as how those similarities have evolved to serve different functions. Such structures are referred to as *homologous*. One might conclude that God used similar structures to serve different functions because the underlying design was sound and, therefore, worthy of multiple applications. However, the existence of *analogous* structures—those that serve the same function but with wholly different designs—and, as we saw in Chapters 6 and 7, the sometimes inferior nature of both homologous and analogous structures suggests that God was likely not *directly* involved.

The forelimbs of terrestrial vertebrates are examples of homologous structures. The same basic skeletal structure found in our own arms and hands is also found in the forelimbs of bird wings, bat wings (in a radically different way than bird wings), whale, dolphin, seal, and manatee flippers, and even the forelimbs of horses, cows, elk, deer, and most other terrestrial vertebrates. The illustration below shows how the same basic bone structures are present in various appendages of starkly different shapes and functions.

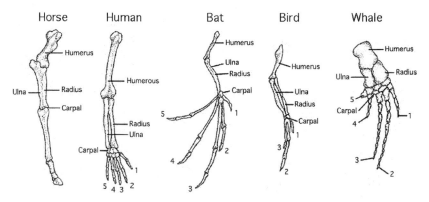

As noted in the previous chapter, the discovery of several ancient fish species fossils that exhibited a number of rudimentary characteristics of terrestrial animals during the time just before amphibians began to appear, strongly suggests that amphibians evolved from bony fishes. We also saw how anatomical similarities between birds and theropod dinosaurs suggest that birds are evolutionary descendants of that suborder of dinosaurs. Fortunately, we no longer have to rely solely on anatomical analysis of fossils to reach conclusions about which species descended from which—about the true architecture of the "tree of life." Advances in research over the last several decades have provided a great deal of very compelling supporting evidence from the fields of biochemistry and genetics.

Remarkably, scientists have recovered tiny amounts of a protein collagen from the thighbone of a *Tyrannosaurus rex* that lived about 68 million years ago where the state of Montana resides today. As was reported in the journal *Science*, an analysis of the protein's sequence of amino acids revealed that it most closely resembled that of modern-day chickens, supporting the paleontological evidence that birds are descendants of theropod dinosaurs. Paleontologist Mary Schweitzer of North Carolina State University, who recovered the cells from the *T. rex* bones, expressed her optimism that (just as we saw in the case of Neanderthals in the last chapter) the recovery of cells from the bones of extinct species will increasingly provide information about evolutionary relationships.[1]

We need not rely on the very rare recovery of organic cells from extinct species, however, to find evidence of evolution in the biochemistry of organisms. The newly developed capability of scientists to map entire genomes, along with newly developed software capable of analyzing, comparing, and sorting massive amounts of genetic data on supercomputers, have enabled scientists to produce more refined maps of evolutionary ancestral relationships among species.

This work has confirmed many of the previous assumptions arrived at through the work of paleontologists, and it has yielded some new insights as well. In constructing a "tree of life" consisting of 13,533 species of plants, Stephen Smith and his colleagues from the National Evolutionary Synthesis Center in North Carolina found that ferns, long thought to have evolved very little for hundreds of millions of years, "have actually been evolving faster than younger groups of plants, like conifers and flowering plants."[2]

In another study, researchers at Pennsylvania State University discovered that a significant rearrangement of the family tree of certain scaly reptiles was necessary. In a genetic analysis of the largest living order of reptiles known as *Squamata*, which includes lizards and snakes, biologists S. Blair Hodges and Nicolas Vidal found that the 1,400 currently living species of primitive-looking iguanas are most closely related to snakes and other more recently evolved types of scaly reptiles. As a result, iguanas, which had been placed near the bottom of the evolutionary tree of *Squamata* according morphological criteria, were moved into a group near the top of the tree. Appearances can sometimes be deceiving as organisms adapt to new environments, but a species' genetic history is well preserved in its genome. The same study also showed that venom, previously thought to have been a relatively recent evolutionary development, evolved in these reptiles about 200 million years ago.[3]

Evolutionary trees of life are being constructed on many fronts. Most are limited to small groups of species, but a few more ambitious projects are underway as well. The National Science Foundation is funding an endeavor, aptly named "Assembling the Tree of Life," that aims to construct a tree that encompasses "all living things." According to its website, the AToL project promotes collaborations between Universities to investigate evolutionary relationships among groups of species, and to promote research into computational tools for assembling the information and making it available to researchers and to the general public.

One of the difficulties with the very large "trees" that are being developed is finding a way for observers to be able to see the overall structure of the tree as well as its finer details and individual species. Devising a way to see a tree that includes the 1.75 million known species is no small undertaking. (Indeed, estimates of the number of living species that have not yet been identified range from about 2 million to 100 million.) Illustrations of that sort will naturally have to be in the form of interactive computer applications.

Biologist David Hillis has even expressed a longing for a hand-held device that would enable scientists to genetically analyze specimens in the field and place them in their correct position in the tree of life, even if they may be previously undiscovered species.[4] Developed by Dr. Hillis, Dr. Derrick Zwickl, and Dr. Robin Gutell at the University of Texas in Austin, the tree below illustrates the evolutionary relationship of only 3,000 species based on a single gene, but it is nevertheless intended as a representative sampling of all of life. It is recommended that the illustration be displayed at a scale of at least four and a half feet across in order to see the individual species that are listed at the perimeter of the sphere.

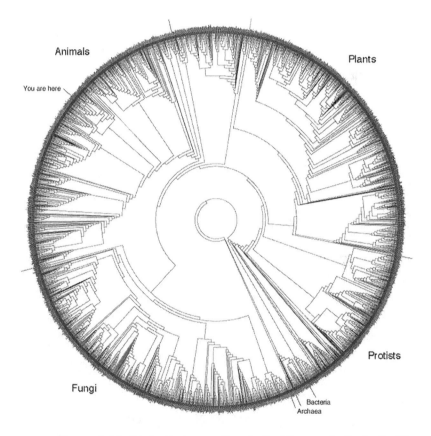

One might think that genetic similarities and dissimilarities among all the species of the world do not necessarily say that much about evolution. God could certainly have made each species individually but similarly to others. The only reasonable explanation for some of those similarities and dissimilarities, however, is that they are the result of evolutionary processes.

The physical characteristics and to some extent the behavior of all organisms, from the tiniest bacteria to great whales, from pansies to giant redwoods, are determined by the genes within their each and every cell. Genes carry the instructions for the production of proteins necessary for the development and the function of all living things. Similar to the way all computer programs operate with a binary language (a series of only two numbers), the genes of all organisms (and some viruses) carry instructions by means of various arrangements of only four molecules: *adenine, guanine, cytosine,* and *thymine.* These four molecules, strung together in a great many different ways, constitute the genetic code within DNA, which is then organized into long structures called chromosomes. Humans, for example, have two sets of twenty-three chromosomes that carry a total of about 20,000 to 25,000 genes.

When organisms reproduce, those genes of coded instructions are transferred, or copied, into the progeny. As described in Chapter 7, however, mistakes do occasionally occur as genetic information is passed from one generation to the next, such as in the case of Down's syndrome, where entire chromosomes are damaged or improperly transferred, or cystic fibrosis, where faulty genes are inherited from both parents. Most gene mutations are either injurious or have no immediate effect. If it is injurious, the organism will usually die or is weakened enough to inhibit its reproduction, thus preventing the mutation from being propagated through the population. Those mutations that have no immediate effect may lie dormant for many generations, or they may become either injurious or beneficial as other mutations occur and interact with them. Only occasionally are mutations beneficial. Naturally, beneficial mutations are most likely to be preserved as they strengthen their carriers and/or enable them to adapt to a new environment.

As we have seen, if two populations of a species become separated by a barrier of one kind or another, and their respective gene pools become isolated from one another, then gene mutations will be prevented from passing between the two groups. Over time, as many thousands of generations and mutations occur, the populations will naturally become less and less similar. If the two populations remain isolated long enough, their genetic differences will prevent them from interbreeding—they will have become two separate species. Even though these two species may be too genetically different to interbreed, they will nevertheless retain a great many genetic similarities, including the presence of many distinguishable "neutral" genes, along with many other types of non-coding DNA, sometimes called "junk DNA" (because it serves no apparent function).

Some molecular biologists believe that as much as 95 to 97 percent of human DNA can be classified as non-coding "junk." It is unlikely, however, that such a large percentage of the genome has no function at all. In fact, new studies have suggested that some non-coding DNA may influence the behavior of coding DNA (genes) in important ways.[5] Nevertheless, it is quite clear to geneticists that much of the genome consists of inactive remnants of the previously functioning genes of evolutionary ancestors. It is also clear that genomes contain very distinctive anomalies that have been passed down through hereditary lineages over a multitude of generations.

Occasionally a gene has been seen to appear in duplicate on a chromosome. The duplication is not needed. One gene could serve the intended function, just as it does in most other species. The duplication is an error, though it is not an injurious error. Since it is not harmful, it can remain in the gene pool over many generations. In fact, this error has been seen to have been passed down through consecutive evolutionary descendent species. Furthermore, in a few cases, one of these duplicate genes has been damaged and "scarred" to the point of dysfunction. If it were not for the duplication, the scarred gene would have been purged from the gene pool long ago. But since a duplicate exists, the "marked" gene can remain in the gene pool and, luckily for geneticists, be followed through multiple descendent species. The existence of such "marked" genes provides an effective tool for scientists to determine which species or groups of species share recent common ancestry.[6]

There are other ways in which "marked" genes can offer compelling evidence of common ancestors among disparate species. About thirty years ago it was discovered that within the code of genes inside DNA—within those long stretches of varied arrangements of four molecules that dictate the production of proteins—there are often stretches of meaningless gibberish that serve no function. Comprising most of the so-called junk DNA in animals (but not plants), these *introns* are stretches of non-instructions that begin and end with "signals" that tell the cell to ignore that particular section of genetic code. Since the intron is ignored by the cell, it does no harm. The presence of identical introns in the genomes of morphologically similar species naturally provides additional evidence of their relatively recent kinship.

In addition to introns, which are found in most genes, there are a number of less frequent mutations that can become inserted into introns. Because these anomalies reside within the lengths of introns they are harmless and can be copied generation after generation for many millions of years. Such markers provide additional opportunities for geneticists to refine or confirm phylogenic lineages. For example, a particular SINE (short interspersed element) designated CHR-1 has been found within a specific intron of a particular gene shared by a group of related animals—even-toed ungulates. As we saw in the last chapter, paleontological and morphological evidence strongly suggests that modern marine mammals are descendants of early even-toed ungulates. As it turns out, the SINE CHR-1 anomaly is not only found in the DNA of today's hippopotamuses, giraffes, camels, pigs, sheep, goats, cattle and other even-toed ungulates, it is also found in the DNA of cetaceans—that is, today's whales, porpoises, and dolphins.[7]

In addition to mutations resulting from genetic reproduction errors, viruses can also sometimes create markers within introns. Occasionally, a viral infection can leave behind a so-called "silenced" version of its reproductive instructions within a host's own genes. When such an anomaly is inserted into an intron, it does no harm to the host and can remain in DNA that is passed from generation to generation for many millions of years. For example, all Eastern Hemisphere monkeys as well as apes carry a viral scar designated HERV-K64. Monkeys in the Western Hemisphere, however, do not have this anomaly in their genes. This indicates that the HERV-K64 anomaly entered the gene pool after the ancestors of Western Hemisphere monkeys had become separated from those of Eastern Hemisphere monkeys, but before apes had evolved from those ancestors that they have in common with Eastern Hemisphere monkeys. A different viral scar, designated HERV-K18, has been found in apes, but not in any monkeys. This indicates that the HERV-K18 anomaly entered the gene pool of an ancestor species to all apes after its lineage had been separated from the lineages of all monkeys.[8]

Scientists have also been able to see numerous indicators in our own genome of our relatedness to other species. Even creatures as seemingly unrelated to humans as mice share many genetic similarities with humans. This is, of course, why mice are so commonly used in medical research. Not surprisingly, a few non-functioning similarities between the mouse and human genomes provide compelling evidence that we share ancient ancestors.

"Ancient repetitive elements" (AREs) arise from so-called "jumping genes" that copy and insert themselves in additional locations within DNA. These are aberrations that usually contribute no functionality to the genome. Identical AREs are found in the same positions within corresponding stretches of DNA in the genomes of both humans and mice, as well as other mammals. Some of these AREs were truncated when they were originally copied into the gene pool, removing any possibility that they could serve any function. The only reasonable explanation for why such identical anomalies are found within the genomes of both humans and mice is that we share ancestors within which those anomalies arose many millions of years ago.[9]

Though the genomes of humans and mice are notably similar, a comparison of the human and chimpanzee genomes reveals an even more astounding degree of similarity. Humans and chimpanzees (along with bonobos) share about 96 percent to more than 98 percent (depending on how it is calculated) of their DNA characteristics. (The DNA among all humans is about 99.9 percent identical.) Just as with mice, the similarities between the functioning DNA of chimpanzees and humans alone do not prove that the two species are related, but there are a number of interesting circumstances that indicate we are.

For example, chimpanzees (along with gorillas and orangutans) have twenty-four pairs of chromosomes, while humans only have twenty-three pairs. Most interesting is that a side-by-side comparison of the human and chimpanzee genomes strongly suggests that chromosome #2 in humans resulted from the fusion of the 2nd and 3rd chromosomes found in chimpanzees, within a population of distant ancestors. The DNA sequences along human chromosome #2 are virtually identical to those of the two chimpanzee chromosomes if they were attached end-to-end. Specific DNA sequences that occur at the ends of all primate chromosomes are found just where evolutionary theory would predict if the two short chimpanzee chromosomes were to become fused together, right in the middle of human chromosome #2.[10]

A gene known as MYH16 dictates the production of a protein that plays a role in the development and ultimate strength of jaw muscles in all primates. In humans, however, the gene is inactive as a result of damage by mutation. The absence of the protein produced by the gene is likely the reason for the much weaker jaw found in humans. Given that jaw muscles are anchored to the skull, it has been speculated that the weakening of jaw muscles in our human ancestors may have, over time, helped to allow for the upward expansion of the skull and our larger braincase.[11] While this alone could not account for modern humans' larger brains and intellect, it clearly could have been one of the instruments in the great concert of events that facilitated human evolution.

We saw in Chapter 7 how imperfections in organisms well illustrate how they have evolved from the ground up, rather than having been *directly* created from the top down by an infallible God. Another example of imperfection in the physiology of human beings has resulted in our need to consume foods that are rich in vitamin C. In this case, however, the imperfection is not the result of how we were structurally put together. It is a result of the vulnerability of our genes to mutation.

Most mammals naturally produce ascorbic acid (vitamin C) by means of a series of five enzymes in the liver that make it from ordinary sugars. While we have most of the necessary enzymes in our livers, we lack one called gulonactone oxidase, or "GLO." We have the same gene found in other mammals that produces GLO, but ours is broken. It has been damaged by so many mutations that it no longer functions. It has become another example of "junk" DNA.

Evidently the fatal damage to our GLO gene occurred a very long time ago. We can see this because we are not the only mammals to carry this defective gene. A number of our closest evolutionary relatives also carry the very same inactive gene, including chimpanzees, bonobos, gorillas, and orangutans. It is pretty clear that the gene became damaged in ancestors that we share with these primates—ancestors that had become genetically separated from the ancestors of most other primates.[12]

The science of genetics offers many more evidentiary examples of evolution and includes a number of issues of greater complexity than can be effectively discussed here. But what we have seen in these few examples can readily be understood as compelling evidence of common ancestry among the Earth's organisms. The way in which genes have been "marked" by various anomalies has enabled scientists to clearly determine the common ancestral lineages of disparate species. In most cases, these findings have supported assumptions about evolutionary history that had been previously derived from the findings of paleontologists. Occasionally a few of the branches of the tree of life, as we understood it, have had to be rearranged. But in each of these cases, our growing knowledge of genetic "footprints" has furthered our understanding of how the phylogenic tree of life is configured—that is, the relatedness of species and how biological evolution, as the instrument of life's creation, has shaped our world.

Part 4

The Politics of Evolution

10

"Creation Science" and Intelligent Design Theory

T he renowned paleontologist and Harvard University professor Stephen Jay Gould often recounted a legendary story of the aristocratic wife of an English lord who, upon hearing of Darwin's new theory about evolution, exclaimed to her husband: "Oh my dear, let us hope that what Mr. Darwin says is not true. But if it is true, let us hope that it will not become generally known!" Professor Gould went on to suggest that the concerned gentlelady's sentiment well illustrates an attitude that has persisted among a few vocal opponents of Darwinian theory ever since it was first made public. Indeed, from the advent of so-called "creation science" through the development of the more recent "Intelligent Design" or "ID" theory, we find that, even aside from those who simply cling to the narrow theology of Biblical literalism, most of the proponents of these concepts place much more emphasis on why they believe biological evolution *should not* be true than on why it *is not* true. In keeping with the second part of our lady's sentiment, the very titles "creation science" and "Intelligent Design theory" are terms that have resulted from nearly a century of political struggle to remove the teaching of biological evolution from American public schools.

In the early part of the twentieth century a number of states, particularly among the southern "Bible Belt" states, enacted laws against the teaching of biological evolution in their public schools. The first and most famous of these statutes was the Tennessee law that resulted in the so-called Scopes "monkey trial." The 1925 Butler Act made it unlawful to "teach any theory that denies the story of the Divine Creation of man as taught in the Bible, and to teach instead that man has descended from a lower order of animals." The American Civil Liberties Union sought to challenge the statute on the basis that it violated schoolteachers' constitutional right of free speech and announced that they would defend anyone who was willing to break the law. Primarily in an effort to gain publicity for their small town of Dayton Tennessee, civic leaders encouraged football coach and physics teacher John Scopes to participate in the test case. Scopes had taught biology as a substitute teacher and admitted that he had taught chapters on human evolution from a textbook entitled *A Civic Biology* (1914).[1]

The ACLU's plan was somewhat diverted when, first the prominent Democratic politician and anti-evolution crusader William Jennings Bryan offered to assist with the prosecution, and then the equally prominent defense attorney Clarence Darrow offered to square off against him. Since Darrow had issued press releases announcing his offer, the ACLU had little choice but to accept it. The trial became famous mostly as a result of Darrow's success in getting Bryan himself on the stand, and then forcing him to admit the embarrassing implausibility of a literal interpretation of the Scriptural creation stories. Nevertheless, Scopes, by his own admission, had violated the statute and was ultimately found guilty and assessed a fine of $100. This was the outcome the ACLU had expected and hoped for so that they could appeal the case on constitutional grounds. Their plan was thwarted, however, when the Tennessee Supreme Court overturned the case on a technicality having nothing to do with the United States Constitution. The conviction was overturned because the judge in the original case had assessed the $100 fine, while Tennessee law only allowed for juries to set fines above $50.[2]

Similar statutes forbidding or restricting the teaching of biological evolution were debated in as many as twenty states and enacted in Mississippi, Arkansas, Oklahoma, and Florida by the end of the 1920s. As a result of the public unpopularity of teaching evolution and ongoing political pressure applied to textbook publishers, evolution was scarcely mentioned in most American public schools before the 1960s.

Then the Soviet Union's 1957 launch of the first man-made satellite, Sputnik, spawned a renewed emphasis on science education in the United States. Along with the physics and mathematics required for aerospace engineering came a new emphasis on other sciences too, including biology. New textbooks began to once again cite evolution as the foundation of biological science, despite anti-evolution laws still on the books in a number of states.

It was not until 1968 that the United States Supreme Court ruled, in a case involving Arkansas' anti-evolution statute, that all such laws were unconstitutional. The opinion in the case of *Epperson v. Arkansas* stated that Arkansas's law was "an attempt to blot out a particular theory because of its supposed conflict with the Biblical account, taken literally." The statute was deemed in violation of the "establishment clause" of the Constitution's First Amendment. Then a 1975 ruling by a Federal Appeals Court, in *Daniel v. Waters*, struck down Tennessee's replacement for the Butler Act, which mandated equal time in biology classes for a literal interpretation of *Genesis*. The decision stated that Tennessee's law was a,

clearly defined preferential position for the Biblical version of creation as opposed to any account of the development of man based on scientific research and reasoning. For a state to seek to enforce such preference by law is to seek to accomplish the very establishment of religion which the First Amendment to the Constitution of the United States squarely forbids.

It was the Federal courts' refusal to allow religious instruction in public school science classrooms that spawned the idea of "creation science." If the courts were not going to allow a literal understanding of the Bible's account of creation, as religion, to affect science curriculum, then there were those who were determined to turn a literal understanding of the *Genesis* stories into a science. There would be no more talk of the inerrant Bible's book of *Genesis*, just the purported scientific evidence of a sudden, Special Creation.

A 1961 book entitled *The Genesis Flood* became the primary manifesto of the "creation science" movement and today remains a revered text among many of its advocates. Written by conservative Old Testament scholar John C. Whitcomb, Jr. and hydraulic engineer Henry Morris, *The Genesis Flood* argues that the Earth was created in six twenty-four hour days, and that the entire visible universe is only a few thousand years old. The book maintains that the characteristics of the geological formations found on Earth, as well as the many fossils of extinct species that have been found in those formations, can be accounted for by the Bible's story of Noah and the Great Flood. It maintains, ironically contrary to Scripture, that Noah had failed in his mission and was unable to save all of the species on Earth. As we might expect, the book also claims that all of the modern methods of determining the age of geologic formations that reveal a 4.5 billion year old Earth are flawed.

In 1972 Mr. Morris founded the Institute for Creation Research for the purpose of seeking physical evidence of the six-day creation story described in the Bible and providing that evidence and other support to those who struggle against the teaching of biological evolution in American public schools. The organization remains active today and can be seen at www.icr.org.

Today most creationists do not subscribe to the "young-Earth creationism" advocated by Mr. Whitcomb, Mr. Morris, and the Institute for Creation Research. The overwhelming evidence of an ancient Earth has induced many to concede that our planet is billions of years old. The term "creationist" or "creationism" can refer to a rather wide variety of beliefs in divine creation as long as they exclude evolutionary processes. Most creationists believe that while the Earth may be ancient, human beings were nevertheless created directly by God relatively recently, a position referred to as "old-Earth creationism." (To be clear, there are lots of Christians who believe that God created the world, but who are not "creationists," as we saw in the introduction to this book.) Regardless of their varying positions on the age of the Earth, creationists are united in their rejection of Darwinian evolution, and many are active in efforts to either remove biological evolution from public school biology classes or to secure equal time for the teaching of "creation science."

The trouble with "creation science"—the reason the term is always in quotes in this text and the reason its proponents have had so little success in getting it into American science classrooms—is that it is not science at all. It is not mainstream or even sound Christian doctrine either. It is an especially narrow religious ideology posing as science.

Objections to teaching "creation science" in science classrooms are not exclusive to secularists. Because it is ultimately injurious to Christianity, many mainstream Christians have also objected to the teaching of this unorthodox religious doctrine in public schools. In 1981 Arkansas enacted the "Balanced Treatment Law" which required the state's public schools to provide equal time for the presentation of "creation science" whenever evolution was taught. Supported by the ACLU, numerous clergymen and church groups of various denominations filed suit, arguing that the law sought to establish a very narrow fundamentalist religion by the state, at the exclusion of mainstream Jewish and Christian belief. The plaintiffs included the Union of American Hebrew Congregations, the American Jewish Congress, the American Jewish Committee, the Arkansas head of the Presbyterian Church, individual clergy from the United Methodist, Southern Baptist, and Presbyterian Churches, as well as resident Bishops of the United Methodist, Episcopalian, Roman Catholic and African Methodist Episcopal Churches.[3]

In overturning the law, Federal Judge William Overton noted that the theory of Special Creation as advocated by "creation science" was necessarily dogmatic and prohibitive of any revision, and therefore, not a scientific theory. Judge Overton ruled that,

The 'creationists' methods do not take data, weigh it against opposing scientific data, and thereafter reach the conclusions stated in Section 4(a). Instead, they take the literal wording of the book of *Genesis* and attempt to find scientific support for it.

The judge concluded that, "'creation science' has no scientific merit or educational value as science."

In 1985, a Louisiana "Balanced Treatment" statute was struck down by a Federal District Court because, as the ruling stated, "it promotes the beliefs of some theistic sects to the detriment of others." After the verdict had been upheld upon appeal, the case of *Edwards v. Aguilard* was then heard by the United States Supreme Court. In a seven to two decision, the High Court ruled that,

The Act violates the Establishment Clause of the First Amendment because it seeks to employ the symbolic and financial support of government to achieve a religious purpose.

In light of the *Edwards v. Aguilard* ruling, "creation science" supporters concluded that a new tactic needed to be developed. Instead of simply invoking Scripture, they needed to directly confront evolution on the basis of the science. But in order to do that, they would have to change the very definition of science and the principles of the scientific method.

Phillip E. Johnson, law professor emeritus of the University of California at Berkley, has long been active in the effort to rebut Darwinian evolution. An author of several books on the subject, he has alleged that evolutionary theory is largely based on what he sees as the materialistic philosophical assumptions of the scientific community. In 1992 and again in 1993, Johnson gathered a group of like-minded individuals for meetings to formulate a strategy to confront Darwinian evolution. The result would become known as the "Intelligent Design" or "ID" movement.

A politically conservative "think tank" called the Discovery Institute soon adopted Johnson's cause and established a branch called the Center for the Renewal of Science and Culture to provide financial, intellectual, and political support for what was termed "Intelligent Design theory."

In an endeavor to attract funding, Johnson produced an outline of the strategy that was to be employed to confront Darwinian evolution in particular, as well as the secular nature of the scientific method in general. "The Wedge" document was intended to be kept secret, but was leaked in 1999 and the Discovery Institute was eventually forced to admit that it was its source. The document plainly stated the objectives of the Center for the Renewal of Science and Culture and its Intelligent Design movement:

> The Center seeks nothing less than the overthrow of materialism and its cultural legacies. ...we are convinced that in order to defeat materialism, we must cut it off at its source. That source is *scientific* materialism.

The document explained that with a small wedge it is possible to topple a giant tree. Similarly, their aim was to begin to topple the materialistic worldview of greater society by first offering a theistic alternative to Darwinian evolution. After describing Johnson's own books, along with one by Lehigh University biochemist Michael Behe that was also critical of evolutionary theory, as the thin edge of the wedge, the document continued.

> We are building on this momentum, broadening the wedge with a positive scientific alternative to materialistic scientific theories, which has come to be called the theory of intelligent design (ID). Design theory promises to reverse the stifling dominance of the materialist worldview, and to replace it with a science consonant with Christian and theistic convictions.

The strategy consisted of three phases: I) Development of an alternative theory through research and establishing it through writing books and articles. II) "Publicity and opinion-making." III) "Cultural confrontation and renewal." As a part of phase three, the intent was to "pursue possible legal assistance in response to resistance to the integration of design theory into public school curricula." With this, however, they encountered some difficulty.

In December 2004 a group of parents filed suit in federal court against the Dover, Pennsylvania school board after it had included ID theory instruction and materials in the district's science classrooms. As part of their defense, attorneys for the board intended to show that ID was a legitimate scientific theory and not simply the product of religious doctrine. ID theorists were handed the opportunity to testify that they had sought. The most prominent ID theorist to testify was Professor Behe, who has authored a couple of books and numerous articles espousing the concept of "irreducible complexity." Federal Judge John E. Jones III (a conservative Republican, appointed by President George W. Bush) was unconvinced. Within his written ruling, the judge cited Behe's testimony:

On cross-examination, Professor Behe admitted that: "There are no peer-reviewed articles by anyone advocating for intelligent design supported by pertinent experiments or calculations which provide detailed rigorous accounts of how intelligent design of any biological system occurred." [22:22-23 (Behe).] Additionally, Professor Behe conceded that there are no peer-reviewed papers supporting his claims that complex molecular systems, like the bacterial flagellum, the blood-clotting cascade, and the immune system, were intelligently designed. [21:61-62 (complex molecular systems), 23:4-5 (immune system), and 22:124-25 (blood-clotting cascade) (Behe).] In that regard, there are no peer-reviewed articles supporting Professor Behe's argument that certain complex molecular structures are "irreducibly complex." [21:62. 22:124-25 (Behe).] In addition to failing to produce papers in peer-review journals, ID also features no scientific research or testing.[4]

Brown University biology professor Dr. Kenneth R. Miller, one of the lead witnesses for the plaintiffs, later described Judge Jones' expressed frustration with,

the 'breathtaking inanity' of the Dover Board of Education, the persistent attempts of the ID movement to obscure its religious roots, and the willingness of self-professed people of faith to come into his courtroom and lie under oath.[5]

With the declared intent of the Dover school board's attorneys to argue that ID is a legitimate scientific theory, at least a couple of their witnesses may have undermined their case by admitting that the definition of science would have to be altered in order for ID to be science. University of Idaho microbiologist and Discovery Institute fellow Scott Minnich confirmed this view when asked if, "the rules of science have to be broadened so that supernatural causes can be considered."[6] Another ID witness, Steven William Fuller, described the ID movement's intent to "change the ground rules of science to include the supernatural."

Of course, as we saw in Chapter 4, confusing the quest for scientific knowledge with that of spiritual knowledge is very often injurious to both. Whenever scientific research is predicated upon religious or philosophical assumptions—whenever the findings of science are shaped by judgments of value—objectivity, and therefore reliability, is lost.

Proponents of teaching ID theory in public schools as a "balance" to Darwinian theory received a powerful endorsement in 2005 when then President George W. Bush, in response to a question, said, "both sides ought to be properly taught." Nevertheless, most school boards and state legislatures have been able to resist efforts to insert ID into science classrooms. As the National Academy of Sciences has pointed out,

> The claim that equity demands balanced treatment of evolutionary theory and special creation in science classrooms reflects a misunderstanding of what science is and how it is conducted. ...claims of supernatural intervention in the origin of life or of species are not science because they are not testable by the methods of science.

While science cannot, as a matter of principle, "prove" that anything is absolutely true, it can certainly prove that something is false. In fact, a proper scientific theory must be falsifiable. The proponents of ID theory assert that, in principle, specific biological structures that they currently describe as evidence of an intelligent designer could be shown to have been the result of Darwinian natural selection—that, in fact, ID theory is falsifiable. But ID theory rests on a broader and more dogmatic claim. ID theorists insist that, since no one has actually seen speciation or the development of complex biological structures occur in real time, it cannot be proven that such events were the result of Darwinian natural selection, and therefore it should be concluded that these events have been the result of an intelligent agency. Since deductive reasoning is to be excluded and since it is impossible for any one person (or even several generations of people) to see the development of complex biological structures in real time, ID theory's premise will always be viable.

Furthermore, regardless of what can be demonstrated regarding the origins of any particular biological structure, the ID thesis proclaims that any and all complex biological structures that cannot be demonstrated to have been the result of Darwinian natural selection are assumed, by default, to have been the result of an intelligent cause. Since ID theory's premise is not dependent on the existence of affirmative and testable evidence, but instead is solely dependent on a lack (either real or imagined lack) of evidence to dispute its central claim, it will always be viable. It cannot be proven false. Therefore, Intelligent Design theory is not a scientific theory and has no place in a science classroom—a religion or philosophy class perhaps, but certainly not a science class.

In order to get their ideas into public schools, the Discovery Institute and its ID proponents continue to insist that they do not promote religion. They make no public proclamations as to who or what the intelligent designing cause of complexity might be—it could be space aliens, for all they know. The dishonesty of this claim is remarkable. As we have seen, their true sentiment has been well documented.

Leading ID proponent William Dembski has written that, "while not directly proving that God exists, intelligent design is far more friendly to theism than Darwinism." Many people disagree. In addition to its not following the basic principles of science, there are several reasons why Intelligent Design theory is not nearly as friendly to Christianity as is Darwinian theory.

With the use of terms like "specified complexity" and "irreducible complexity," ID theorists rest their case primarily on the existence of structures in nature for which no natural cause has yet been identified. Their stated objective is to demonstrate that some structures could not have been the result of "purposeless" Darwinian natural selection. Fair enough. But of course Darwinian theory has never claimed that natural selection is the only organizing principle in nature. As we have seen, natural selection operates in conjunction with many other more fundamental natural organizing principles. Most pertinent to ID theory's general thesis, however, is its dependence on *structures in nature for which no natural cause has yet been identified*. Much like Newton and Paley before them, ID theorists have merely discovered an Intelligent Designer of the gaps.

Dr. Dembski has cited a freshman course at Cornell University in which Professor Will Provine had stated, "Evolution is the greatest engine of atheism ever invented." What Dr. Dembski and Professor Provine have both evidently overlooked is that evolution could never have become an "engine of atheism" without either one or both of two things having come first—undue Biblical literalism and a belief in God grounded in the notion that some structures in nature could have no natural explanation. As we saw in Chapter 4, it was the purported "scientific" evidence of God's existence based on gaps in our understanding of natural phenomena that established the first rational basis for atheism.

The way it has been presented by many of its proponents, ID theory poses an even more direct assault on the most fundamental principle of Christianity—monotheism. Whether stated in terms of "specified complexity," "irreducible complexity," or just complexity in general, ID theorists contend that the immense organized complexity found in living organisms necessarily requires an "intelligent cause." As leading ID proponent David Berlinski has written:

> The structures of life are complex, and complex structures get made in this, the purely human world, only by a process of deliberate design. An act of intelligence is required to bring even a thimble into being; why should the artifacts of life be any different?[7]

We saw in Chapter 6 how a great many complex organized structures arise through natural processes. If it is the intention of ID theorists to simply dismiss what we know about how organized complexity can emerge from natural causes, and to insist that great complexity can only exist if it is directly designed and produced by a supernatural, intelligent agency, then they necessarily deny the monotheism of Christianity. Using Dr. Berlinski's logic, why should the intelligent cause be any different than the thimble or the "artifacts of life"? An immutable God (the intelligent cause we all know is at issue) is, by definition, irreducibly complex. By Dr. Berlinski's reasoning the intelligent cause of complex organisms would itself require an intelligent cause for its existence. As an irreducibly complex entity, God Himself could not exist without having been created by an even more complex and more capable Creator. That Creator would then, of course, be required to have been created by an even more complex and powerful God, and on and on. The very first rule of Christianity would be doomed.

There are a great many uncertainties in our understanding of the processes of evolution. God might very well be playing an active role on a level that, by design, is undetectable. Despite the declarations of a few outspoken atheists, such as Richard Dawkins and other so-called New Atheists, evolutionary theory makes no claim otherwise. It is outside the competence of science to make any judgments about the supernatural at all. Science can only judge that which is detectable in nature. What science has detected and effectively confirmed through testing is that, while it is certainly not the only organizing principle in nature, Darwinian natural selection is by far the most prominently detectable organizing process in biology, accounting for most of the physical and behavioral characteristics of the Earth's living organisms.

11

"Darwinism"

The persistent use of the term "Darwinism" by Intelligent Design theorists and others is indicative of a widely-held belief that Darwinian evolutionary theory is synonymous with a godless naturalistic or materialistic philosophy that subscribes to the notion that, whether in economics, foreign relations, race relations or any number of other human relations, "survival of the fittest" is the natural order of the world and humanity should just embrace that reality. Though the term "Darwinism" was first coined by Darwin's friend Thomas Henry Huxley and can be used simply as a reference to natural, Darwinian evolutionary processes, the "ism" part of the term can imply the inclusion of a philosophical component that has little to do with Darwin's study of biological processes. As David Berlinski has written, "The term 'Darwinism' conveys the suggestion of a secular ideology, a global system of belief." We find that, in fact, most of the writing of ID theorists is dedicated to the loathing of so-called "Darwinian philosophy," with the processes of biology scarcely mentioned.

The 2004 book *Uncommon Dissent: Intellectuals Who Find Darwinism Unconvincing*, edited by William A. Dembski, contains a collection of essays written by sixteen of the world's leading ID proponents. Only four of the sixteen are biologists. Philosophy is the primary topic of discussion. Writer and theologian Nancy R. Pearcey explained that the general public is passionate about a theory of biology because:

They know that when naturalistic evolution is taught in the science classroom, then a naturalistic view of ethics will be taught down the hallway in the history classroom, the sociology classroom, the family life classroom, and in all other areas of the curriculum...

Darwinism functions as the scientific basis for an overall naturalistic worldview. ... If you start with impersonal forces operating by chance (in other words, naturalistic evolution), then over time you will end up with naturalism in moral, social, and political philosophy."[1]

Ms. Pearcey's assertion is unquestionably true—except that it did not take any time at all for Darwin's discoveries to be used to support a variety of philosophical points of view. Immediately after Darwin and Alfred Russel Wallace's discovery of natural selection as the primary mechanism of biological evolution it was adopted by a number of other individuals and factions as scientific evidentiary support for the philosophical justification of very often self-interested and repressive ideologies. The idea of "survival of the fittest" as an unyielding and noble Law of Nature became an underpinning for extreme *laissez-faire* capitalism, imperialism, racism, eugenics, fascism, and even Nazism.

Extracting a wholly different principle from Darwin's observations than those on the political right, Russian anarchist Prince Peter Kropotkin pointed to how Darwin had demonstrated that cooperation among the members of a species could overcome the disadvantages of competition and thus secure their safety and prosperity.[2] Karl Marx declared that Darwin's book "serves me as a basis in natural science for the class struggle in human history." As professor Douglas Futuyma aptly noted in his book *Science on Trial*, "just as the devil can cite Scripture to his purpose, advocates of any political philosophy whatsoever could find something in evolution to support their ideas."

The phrase "survival of the fittest" did not originate with Charles Darwin (though he had no objection to it). An English philosopher of sociology named Herbert Spencer first used the phrase in a book in which he drew parallels between his own theories and Darwin's discoveries in biology. Spencer had already developed a theory of evolution well before the publication of *On the Origin of Species*. But it had nothing to do with biology. It was a theory of sociology. After discovering Darwin's work, however, Spencer sought to synthesize his ideas concerning sociology with the very latest findings of the physical sciences of biology and physics into one coherent structure that would account for the natural, and therefore the correct, order of everything. Spencer and others' application of Darwinian principles to social philosophy would come to be known, mostly pejoratively, as "Social Darwinism."

Spencer's theory of what amounted to "social selection," which he derived in part from having read the work of Thomas Malthus, just as Darwin and Wallace had done, appeared in articles some six years before Darwin and Wallace jointly published their discovery of natural selection. Spencer argued that pressures upon the subsistence of populations had led to the improvement of the human condition, as individuals with superior intelligence, skill, ingenuity, and self-control had adapted through technological innovation in order to survive, while less capable populations or individuals had simply perished or were subjugated.

As a result of his belief in this natural evolution of human progress, Spencer promoted an ultra-conservative political philosophy that emphasized the rights and the freedom of individuals at the exclusion of any collective initiatives. He opposed all government aid to the poor. He believed the poor to be inferior and unfit, and wrote that, "The whole effort of nature is to get rid of such, to clear the world of them, and make room for better." He attributed their position in life to stupidity, vice, and idleness. "If they are sufficiently complete to live, they *do live*, and it is well they should live. If they are not sufficiently complete to live, they die, and it is best they should die."

Despite such declarations, Spencer insisted that he was not opposed to private charity to the unfit. He supposed that such charity was beneficial to the character of the donors. He was merely opposed to compulsory state initiatives for the poor. Similarly, Spencer opposed public education, state banking, and government postal systems. He was also opposed to tariffs and any kind of regulation of business enterprise, with perhaps the exception of the occasional suppression of local moral or sanitary nuisances.[3]

Spencer's opposition to tariffs, business and industrial regulation, and costly government programs made him especially popular and influential among a few sociologists and many prominent industrialists in the United States. In an address to a Sunday-school class, John D. Rockefeller explained that,

> The growth of a large business is merely a survival of the fittest. ... The American Beauty rose can be produced in the splendor and fragrance which bring cheer to its beholder only by sacrificing the early buds which grow up around it. This is not an evil tendency in business. It is merely the working-out of a law of nature and a law of God.[4]

Andrew Carnegie sought out Spencer and became a close friend. In his autobiography, Carnegie explained how reading Darwin and Spencer had enabled him to be consoled as he considered the demise of Christian theology.

> I remember that light came as in a flood and all was clear. Not only had I got rid of theology and the supernatural, but I had found the truth of evolution. 'All is well since all grows better,' became my motto, my true source of comfort. Man was not created with an instinct for his own degradation, but from the lower he had risen to the higher forms. Nor is there any conceivable end to his march to perfection. His face is turned to the light; he stands in the sun and looks upward.[5]

Carnegie of course also took comfort in applying the laws of nature to sociology and the practices of business competition. In an article in the *North American Review*, he sought to ameliorate the harshness of natural selection as applied to social ethics.

It is here; we cannot evade it; no substitutes for it have been found; and while the law may sometimes be hard for the individual, it is best for the race, because it insures the survival of the fittest in every department.

Despite its respectability among many, a number of social philosophers pushed back against Spencer's brand of dispassionate *laissez-faire* economics. Lester Ward, for example, pointed out that superior plants and animals are often produced, not by blind natural forces, but by the human intervention of domestication. Furthermore, Ward observed, to allow large corporations to become monopolies as they overpower all of their competitors is to, in fact, stifle the very benefits of competition that *laissez-faire* purports to engender.

Its credibility had waned to some extent by the beginning of the twentieth-century, but Herbert Spencer's extreme version of *laissez-faire* economics remained a powerful influence in the United States until the Great Depression and the subsequent New Deal. Of course Spencer's ideas associated with what he and others believed was the noble and universal principle of "survival of the fittest" did not just apply to economics. The same ideas were used to justify racism and imperialism.

Many prominent thinkers in the United States and Europe thought it was not only acceptable, but a moral duty that the most powerful nations should subjugate weaker nations and primitive peoples. It was "the white man's burden" to see to it that "inferior" peoples were instructed on how they would be governed and to see to it that their natural resources would be put to good use. Furthermore, if powerful nations retreated from this responsibility, then others would take their place and become more powerful competitors. In his 1899 book, *The Strenuous Life*, Theodore Roosevelt warned of the consequences if the United States failed to live up to its "responsibilities" in securing its power and authority over Hawaii, Cuba, Puerto Rico, and the Philippines, three of which it had just won control of in the Spanish-American War.

> If we stand idly by, if we seek merely swollen, slothful ease and ignoble peace, if we shrink from the hard contests where men must win at hazard of their lives and at risk of all they hold dear, then the bolder and stronger peoples will pass us by, and will win for themselves the domination of the world.[6]

As John Barrett, former minister to Siam put it, "The rule of the survival of the fittest applies to nations as well as to the animal kingdom." Many people in the United States and Europe simply believed that, by virtue of the laws of nature, world supremacy and domination was, "destined to belong to the Aryan races and to the Christian faith."[7]

It certainly has not helped Darwin's reputation that it was his cousin, Francis Galton, who coined the term "eugenics" in 1883. Galton was a respected scientist and his idea of eugenics was well fitted to popular nineteenth-century and early twentieth-century sensibilities. Today, thankfully, such ideas are seen as horribly immoral. Galton and others believed that the human race could be "perfected" by discouraging, or in some cases out-right preventing, the reproduction of "undesirables"—not just those inferior people of color, but also the poor, intellectually retarded, or mentally disturbed—while encouraging the procreation of "desirables."

In the United States eugenics grew into a popular movement after the turn of the twentieth century and endured for several decades. It was widely believed that I.Q. tests scientifically demonstrated that non-whites and immigrants were less intelligent than upper class white people, and therefore, inferior. (We now know, of course, that cultural biases and language unfamiliarity skew the results of such tests.) As a result of the newly popular I.Q. test and other bigoted criteria in determining who was "unfit," immigration into the United States from eastern and southern Europe was curtailed, and compulsory sterilization laws were enacted in thirty states. The United States Supreme Court upheld the legality of eugenic sterilization in a 1927 decision written by Oliver Wendell Holmes, which included the infamous sentence, "Three generations of imbeciles are enough."

Sterilization was aimed primarily at criminals and the mentally ill, but was often used for the "offenses" of being developmentally disabled, black, Hispanic, native-American, epileptic, physically deformed, or just plain poor. So-called "voluntary" sterilization programs persisted until the 1970s, but collusion was often used to sterilize people without their knowledge or consent, and such programs eventually fell into disrepute.

Though they began in the United States, eugenic sterilization programs quickly spread to a number of European nations. The editors of the *New England Journal of Medicine* wrote in 1934, a year after Hitler had become chancellor, that "Germany is perhaps the most progressive nation in restricting fecundity among the unfit."[8] Of course Nazi Germany then went on to become the most infamous perpetrator of compulsory sterilization programs. The Nazis forcibly sterilized hundreds of thousands of people before going on to murder millions with their purported justification of preserving Aryan genetic superiority as a moral imperative based on a philosophical principle of "survival of the fittest."

Among the most forceful critics of Social Darwinism from its start in the nineteenth century were clergymen. Like their predecessors who had criticized slavery, religious leaders criticized the *laissez-faire* industrialism that they saw as callously unfair to the working class. In the cities they witnessed the despair of those whose wages were insufficient to enable them to escape the slums, and they saw the lack of a safety net for the unemployed. As a result, religious organizations and individuals through the first half of the twentieth century more predominately tended to promote the causes of the political left—that is, the advocates of societal intervention. They fought against Spencer's idea of unencumbered individualism and his "winner take all" ideology. They sought government intervention to ensure fairness and opportunity for all. They fought for a minimum wage, limited working hours, the right to unionize, an end to child labor, and women's suffrage. They advocated a society that was guided by human compassion and fairness, rather than an amoral naturalistic system. As noted in Chapter 3, Christianity teaches us that we have a responsibility to rise above the mechanics of the natural world and to aspire to a morality that transcends nature.

Of course social Darwinism also runs counter to American founding principles. Though the rights and freedom of the individual— individualism—is a cherished tradition in the United States, citizens are nevertheless promised fairness of opportunity regardless of their "fitness" in relation to other citizens. This idea and its reasoning was articulated by Thomas Jefferson in his first draft of the Declaration of Independence when he described the principle "that all men are created equal" as a "sacred" truth. (It was the impious Benjamin Franklin who urged the substitution of "self-evident" for "sacred.") It had not escaped Jefferson's attention that, in fact, men possess quite a wide range of physicality, intellect, initiative, and moral aptitude. He simply meant that, since all men are created by God, we are all "equal in the possession of a common humanity," and that natural law, therefore, dictates that all men are entitled to the same inherent natural rights.[9] The social Darwinist idea of "winner take all" is therefore not just immoral and un-Christian, it is also definitively un-American.

Spencer's "survival of the fittest" expression of a "winner take all" ideology is not really Darwinian either. It is unfortunate that Darwin used the phrase after Spencer had introduced it because it is rather misleading as a description of how his discovery, natural selection, works. It implies that only the "fittest" survive, when in fact that is very often not the case. As mentioned in Chapter 6, "survival of the viable" is perhaps a more apt phrase, since the only fitness requirement for survival is viability, not superiority to other individuals or other species. Furthermore, fitness for survival and prosperity also applies to whole populations, as constituent individuals act in cooperation with one another for the benefit of the entire population.

In any case, the use of the mechanics of biological evolution as justification for repression or indifference to the plight of others is an artificial construct that neglects our natural moral tendencies of altruism. Even more so, it neglects the higher order of moral reasoning that has proceeded from religious and cultural development, and that has facilitated the growth of orderly, productive, and virtuous societies. The advocacy of so-called "survival of the fittest" social and economic principles persists even today among a number of individuals and factions, but proponents rarely use that phrase or attempt to justify such ideologies with analogies to Darwinian biological processes. Fortunately, that has fallen into disrepute.

Today's discussions of "Darwinian philosophy" have more to do with the ultimate meaning of life and the existence of a loving and benevolent God. A few acclaimed evolutionary scientists have pointed to Darwinian evolution as ample evidence that there is no Creator God. Chief among them, Richard Dawkins has claimed that, "Darwin made it possible to be an intellectually fulfilled atheist." In his book *The Blind Watchmaker*, Dawkins also used the term "Darwinism" and expressed his desire to persuade readers of the truth of a "Darwinian world-view" that explains the mystery of human existence through scientific discovery alone. In their zeal to emphasize that natural phenomena can account for the emergence and the characteristics of all living organisms, including humans, academicians commonly conclude that the human species "has no purpose." As a result, a Godless, existential philosophic bent does indeed creep into many science classrooms.

As if it were the latest trend in pop culture, evolutionary theory has also been used to sell books on a multitude of human interests, including many topics that are well outside the competence of evolutionary explanations. As we have seen, in the cases of business and politics, not only are evolutionary explanations often misapplied, they can lead to dangerously amoral or even immoral conclusions. A few theorists have even alleged evolutionary explanations for criminality, as if to suggest a mitigation of culpability.

The proponents of "creation science" and Intelligent Design theory, among others, are quite right to criticize the scientific community and pop authors either for inadvertently mixing hard science with philosophy and pop culture or for deliberately using Darwinian evolutionary theory to promote personal philosophical or theological opinions. But they are factually as well as tactically mistaken to assert that natural evolutionary processes are not real. Whether by critics or proponents, it is an error to believe that Darwinian evolutionary theory is inseparable from materialistic or naturalistic philosophies that deny a living God. Evolutionary theory is only concerned with the fundamental physical and behavioral mechanics of biology. Even if they may bear his name, so-called "social Darwinism," or "Darwinian philosophy" have very little to do with Charles Darwin or his discoveries.

Nevertheless, many people have great difficulty reconciling the *seemingly* blind, materialistic forces of nature that shape our world with the idea of a providential God who has created the universe and humankind for noble and loving purposes. Sadly, their philosophic outlook on life is therefore dependent on their choosing one of only two fundamental points of view. Indeed, we find that the essays of ID theorists reflect visions of only two possibilities for the world. As Robert C. Koons put it:

> The Western philosophical tradition has thus bequeathed to us two competing metaphysical models: one in which everything is to be explained ultimately in terms of blind and purposeless forces (the materialistic model); and one in which purpose-

fulness is a fundamental and irreducible reality (the teleological model).[10]

The teleological model, in this case, being one in which God either regularly or occasionally supersedes the very forces of nature that He set in place in order to assure His desired outcome. As mentioned in the introduction, proclamations of only those two possibilities may simply underestimate the power and the capabilities of God. A transcendent God need not be confined to such narrow parameters.

As we have seen, for an omniscient, omnipresent, and omnipotent God, the possibilities are limitless. The will of a God Who transcends space and time cannot be thwarted by any contingencies that may arise from the outcomes of indeterminate events (or choices made by human beings with free will). Life can surely have arisen, evolved, and speciated on Earth through purely natural processes — processes that might appear from our perspective to be blind and purposeless — without the outcome being at all surprising or purposeless to God. According to Scripture, His plan is perfect and complete, regardless of the many contingencies and outcomes that may arise within it. God is certainly not constrained by the limits of the imaginations of those who can envision the possibility of only two philosophic absolutes for the world.

We have also seen that, reasonably understood, Scripture does not demand a young Earth or the *direct, supernatural* creation of atoms, molecules, stars, planets or living organisms. According to Scripture, God's creation is nature itself.

A providential and transcendent God need not control everything that happens. Indeed, a world in which we can be saved through a confession of faith necessarily accommodates an alternative choice for which God cannot be held responsible. As human beings, created in the image of God, we can only be held accountable if we have free will. And we can have free will only if the world operates and evolves, at least in part, independently of God's direct control.

Accordingly, an enormous body of physical evidence has revealed that the modern character of our entire physical universe is the result of billions of years of natural evolutionary change—from the initial point from which space, time, matter, and energy have emanated, through to the living organisms that we see around us today.

Paleontologists have unearthed a multitude of fossils that were formed over 3.6 billion years of the Earth's 4.6 billion year history. The discovery of these fossils has revealed a clear pattern of evolutionary development of life on Earth—from the simple prokaryotic single-cell organisms that first appeared some 3.6 billion years ago, to the more complex eukaryotic single-cell organisms that only emerged 2.4 billion years later (1.4 billion years ago), to the first multi-cellular organisms that evolved from those single-eukaryotic-cell organisms soon after, to many of the first representatives of today's phyla around 570-600 million years ago, then on to fishes and the first land plants about 450 million years ago, to amphibians 380 million years ago, to reptiles 325 million years ago, to dinosaurs and mammals 225 million years ago, and then eventually, with the extinction of the dinosaurs 65 million years ago, to the flourishing of mammals and to the many mammals, including us, that we see in the world today.

Modern geneticists have not only confirmed much of what paleontologists have gleaned from the fossil record, they have gone even further in many areas in confirming the evolutionary history of life on Earth. The "marked" genes with which scientists have been able to track common ancestral lineages across a variety of species should eliminate any doubt in all but the most determined deniers of evolution.

If we simply take notice, evidence of evolution can be observed in the world all around us—in the food we buy, in our home landscapes, in our pets, in infectious and heritable diseases, and even in our own anatomy. We can rather easily see it in the structural order of the entire natural world.

We can also see an elegance and beauty in nature's structural order that, for the believer, declares the glory of God's work. The spiritual insight of knowing God through a personal relationship with

Jesus Christ enables the Christian to witness the otherwise "invisible qualities" of God in all of nature.[11]

If indeed God created the natural universe, with all of its natural laws—the laws of gravity, motion, thermodynamics and all the other laws of physics—did He not create all of the natural possibilities within the realm of the physical universe—every atom and every molecule interlocked within the universal laws that govern natural consequences? Can there be any legitimate claim of certainty that God did not, upon setting the physical universe in motion, perhaps with a big bang, sufficiently set the parameters and the course for natural events within His created spatial dimensions of space and time? We certainly need not suppose that God created a natural world that is inadequate to His purposes.

Wherever we might declare a line between God's direct supernatural action and the subsequent natural processes that follow, we clearly need not concede that a natural environment which can support the systematic evolutionary development of complex organisms would require an ideological Naturalism or Materialism that excludes an active, living God. As Scripture informs us, we "cannot fathom what God has done from beginning to end." Rather, the believer is to confidently receive the Spirit and have faith in His benevolent stewardship. Even if we cannot demonstrate God's role through scientific analysis—even if all we can find are natural processes that account for the evolutionary propagation of life on Earth—we certainly need not retreat from a conviction of God's providence and our marvel at the glory of God's creation.

* * * *

Acknowledgements

M ost of all, I would like to thank my wife Ginny for her
patience, her love, and her gracious support of my disparate
pursuits. I thank Linda Guthrie and Bob Hartley for giving me the idea
to write this book. Their love and encouragement has been a great
comfort to me for many years. I also want to thank my brothers-in-law,
Dr. Artie Sudan and Philip Sudan esquire. Their love and fellowship
have been a treasure to me, and their extensive knowledge of and
passion for Scripture have inspired me to learn more. My sister Karen's
mastery of the English language has also been greatly helpful. For their
willingness to appraise preliminary drafts and to offer invaluable
insight and practical suggestions, I am also immensely grateful to Richard "Rusty" Rutherford, Eric Sawyer, and Reverend Kristin Huffman.

A not so uncommon scoff in academia pronounces that, "to use
the work of one person is plagiarism, while to use the work of many is
scholarship." Given that I have no academic background in either
science or theology, I have naturally had to rely heavily upon the work
of those who do. To craft this book, I have benefited enormously from
the informed writings of many people. Among the most notable
contemporary authors are Karen Armstrong, Douglas Futuyma, Richard
Fortey, Kenneth Miller, Carl Zimmer, Ernst Mayr, Francis Collins,
Darrell Falk, Keith Miller, Richard Dawkins, Stephen Jay Gould, Bill
Bryson, Jonathon Miller, G.J. Sawyer, and Viktor Deak. I am particularly indebted to Dr. Simon Conway Morris of Cambridge University
and Dr. Owen Gingerich of the Harvard-Smithsonian Center for Astro-
physics for their extraordinary kindness in scanning the entire manu-
script and pointing to a number of needed corrections. Finally, I want to
thank my editor, Susan Leon. Her enthusiasm for the project and her
insightful suggestions have been invaluable. Of course any errors that
may remain are mine alone.

About the Author

B ruce Glass is a businessman, artist, and author. For the past twenty-five years he has been engaged in the business of commercial photography. As seen with this book, he also has a keen interest in matters of philosophy, faith, and science. He and his wife Ginny live in Houston, Texas.

Notes

Notes for the Introduction

[1] David Quammen, "Was Darwin Wrong?" *National Geographic*, November 2004, p. 6

[2] Carl Zimmer, *Evolution: The Triumph of an Idea*, (New York 2001), p. 338

[3] Keith B. Miller, "An Evolving Creation: Oxymoron or Fruitful Insight?, *Perspectives on an Evolving Creation*, edited by Keith B. Miller (Grand Rapids 2003), p. 4

[4] Jerry Adler, "Doubting Darwin," *Newsweek*, February 7, 2005

[5] Darrell R. Falk, *Coming to Peace With Science: Bridging the Worlds Between Faith and Biology*, (Downers Grove, IL 2004), p. 232

[6] Carl Zimmer, *Evolution: The Triumph of an Idea*, (New York 2001), p. 338

[7] Keith B. Miller, "An Evolving Creation: Oxymoron or Fruitful Insight?, *Perspectives on an Evolving Creation*, edited by Keith B. Miller (Grand Rapids 2003), p. 4

[8] Jim Seghers, "Pope John Paul II on Evolution and Mary," *Totus Tuus Ministries*, August 28, 1999

[9] C.S. Lewis, *Miracles* (1947), reprinted in *The Complete C.S. Lewis Signature Classics*, (New York 2002), p. 272

Notes for Chapter 1 – God's Word

[1] Thomas Aquinas, *Summa contra gentiles* 1.5.3 in *Thomas: Selected Writings*, trans. R. McInery (Harmondsworth, U.K., 1998), as cited in Karen Armstrong's *The Case For God*, p. 142

[2] Everett Ferguson, *The History of Christianity*, edited by Dr. Tim Dowley, (Oxford 1990), p. 107

[3] Karen Armstrong, *The Case For God*, (New York 2009), p. 96

[4] Augustine, *On Genesis*, (New York 2002) (published by the Augustine Heritage Institute) p. 285

[5] Everett Ferguson, *The History of Christianity*, edited by Dr. Tim Dowley, (Oxford 1990), p. 112

[6] Webster's II New Riverside University Dictionary, (1984, 1988, 1994) p. 702

[7] Everett Ferguson, *The History of Christianity*, edited by Dr. Tim Dowley, (Oxford 1990). pp. 104-106

[8] David F. Wright, H. Dermot McDonald, *The History of Christianity*, edited by Dr. Tim Dowley, (Oxford 1990), pp. 104-112

[9] Timothy Ferris, *Coming of Age in the Milky Way* (New York 1988), p. 45

[10] Augustine, *On Genesis*, (New York 2002) (published by the Augustine Heritage Institute) p. 211

[11] Mark Knoll, ChristianityToday.com, *The Rise of the Evangelicals*, August 8, 2008

[12] Karen Armstrong, *The Case For God*, (New York 2009), p. 238

[13] Keith B. Miller, "An Evolving Creation: Oxymoron or Fruitful Insight?" also Mark A. Knoll and David Livingstone, "Charles Hodge and B.B. Warfield on Science, the Bible, Evolution, and Darwinism," *Perspectives on an Evolving Creation*, edited by Keith B. Miller (Grand Rapids 2003), pp. 4, 61-71

[14] Rick Warren, *The Purpose Driven Life* (Grand Rapids 2002), Appendix 3, p. 325

[15] Karen Armstrong, *The Case For God*, (New York 2009), p. xi

[16] Ibid., p. 32

[17] In addition to the two distinct creation stories found in *Genesis*, the Bible also makes reference to creation having begun with a great sea battle in which God prevailed over a sea monster or dragon named Rahab and/or the multi-headed Leviathon. (for example, *Psalm* 47:13-17, *Psalm* 89:10-11, and *Isaiah* 51:9)

[18] Peter Enns, *The Evolution of Adam: What The Bible Does and Doesn't Say About Human Origins*, (Grand Rapids 2012), p. 25. For a more detailed account of the Documentary Hypothesis, as well as a more thorough analysis and interpretation of the creation stories, Enns' book is an excellent source.

[19] Walter Brueggemann, *Genesis: in Bible Commentary for Teaching and Preaching*, James L. Mays, Series Editor, (Louisville 1982), pp. 17, 30

Notes for Chapter 2 – God's Creation

[1] William Paley, *Natural Theology*, pp. 5-6

[2] www.philosophy.lander.edu, Lander University, Greenwood, South Carolina

[3] D. Ratzsch, "Teleological Arguments for God's Existence," *Stanford Encyclopedia of Philosophy*, 2005 – www.plato.stanford.edu/entries/teleological-arguments

[4] John D. Barrow and Frank J. Tipler, *The Anthropic Cosmological Principle*, (New York 1986) p. 23

[5] Ibid., p. 28

[6] Stephen W. Hawking, *A Brief History of Time: From the Big Bang to Black Holes* (1988), pp. 121-122

[7] Kenneth R. Miller, *Finding Darwin's God*, (New York 1999), p. 228

[8] Ibid.

[9] Simon Conway Morris, *The Crucible of Creation*, (Oxford 1998), p. 14

[10] Martin Luther, "Psalm 147," in *Luther's Works*, volume 14 (St. Louis: Concordia 1958), footnote # 9

[11] Robert John Russell, "Special Providence and Genetic Mutation: A New Defense of Theistic Evolution," *Perspectives on an Evolving Creation*, edited by Keith B. Miller, (Grand Rapids 2003), p. 363

[12] C.S. Lewis, *Miracles* (1947), reprinted in *The Complete C.S. Lewis Signature Classics*, (New York 2002), p. 309

[13] Karen Armstrong, *The Case For God*, (New York 2009), p. 146-147

Notes for Chapter 3 – God's Providence

[1] It might be useful to note that neither Jews nor Eastern Orthodox Christians interpret Genesis 3 in that way. The idea of our inheritance of a "fallen world" as a result of the "original sin" committed by Adam and Eve is exclusive to Western Christianity.

[2] Thomas Aquinas, *Aquinas's Shorter Summa*, Sophia Institute Press (Manchester, NH 1993) p. 154

[3] Ibid., p. 157

[4] Kenneth R. Miller, *Finding Darwin's God*, (New York 1999), pp. 207-213

[5] C.S. Lewis, *Miracles* (1947), reprinted in *The Complete C.S. Signature Classics*, (New York 2002), p. 277

[6] Augustine, *On Free Choice of the Will*, Translated by Thomas Williams (Indianapolis 1993) p. 111

[7] Augustine, *On Genesis*, (New York 2002) (published by the Augustine Heritage Institute) p. 408

[8] Nell Greenfieldboyce, "Cagebreak! Rats Will Work To Free A Trapped Pal," NPR, 12/9/2011

[9] Jessica C. Flack and Frans B.M. de Waal, "Any Animal Whatever," *Evolutionary Origins of Morality*, edited by Leonard D. Katz (Bowling Green, OH 2000), p. 19

[10] Ernst Mayr, *What Evolution Is*, (New York 2001), pp. 257-260

[11] Ibid.

[12] Thomas Aquinas, *Aquinas's Shorter Summa*, (Manchester, NH 1993, 2002), p. 225

[13] Augustine, *On Free Choice of the Will*, Translated by Thomas Williams (Indianapolis 1993) p. 120

[14] Michael Dowd, *Thank God for Evolution*, (New York 2007), pp. 57, 59

Notes for Chapter 4 – Layers of Understanding

[1] Brian Greene, *The Elegant Universe*, (New York 1999), 108-111

[2] Bill Bryson, *A Short History of Nearly Everything*, (New York 2003), p. 162

[3] New Advent Catholic Encyclopedia, http://www.newadvent.org/cathen/13548a.htm

[4] Paul Strathern, *St. Augustine In 90 Minutes*, (Chicago 1997), pp. 45, 47

[5] Karen Armstrong, *The Case For God*, (New York 2009), pp. 144, 193

[6] Paul Strathern, *Aristotle In 90 Minutes*, (Chicago 1996), pp 52-53

[7] Karen Armstrong, *The Case For God*, (New York 2009), pp. 161-208

[8] Ibid., pp. 197-198, 203

[9] Ibid., p. 203

[10] Ibid., pp. 198-199

[11] Ibid., p. 214

Notes for Chapter 5 – The Awakening of Evolutionary Science

[1] Columbia University Press Encyclopedia

[2] Douglas J. Futuyma, *Science on Trial*, (Sunderland, MA 1995), pp. 25-26. Futuyma attributed this history to J.C. Greene in *The Death of Adam: Evolution and its Impact on Western Thought* (Ames: Iowa State University Press, 1959).

[3] Ernst Mayr, *What Evolution Is*, (New York 2001), p. 82

[4] Ibid., p. 86

[5] Carl Zimmer, *Evolution: The Triumph of an Idea*, (New York 2001), pp. 38-39

[6] Ibid., p. 39

[7] Ibid., pp. 16-17

[8] Ibid., p. 24

[9] Douglas J. Futuyma, *Science on Trial*, (Sunderland, MA 1995), p. 31

[10] Ernst Mayr, *What Evolution Is*, (New York 2001), pp. 74-82

[11] Douglas J. Futuyma, *Science on Trial*, (Sunderland, MA 1995), p. 24

[12] Jonathan Miller, *Darwin for Beginners*, (New York 1982), p. 135

[13] Ibid., p. 152-156

[14] Douglas J. Futuyma, *Science on Trial*, (Sunderland, MA 1995), p. 39

Notes for Chapter 6 – "Let the Land Produce Living Creatures"

[1] Howard J. Van Till, "Is the Universe Capable of Evolving?" *Perspectives on an Evolving Creation*, edited by Keith B. Miller (Grand Rapids 2003), pp. 317-318

[2] Richard Fortey, *Life: A Natural History of the First Four Billion Years of Life on Earth*, (New York 1997), pp. 41-43

3 University of California Museum of Paleontology,
http://evolution.berkeley.edu/evolibrary/article/_0_0/endosymbiosis_04

4 Richard Dawkins, *The Blind Watchmaker*, (New York 1996), p. 14

5 Carl Zimmer, *Evolution: The Triumph of an Idea*, (New York 2001), p. 193

6 Ibid., pp. 235-239

7 Today many people have noted that the most intellectually capable people in the world tend to have fewer children than less intelligent people, possibly reversing the evolutionary trend toward greater intellect. Of course this appearance likely has more to do with education that actual intelligence. Unfortunately, Darwin even suggested that poor and less capable people should not marry and propagate. He did not advocate prohibition of it, but this idea among other socially unacceptable musings have been used by critics in their efforts to discredit all of his work. We should keep in mind that in the Victorian age in which Darwin lived and worked such suggestions were considered morally responsible. Today we know to use extreme caution in advocating any public policy regarding such observations. Thankfully, human freedom has become the highest ideal of moral values.

8 Ernst Mayr, *What Evolution Is*, (New York 2001), pp. 224-225

Notes for Chapter 7 – Clues All Around Us

1 Jonathan Miller, *Darwin for Beginners*, (New York 1982), pp. 8-9. Mr. Miller cleverly used the example of these kinds of puzzle drawing to illustrate how other scientists, given the same evidence, had not seen what Darwin saw.

2 Peter Tyson, "A Potpourri of Pooches," *Dogs and More Dogs*, PBS/NOVA/WGBH, www.pbs.org.

3 Stephen J. Gould, *The Panda's Thumb*, (New York 1980), p. 205

4 www.farm-direct.co.uk/

5 www.nativetech.org/cornhusk/cornhusk.html

6 Dorothy Hinshaw Patent, *Evolution Goes On Every Day*, (New York 1977), pp. 41-43

7 Carl Zimmer, *Evolution: The Triumph of an Idea*, (New York 2001), p. 200

8 Ibid., p. 201

9 Ibid., pp. 201-202

10 Ibid., pp. 203-204

[11] David Quammen, "Was Darwin Wrong?" *National Geographic*, November 2004, p. 21

[12] Ibid., pp. 21, 30.

[13] World Health Organization website: Avian influenza fact sheet. Jan. 15, 2004

[14] D.V. Desai, Hiren Dhanani: Sickle Cell Disease: History And Origin. The Internet Journal of Hematology, Volume 1 Number 2, 2004.

[15] Ernst Mayr, *What Evolution Is*, (New York 2001), pp. 27-30

[16] Douglas Theobald Ph.D., Dept. of Biochemistry, Brandeis University. "The TalkOrigins Archive"

[17] Michael John Denton, "An Anti-Darwinian Intellectual Journey," *Uncommon Dissent*, William A. Dembski editor (Wilmington, DE 2004). P. 156

[18] Charles Darwin, *Origin of Species*, (Norwalk CN 1991, by Easton Press Publishing), p. 168

[19] World Book Encyclopedia. 233 Michigan Ave., Ste. 2000, Chicago, IL 60601.

Notes for Chapter 8 – The History of Life

[1] Stephen Jay Gould, *Wonderful Life: the Burgess Shale and the Nature of History*, (New York 1989), pp. 57-58

[2] Richard Fortey, *Trilobite: Eyewitness to Evolution*, (New York 2001), p. 139

[3] David J. Bottjer, "The Early Evolution of Animals," *Scientific American*, August 2005, pp. 42-47

[4] Richard Fortey, *Life: A Natural History of the First Four Billion Years of Life on Earth*, (New York 1997), p. 101

[5] Richard Fortey, *Trilobite: Eyewitness to Evolution*, (New York 2001), pp. 85-92, 98-99, 111

[6] Richard Fortey, *Life: A Natural History of the First Four Billion Years of Life on Earth*, (New York 1997), p. 150

[7] Ibid., p. 227, 228-229

[8] Mark A. Norell & Xu Xing, "The Varieties of Tyrannosaurs," *Natural History*, May 2005, pp. 36-7

[9] Darrel R. Falk, *Coming To Peace With Science: Bridging the Worlds Between Faith and Biology*, (Downers Grove, IL 2004), pp. 116-117

[10] Steven Mithen, *The Prehistory of the Mind: The Cognitive Origins of Art, Religion and Science*, (New York 1996), p. 17

[11] Jamie Shreeve, "The Birth of Bipedalism" *National Geographic*, July 2010, pp. 63-66

[12] G.J. Sawyer, Esteban Sarmiento, and Richard Milner, *The Last Human: A Guide to Twenty-two Species of Extinct Humans*, (Yale University Press 2007), pp. 107-112

[13] Ibid., pp. 151-153

[14] Ibid., pp. 158-163, 168-173

[15] Mike Morwood, Thomas Sutikna, Richard Roberts, "The People Time Forgot" *National Geographic*, April 2005, p. 11

[16] G.J. Sawyer, Esteban Sarmiento, and Richard Milner, *The Last Human: A Guide to Twenty-two Species of Extinct Humans*, (Yale University Press 2007), pp. 176-180

[17] Ibid., p. 210

[18] Stephen S. Hall, "Last of the Neanderthals" *National Geographic*, October 2008, pp. 40-42

[19] Ibid., p. 50

[20] Gary Stix, "Traces of a Distant Past" *Scientific American*, July 2008, pp. 56-63

[21] Bill Bryson, *A Short History of Nearly Everything*, (New York 2004) p. 337

Notes for Chapter 9 – The Tree of Life

[1] Sharon Begley, "T. *rex* and His Family," *Newsweek*, April 23, 2007, P. 12

[2] Carl Zimmer, "Crunching the Data for the Tree of Life," *The New York Times*, February 10, 2009

[3] A press release issued by Penn State University on November 22, 2005.

[4] Carl Zimmer, "Crunching the Data for the Tree of Life," *The New York Times*, February 10, 2009

[5] F. Flam, "Hints of a Language in Junk DNA," *Science*, 266:1320, 1994

[6] Darrell R. Falk, *Coming to Peace With Science: Bridging the Worlds Between Faith and Biology*, (Downers Grove, IL 2004), pp. 183-188

[7] Ibid., pp. 189-191

[8] Ibid., pp. 192-193

[9] Francis S. Collins, *The Language of God*, (New York 2006), pp. 134-137

[10] Ibid., pp. 137-138

[11] Ibid., pp. 138-139

[12] Kenneth R. Miller, *Only A Theory: Evolution and the Battle for America's Soul*, (New York 2008), pp. 97-99

Notes for Chapter 10 – "Creation Science" and Intelligent Design Theory

[1] Carl Zimmer, *Evolution: The Triumph of an Idea*, (New York 2001), p. 318

[2] Ibid., pp. 319-320

[3] Lenny Flank, "What Is The Position of Other Churches on Evolution?" internet article 1995

[4] *Kitzmiller v. Dover* decision, p. 88, as cited in Kenneth R Miller's *Only A Theory: Evolution and the Battle for America's Soul*, (New York 2008), pp. 178-79

[5] Kenneth R. Miller, *Only A Theory: Evolution and the Battle for America's Soul*, (New York 2008), p. 209

[6] The words quoted here were not Minnich's directly. They were within a question posed to him by plaintiff's attorney Steve Harvey. In his answer, Minnich confirmed that they accurately described his view. See endnote on page 234 of Kenneth R. Miller's *Only A Theory*.

[7] David Berlinski, "The Deniable Darwin," *Uncommon Dissent: Intellectuals Who Find Darwinism Unconvincing*, edited by William A. Dembski (Wilmington, DE 2004), p. 269

Notes for Chapter 11 – "Darwinism"

[1] Nancy R. Pearcey, "Darwin Meets the Berenstain Bears: Evolution as a Total Worldview," *Uncommon Descent: Intellectuals Who Find Darwinism Unconvincing*, edited by William A, Dembski, (Wilmington, Del. 2004), pp. 53, 54

[2] Douglas J. Futuyma, *Science on Trial: The case for Evolution*, (Sunderland, MA 1982, 1995), p. 210

[3] Richard Hofstadter, *Social Darwinism in American Thought*, (Philadelphia 1944, republished by Beacon Press in 1992), p. 41

[4] Ibid., p. 45

[5] Ibid.

[6] Ibid., p. 180

[7] Charles Pearson, *National Life and Character*, (1893), p. 85, (As noted in Hofstadter's *Social Darwinism in American Thought*, p. 186)

[8] David Morgan, "Yale Study: U.S. Eugenics Paralleled Nazi Germany," *Chicago Tribune*, Feb. 15, 2000

[9] Carl Becker, *Proceedings of the American Philosophical Society*, Vol. LXXXVII, No. 3 (1944), pp. 201-210. Reprinted in *Thomas Jefferson, A Profile* edited by Merrill Peterson (New York 1967), pp. 44-46

[10] Robert C. Koons, "The Check Is in the Mail: Why Darwinism Fails to Inspire Confidence," *Uncommon Descent: Intellectuals Who Find Darwinism Unconvincing*, edited by William A, Dembski, (Wilmington, Del. 2004), p. 7

[11] *Romans* 1:20

Index

Made in the USA
Middletown, DE
19 September 2017